The Book of the
Merchant Navy Pacifics

Second Edition; greatly upgraded and expanded including new sixteen page colour section

By
Richard Derry
Ian Sixsmith

Irwell Press Ltd.

ISBN 978-1-906919-34-4

Acknowledgements

This book was first made, in a rather more limited format, back in 2001; that early version, nor this one, would not have been possible without the kind assistance of several people. Thanks must go principally to Eric Youldon, on occasion a lonely torch bearer for the original engines and still winning the argument, or at least steadily rebalancing it. Mark Arscott of Markits is still making those Bulleid wheels along with much else the modeller might require – including now of course 7mm, the modeller's inevitable one-way street of middle age: PO Box 40, Watford, Herts, WD24 6TN, tel/fax 01923 249711). Thanks also to Barry Fletcher, Robert Stevenson, the late D.W. Winkworth, Hamish Stevenson, Brian Bailey, Allan C. Baker, Chris Hawkins, John Fry, the late Alec Swain, Geoff Goslin, Brian Seddon, Alan Hammond and Barry Hoper of the Transport Treasury. In its infancy when the first version of this book appeared, the Transport Treasury is now a powerhouse among negative collections. It can be found at 'Logie Shannoch' (which may or may not be Gaelic for 'Aladdin's Cave') in the hamlet of Drumrossie near Insch, Aberdeenshire, AB52 6LJ. In the earlier Book of the Merchant Navy Pacifics we suggested you write with an s.a.e but though you still can of course, times have changed and you can contact the place quicker at www.transporttreasury.co.uk The tel/fax is 01464 820717.

21C10 BLUE STAR at Eastleigh in wartime black; the 'C' in the number has been reduced to regular size so the photograph dates from November 1942. Two sand fillers, the original forward of the nameplate and one for the front driver – there'd be trouble with that slidebar beneath... Asbestos cloth over trailing truck, letting down somewhat the air-smoothed up-to-dateness of the design, though the paint of the buffer beam, and the burnished buffers, are to Royal Train standards!

First published in the United Kingdom in 2001
This enlarged and expanded edition 2011 published
by Irwell Press Limited, 59A, High Street, Clophill,
Bedfordshire MK45 4BE
Printed by Konway Press

Contents

Bibliography

*B*ulleid's Pacifics by D.W. Winkworth (George Allen & Unwin, 1974 – original and amusing; thought provoking), *Locomotives of the Southern Railway Part 2* by D.L. Bradley (RCTS, 1976 – authoritative and painstaking; every facet laid out), *Loco Profile No.22* by Brian Reed (Profile Publications, 1972 – excellent introduction and thorough outline. Why oh why did they stop publishing them – it was the best 45p you could spend!), *British Pacific Locomotives* by Cecil J. Allen (Ian Allan 1962; broad sweep *par excellence*), *Master Builders of Steam* by H.A.V. Bulleid (Ian Allan 1963; one of the best loco reads there are – with a preface by Bulleid, Ivatt and Stanier!), *Bulleid of the Southern*, another great work by the same author more than a decade later; *Bulleid Power – The Merchant Navy Class* by A.J. Fry (Alan Sutton 1990; puts the C in Comprehensive). Beyond this, there have been umpteen articles from the mainstream railway press since the 1940s, from the *Railway Magazine* to the *Railway Observer* and SLS *Journal* to *The Railway Gazette*, *Railway Engineer*, *Southern Railway Magazine* and so on. Bulleid, like Gresley, even has his own Society with a magazine devoted to his works – *The Leader*, now retitled *Bulleid Express*. Vastly detailed accounts still appear today even in modelling magazines in which the fine old art of 'engine picking' is raised to unprecedented heights – indeed it has got to the point where to know *all* about *all* the Merchant Navys (this is so for the light Pacifics too) is more than mortal man can really hope for. Yet the original volume added something at least to the tale – or brought it together from hitherto obscure sources – and this new volume has a generous crop of those elusive nuggets too. The abiding principle remains, that if it is vital to your modelling, if you find it intolerable for a loco to be less than 100% accurate for a given time then you need to obtain a set of photographs, probably beyond any that can be found in any one book. And then be sure the date on the back of the picture is right! Happy hunting.

A 'Packet' in all its glory at Waterloo on 16 October 1946. 21C4 CUNARD WHITE STAR duly cleaned and decorated at the head of one of four trains for Southampton that day, full of passengers embarking for the maiden voyage of 'Queen Elizabeth' as a trans-Atlantic luxury liner. Pullman coaches, burnished buffers and malachite green livery make for a cheerful glimmer in the post-war austerity gloom. Tail lamp from Nine Elms on ground but route discs not yet set up.

4

1. 'Ten Main Line Locomotives'

Scarcely can a railway board have entered on such a time of frustrating maintenance work, disappointing performance, lows mixed with thrilling highs, uncertainty, expense and worry with such an innocuous phrase – *'Ten New Main Line Locomotives'*. They were two sides of a coin, the Merchant Navy Pacifics – love 'em, hate 'em, scorn versus adulation; seldom could the phrases 'brilliant steaming' be conjoined so often with 'heavy maintenance', or the words 'exhilarating performance' with 'caught fire'*.

It might be that the Merchant Navy Pacifics are the most difficult British express locomotives to write about. The Duchesses, Royal Scots and Princesses and even the BR Standards which have formed the subject of previous 'Books of' in this series enjoyed a fairly consistent perception among enthusiasts and professionals alike. With the products of Bulleid it was different – the opposite in fact was the case. Where one person saw a sublime virtue, another saw a sorry handicap. Even today feelings can run high…

Whichever side of the divide you stand, it is clear that the Merchant Navys (how do you *spell* the plural even, Navys or Navies?) were not an ordinary class of passenger steam locomotive. Contradiction seems to have been their

middle name from the very first. Even when introduced at the height of the Second World War for instance, these locomotives – plainly express Pacifics to anyone with eyes – were classified Mixed Traffic. This is how Bulleid, it has often been said, was able to sneak them past the men at the ministry, overcoming material restrictions and shortages (in fact, not the least heroic part of the whole tale is how Bulleid ever got them built at the time he did). Yet the description, arrived at in 1938 for the benefit of the SR Board, *was true*; Merchant Navys, at least at first and in part, were thoroughly 'mixed traffic' in the way they were worked. On the West of England runs, if not particularly elsewhere, they always had booked turns on perishables, milk and stopping trains.

In fact the suggestion regarding devious 'mixed traffic' labelling has become something of a 'rubber stamp' over the years and needs amending. For instance, the Nine Elms Merchant Navy that worked down on the 3.0pm off Waterloo returned on the 10.42pm freight from Exeter Central Yard to Nine Elms Goods for years – and that's just one example.

So, it is clear that the whole history of the Merchant Navy Pacifics was almost designed for contention, for

having taken the path of unconventionality and individuality with all the controversy it threw up, they were then abruptly and completely reconstituted, into as conventional a steam locomotive as you could wish for. Along the way every detail variation that it was possible to explore and utilise was so explored and utilised, leaving the class an engine-picker's paradise, and a minefield for those who prefer certainty in life.

Bulleid and Modernising the Southern Steam Stock
The class appeared at a time of war, so there was little of the publicity that the LNER A4 streamliners and LMS Pacifics attracted in the 1930s – more significantly there was no series of well-publicised speed runs, or romantic new services. There was no 'Silver Jubilee' for Bulleid's first Pacific, and no stage on which to shine. This was a pity as the technical innovations together with unconventional appearance deserved more.

---

*One has to be careful here – there *were* fires on Merchant Navys, it is true, but they were comparatively rare. It was the light Pacifics that particularly suffered in this regard.

21C2 UNION CASTLE, rolling along with nary a care in the world with an up West of England express at Semley in August 1947; still with the remarkable gunmetal plates on cab and tender, and at the front. It bore these until renumbered and painted blue in early 1950; the Flaman speed recorder with its rodding running back under the cab was put on in 1945 for test runs Waterloo-Bournemouth. Photograph Reverend Cawston Bequest; Canon B.C. Bailey.

CHANNEL PACKET, almost 'as built', but with front numberplate lowered, and the three lower lamps raised – effectively swopping positions since building. There was only one footstep at first, on the nearest side, but a second one (as here) was soon added, also slung under the buffer. Front steps were afterwards always arranged so. Photograph Collection E.S. Youldon.

On 10 March 1941 CHANNEL PACKET was named at Eastleigh by Lord Brabazon. Afterwards 21C1 hauled a three coach guest special to Alresford on the Mid-Hants line where it is seen soon after arrival. His Lordship, with peaked cap, can be spotted among the admirers talking to Bulleid. The engine retains the unlucky horseshoe and has the three bottom lamps and the number plate on original site. These items later swopped positions.

Original condition, March 1941 – metal plates, matt malachite, three yellow lines and that glorious 'widow's peak' as it's often described in the literature. (It is actually the opposite of a widow's peak – but it sounds good.) Note also slightly larger 'C'. Note too the single centrally placed sand filler just forward of the nameplate, and the single sandpipe down to the front of the centre driver.

21C2 in plain malachite at Bournemouth in July 1941, nameplate covered. The second Merchant Navy repeated most of 21C1's early features; very prominent cut-out now at the 'widow's peak', front plate now vertical, single sander.

21C2 UNION CASTLE on a four coach test special at Merstham, 4 July 1941. Light under the 'widow's peak' shows the large hole cut round the chimney. Slightly larger 'C' as with 21C1 previous page; inverted horseshoe.

Bulleid, born in Invercargill at the southern tip of the South Island of New Zealand, served a premium apprenticeship at Doncaster. To summarise his career in a few words, he rose to be Gresley's Assistant on the Great Northern and accounts of his days there, during the momentous times of the Pacifics, 10000 and the Mikados, the Vitry Testing Station and so on make rewarding reading, in *Master Builders of Steam* for instance, by H.A.V. Bulleid (Ian Allan, 1963) and *Bulleid: Last Giant of Steam* by Sean Day-Lewis (George Allen & Unwin, 1963). By the 1930s Bulleid was probably the most prominent 'No.2' on the Big Four and a sudden approach from Sir Herbert Walker of the Southern Railway is said to have come 'out of the blue'. The post of CME of the Southern was his if he cared to apply for it. He did and was appointed and was at his desk in the Waterloo offices in September 1937, a matter of a few months after Walker's approach.

Steam had been neglected on the Southern in favour of electrification and even by 1936 electric train mileage was easily exceeding steam. Yet the longer routes on the former London & South Western Railway were still steam hauled and the heavy boat trains on the Eastern Section still required the best that was available in steam power. The steam stock needed updating, an opportunity in which Bulleid saw more scope for experimentation and innovation than the average, unsuspecting, SR Board member could dream of. Turntable and track considerations soon ruled out 4 8 2s or 2 8 2s so a Pacific it would have to be. Not a 'conventional express passenger engine' to be sure but, as H.A.V. Bulleid puts it, one which could be more aptly described as 'fast mixed traffic'. People have been arguing over the wording ever since. This was in 1938, and the Merchant Navy Pacifics began to grow from a Board agreement to a rather harmless-looking requirement for 'ten new main line steam locomotives'. There was certainly no one on the Board that day who could have thought for the merest second that one day the Southern would have more Pacifics than the LMS!

The design, it was said, was 'experimental' and intended for goods service too... Denied the usual publicity outlets, the Southern had a fair go in its own organ, *Southern Railway Magazine*, under the bald (and bold) headline:

*BIG NEW STREAMLINED ENGINE
FOR SOUTHERN*
A new Southern Railway locomotive of a striking and original design is being introduced into the service. It is the first streamlined – or, as its designer, Mr. O.V. Bulleid, the Company's Chief Mechanical Engineer, prefers 'air smoothed' locomotive of the Southern Railway. The new engine was formally named 'Channel Packet' by the Minister of Transport, Lt. Col. J.T.C. Moore

Preparations for the original volume in 1999-2000 prompted Eric Youldon to an account of the Bulleid valve gear, a more sympathetic ('balanced' he would say) than can usually be found in published accounts. This first appeared in our parent magazine *British Railways Illustrated* in its April 2000 issue. What follows is a slightly amended version:

BULLEID'S CHAIN DRIVEN VALVE GEAR
Some Notes by Eric Youldon

When O.V.S. Bulleid came to draw up his specification for new main line locomotives in the late thirties he was influenced by the amount of time that drivers spent in pits oiling inside gear in conditions that were invariably appalling. He therefore concluded that inside motion should be enclosed and be self-oiling. He also reasoned this would ensure that working parts were protected from dirt and therefore the need for attention between works visits would be minimal. He did concede that when attention was necessary, access problems would arise.

Early thoughts were focussed on a Caprotti drive but wartime material shortages and dependence on an outside supplier ruled this out and so Bulleid decided to develop and patent his own design of valve gear, enclosed in an oil bath. Three cylinder Pacifics were ultimately designed and so the middle connecting rod, crosshead and slidebars were also accommodated within the bath. Any notion (sometimes expressed) that the enclosed mechanism thrashed about wildly in a bath full of oil can be dispelled immediately; the oil level amounted to just eight inches, as shown on the diagram. The only churning effect was caused by the three-throw crankshaft.

The *Railway Gazette* diagram shows the main features of the layout that was used for the Southern Pacifics built 1941 51, which involved a Morse chain drive to a three-throw crankshaft. The initial drive was from the centre coupled axle to an intermediate sprocket and was horizontal to allow for rise and fall of the engine on its springs. The shaft of this sprocket had a second sprocket that drove a further chain extending downwards to a final sprocket mounted on the three-throw crankshaft. Each crank of the latter operated a set of valve gear – one for each piston valve – and its three cranks were spaced out accordingly. Each valve gear consisted of two elements; from the crankpin a vertical eccentric rod rocked the expansion link controlling the radius rod. From the lower end of the eccentric rod a short forward extension was coupled to the combination lever via the union link. These elements corresponded to the eccentric rod and crosshead drives of a conventional set of Walschaerts gear.

The combination lever actuated a plunger linked to the valve rod connected at the other end to the piston valve rocker shaft. Connection to the valve was effected in the centre of the steam chest, which was the exhaust compartment as the cylinders were of the outside admission type.

The intermediate sprocket shaft was adjustable to some extent so that a degree of chain slack could be taken up. The crankshaft had a small sprocket and simple chain drive that operated a pair of pumps for distributing oil at about 20lb/sq.in. from a forty gallon sump. Delivery was by means of a series of small bore pipes that sprayed the working parts and also fed the rubbing surfaces of the inside slidebars. Reversing and cut-off adjustment was effected by steam reverser. The whole gear was small and light in weight and this helped make for free running – one of these engines' characteristics.

Chain stretch beyond the limit of adjustment was obviously an undesirable weakness, but did not affect the length of valve travel, although valve events could be influenced. The whole assembly was a challenge to fitters if the engines (there were 140 of them) were to be kept in good order, but with the backup of a good team of fitters a depot such as Exmouth Junction with some forty Bulleids on its books would daily turn out its Packets and West Countries with the same confidence as their S15s, Woolworths, T9s, Standard Tanks and all the rest.

The question that has to be asked is 'Were the designer's aims realised?' The answer is, yes and no. Simplicity in preparation of working parts was undoubtedly achieved and was much appreciated by many drivers, as revealed in the 'Pistell Testimonial', a collection of highly laudatory and appreciative statements assembled by Driver Pistell in 1966 and presented to Bulleid on his retirement. On the other side of the coin, freedom from fitters' attention was not to be enjoyed on the scale intended and sump draining and oil bath dismantling was resorted to from time to time, although there is little evidence that this significantly reduced mileages covered once early problems had been overcome. Failures out on the road occasionally took place and sometimes with spectacular results but it should be borne in mind that 'ordinary' locomotives had their quota of serious motion failures too. Oil soaked lagging fires were a problem never eradicated which is surprising because the covering of the lagging by sheeting would surely have done the trick.

On the credit side, overheating of the inside big end and main journals of the centre coupled wheels was very rare – there was no need for a heat detector (the 'stink bomb') provided for the middle big end of the ninety locomotives later rebuilt on conventional lines.

When Bulleid heard, in 1956, that the prototype rebuild 35018 was experiencing overheating problems he penned a letter to R.C. Bond (CME, BTC) suggesting he might consider an oilbath but, presumably for diplomatic reasons, it wasn't sent!

Those exotic 'box section', 'boxpok' or 'BFB' wheels. Bulleid spurned proprietary models of this American-type wheel that were available, coming up with cast steel centres. 'BFB' stands for 'Bulleid-Firth-Brown', the latter two names representing the involvement of the Sheffield steel firm of Thomas Firth and John Brown. According to the patent abstract published in *The Railway Gazette* of 16 May 1941, the patent specification for 'B.F.B.' wheels bears the name of Thomas Beaumont and Joseph Fenwick Bridge, both of the Atlas Works, Sheffield, with no mention of Bulleid. So maybe they are actually 'Beaumont-Fenwick-Bulleid' wheels! It matters not – the point is they saved something more than ten per cent in weight and performed well; the rim was shrunk on and secured to the hub not by pins and keys but by a continuous annular corrugated web. They seem to have attracted no criticism and were of course retained in the rebuilt locomotives. One Merchant Navy was built with a set of unique fabricated driving wheels – see the entry under 21C18 BRITISH INDIA LINE. Photograph Collection John Fry.

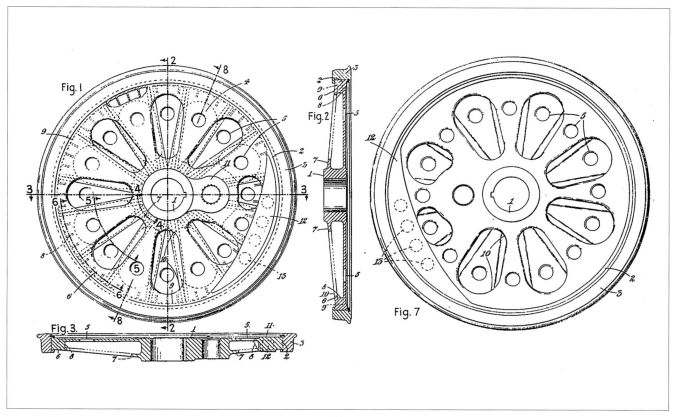

One of the boilers under construction at North British; the attachments/circular holes for the necks of the thermic syphons are low down on the curve of the throatplate. Photograph Collection John Fry.

Brabazon, MC at Eastleigh Works on March 10th and is one of ten which will be known as the Merchant Navy Class, to remind the public of the Southern's close association with the Mercantile Marine. The succeeding engines will be named after famous shipping lines associated with the Southampton Docks as their home port.

There was no mention at this stage of the merchant seaman, for which the naming policy was later claimed. The ten engines were 'being built experimentally' for heavy express passenger and goods services. Besides being the first streamlined Southern Railway engine – apart from the makeshift efforts applied to a Schools in 1938 – CHANNEL PACKET was also 'the first English locomotive to have electric lighting, both for head and tail code lamps and for the gauges and inspection lights in the driver's cabin'. It is not clear if this was just the customary slip of 'English' for 'British' or whether some Scottish or Irish locomotives had once carried electric lights.

'At the naming of 'Channel Packet', the Minister of Transport was accompanied by the Southern Railway Chairman, Mr. R. Holland-Martin, and the General Manager, Mr. E.J. Missenden, together with other Directors and Chief Officers of the Company, officials from the Ministry of Transport, and representatives of the press and news reels. After the naming ceremony Lt. Col. Moore Brabazon, in driver's peak cap, black mackintosh and gloves, drove the locomotive

along some sidings to a train, to which it was then attached for a trial run. With him in the cabin was Driver Tate (noted as the King and Queen's driver when Their Majesties travel on the Southern). Giving his opinion on the new engine, Lt. Col. Moore Brabazon said that he thought it was lovely and that Mr. O.V. Bulleid who had designed it, was not only an engineer but an artist.'

The locomotive's numbering was of course odd to the British eye and 21C1 had to be explained: *'The number, according to the new "Southern" notation, gives the number of the engine, whilst at the same time, the wheel arrangement is indicated. The number of driving axles is indicated by the corresponding letter of the alphabet e.g. C for three.'* It did not quite make so much sense to everyone else of course; not only was it misleading because every other working locomotive in the country had a more familiar, traditional type of number, the system did not even have the doubtful virtue of following continental practice; but then, in 1941 after all, few Britons were going to have much to do with Europe in the near future in any conventional sense... The letter notation as used in Europe utilised letters for the number of coupled axles and numbers for front and rear axles, so a 4-6-0 was 2C0, a 2-8-2 141 and a Pacific 2C1. As it turned out, Southern railwayman (as well as local enthusiasts) took to the strange notation perfectly readily; the engines after all were so different from

anything else that a conventional number almost 'wouldn't do'!

The new locomotive, it could not be denied, incorporated plenty of 'new features'. These were summarised as follows:

(a) Streamlining; another and more accurate description would be 'air smoothed'. The casing enclosing the engine is carried on the main frame instead of on the boiler, as is usually done, and the boiler, consequently, is free to expand inside it. The casing is fabricated by electric welding from rolled sections and one-sixteenth inch steel sheet.

(b) The cab is a continuation of the air-smoothed casing and, like it, is carried on the frame.

(c) The casing forward of the smokebox doorplate acts as an air collector. The large opening over the smokebox door forms the mouth of a funnel tapering to a narrow slot in front of the chimney, discharging a stream of air upwards at high velocity, acting as a screen to the exhaust.

(d) The enclosed space between the frames in front of the smokebox holds the electric light turbo-generator and two mechanical lubricator pumps. This engine is the first English locomotive to be completely lighted by electricity, as both the head and tail lamps are so lighted, in addition to the gauges and the lamps fitted for inspection purposes.

(e) All the cast steel wheel centres, both

SOUTHERN RAILWAY MAGAZINE

with which is incorporated
THE SOUTH WESTERN GAZETTE
(first issued 1881)

Vol. XIX. No. 219.　　　　　　　　　　　　　　　Nov.-Dec., 1941.

NAMED IN HONOUR OF OUR—　　—BRAVE MERCHANT SEAMEN!

ROYAL MAIL

MERCHANT　NAVY CLASS

engine and tender, are the new double-disc patent BFB type.

(f) The driving wheels are fitted with clasp brakes i.e. each wheel has a brake block on each side.

(g) Cab fittings. Both injectors are fitted on the firemen's side, the steam and water controls being arranged in one group on the cab side. The reversing gear is power operated, the steam and hydraulic cylinders being controlled by a single lever.

(h) The tender above the frame is all welded, the profile of the sides being the same as that of the latest 'Southern' carriages. Clasp brakes are fitted to the wheels operated by four 21 inch cylinders through automatic slack adjusters. The tender is filled through covers in the tender cab end at each side, thereby making it unnecessary for the fireman to climb on to the top of the tender.

(i) The boiler – the internal firebox is of steel and is fitted with two thermic syphons. The inner and outer fireboxes are welded. Automatic fire hole doors are fitted. The boiler is lagged with spun glass mattresses.

(j) Valve gear – the Bulleid patent radial valve gear is fitted. The three sets are enclosed in an oil tight casing inside the frames which also encases the middle connecting rod, crosshead and crank. All bearings within this casing are lubricated by a continuous stream of oil pumped by gear pumps from the sump.

It might seem clear that, from the first, the engines were named after the great shipping lines that were so intimately connected with the Southern and its services but it was not so. According to Bradley in *Locomotives of the Southern Railway Part Two* (RCTS 1976) it had been intended that the engines carry British victories of the Second World War. By 1941, sadly, these were not that numerous although a trial plate was made commemorating the sinking of the *Graf Spee*. Later, various capitals of Britain and the Empire were considered but these didn't get anywhere either. It was, Bradley relates, actually the suggestion of the Union Castle Chairman to use merchant shipping lines. Before long someone realised that as everyone was supposed to be in it together the workers ought not to feel left out. 21C1 was already incorporated in the *Southern Magazine* title page but by the time of the third Merchant Navy the engines were being named to mark the (often ultimate) contribution of the merchant seaman keeping the country supplied with food and materials: witness the accompanying illustration.

The first Merchant Navy had three cylinders, one less than the Lord Nelson and thereafter Bulleid departed from most contemporary practice. It is more or less impossible to have a satisfactory Walschaerts motion for an inside cylinder driving the centre axle, whether the valve is set on the top or at the side. (Standard Walschaerts motion could not be accommodated between the frames to drive the second coupled axle because

the leading coupled axle was in the way.) Bulleid did not want divided drive, and he did not want Gresley conjugated gear. He arrived at a separate three-throw crankshaft which allowed all three sets of valve gear to be enclosed in an oil bath, with the projected abolition of the daily preparation time at sheds and less maintenance. He wanted to drive this crankshaft by gears and a propeller shaft as in the rotary-cam poppet valve gears of Caprotti and Lentz but this could not be done because the necessary items were not available – Bulleid doubtless tired of the phrase 'There's a war on'.

So it was that the engines ended up with an enclosed oil bath, as intended, but with *chain driven* valve motion (the aforesaid 'Bulleid patent radial valve gear'). But, however damned the oil bath novelty has become (rightly or wrongly) in retrospect the attractions, *if such a thing could be made to work*, were obvious.

The economics of steam locomotive working were changing rapidly; together with coal quality it was the cost of labour that weighed so heavily against it. Bulleid could, in a way, perhaps be thought prescient in seeking to save the labour of servicing, for the enclosed oil bath would obviate the need for the driver to oil the gear every trip (and save the damage if it were not done properly) at a time of acute labour shortage. It would not be difficult to put a powerful case for the gear, adding up the daily minutes spent oiling and preparing and multiplying it across a

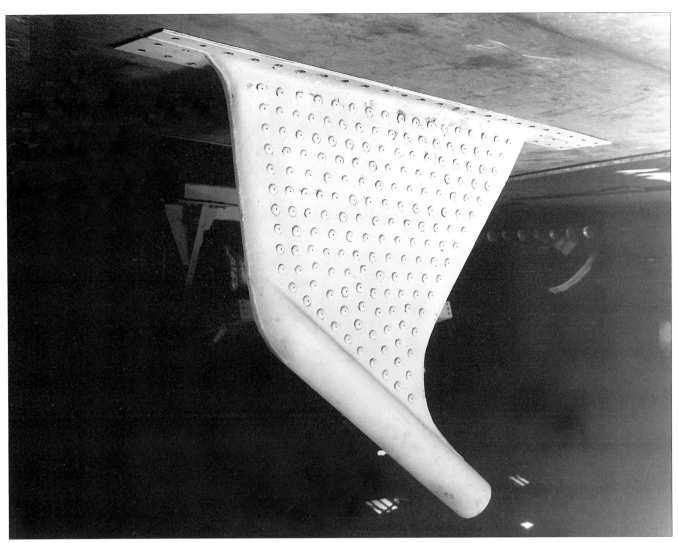

Above. A Nicholson thermic syphon; flattened funnels, they increased the firebox heating surface and supported the brick arch so that it could be higher and therefore give greater air circulation over the fire. They could increase boiler efficiency by up to 10 per cent – at a cost of higher maintenance inevitably. This picture is deliberately reproduced UPSIDE DOWN to show how they sat in the firebox; the long flange attached to the crown sheet and was sufficiently wide to accommodate a row of crown stays. The tube attached to one of those attachments/circular holes seen in the previous boiler view. Through these syphons water circulated back from the body of the boiler through the firebox and back to the boiler via the crown waterspace. You can trace their shape/outline and positioning in the boiler arrangement diagram. Photograph Collection John Fry.

Left. The view into the firebox, between the thermic syphons of 21C4; note the bends in the superheater elements in their flues and the drop plug in down position. The long flange at the top of the thermic syphon, seen previously, is welded to the crown sheet as well as secured by stays. Bulleid used this example to illustrate the ability of his steel firebox design to suffer so little damage following overheating due to low water level. Some 150 roof stays were leaking as a consequence and required recaulking; four superheater flues were leaking and required sealing welds cut away and re-welded. Photograph Collection John Fry.

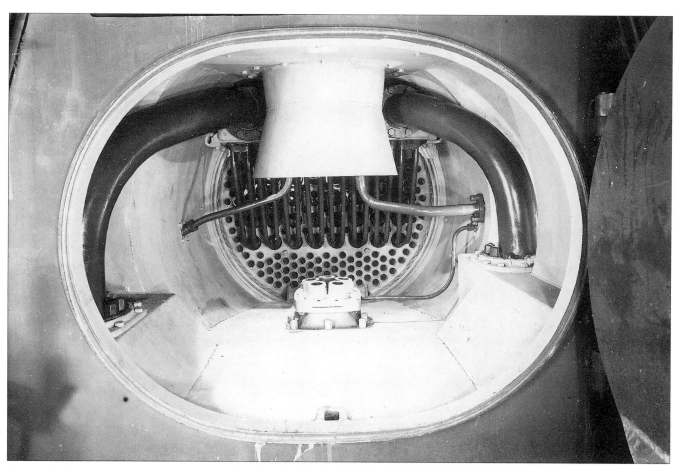

The smokebox interior, painted for the purposes of photography and accordingly in a state of cleanliness it will never acquire again; two of the main steam pipes either side of the petticoat with blastpipe beneath. The much smaller blower pipes enter the petticoat. Photograph Collection John Fry.

Wheeling what is assumed to be CHANNEL PACKET at Eastleigh. No lightening holes in frames... Photograph Collection John Fry.

sizeable fleet of locos, over an entire year. What Bulleid was actually doing, however, was 'writing a long letter on a short piece of paper' and the designs meant to *reduce* labour ended by causing *more* labour than if purely conventional gear had been used. The Bulleid Pacifics are fertile ground for any student of the law of unintended consequences...

Another point to consider when trying to come to a verdict on these brilliant locomotives was the way Bulleid shoe-horned them into a very demanding weight and clearance profile. It must be remembered that they were designed with the Eastern Section boat trains in mind and over there weight and clearance restrictions were formidable. Maximum height above rails was 13ft. 1in. and maximum widths were 9ft. over the cab and 8ft. 10in. across the cylinders. The height of the cab cornice above the rail was 10ft. 11in. As Allen wrote in *British Pacific Locomotives*, 'No other British Pacific design has been subject to such drastic restrictions', and perhaps we should bear it more in mind.

Notable departures were the high pressure 280lb boiler and the welded steel firebox, and the use of thermic syphons. With the unusually high pressure Bulleid was hoping to emulate the sort of superheat limits (400 degrees C) advocated by Chapelon and with the steel firebox he was seeking savings in weight and cost. Eastleigh works, it seems, did not have the wherewithal to construct either of these items, the boilers or the fireboxes; there were certainly delays in getting the designs finally ready and, unpropitiously for Bulleid, drawings were not complete (the work was done at Brighton) until the final weeks of peace. Bulleid had to give the first order, for ten boilers and fireboxes, to an outside contractor, North British, and only on 19 August 1939, perilously late.

It was obviously not a good time to place any major engineering order; war was seen as inevitable, with who knew what horrors in store, from gas to mass bombing, and the Government was increasingly taking hold of industry and transport. It was here, doubtless, that the 'mixed traffic' classification of the engines came in useful – though perhaps we should not make *too* much of this. Remember the LMS could continue to build unashamedly passenger Pacifics despite wartime difficulties, and these included fully streamlined members of the class, awkward to work on in everyday service even in peacetime – see the earlier volume in this series *The Book of the Coronation Pacifics*.

Bulleid desired that the boilers should eventually be built at Eastleigh and according to Brian Reed (*Loco Profile No.22, Merchant Navy Pacifics*, Profile Publications Ltd, 1972) by the summer of 1940 he was pressing for suitable machinery, at a cost of £20,000 or more. Reed rather disapproved of Bulleid's activities and deprecated this sort of expenditure at such a time of national need. They would not be available until May 1941, so in November 1940 another ten Merchant Navy boilers were ordered from North British – an order that was cancelled as Eastleigh acquired the necessary equipment and NBL proved ever more taken up with war work. It is not easy to deliver a verdict on such events all these years on. Government control in wartime might very well be a right and proper thing, but it didn't mean such a system was flawless – indeed it was probably a disruptive disaster in many spheres, especially in the first years. Bulleid, it could be said, triumphed against the odds, getting the engines he needed for his railway – which, after all, was in the Front Line like no other. In any event, the ten boilers ordered from NBL, for the first Merchant Navy Pacifics, eventually left the Hyde Park works and made their way to Eastleigh on specialised LNER wagons, from the end of 1940 to spring the following year.

These first ten boilers had the taper on the underside, on the front ring, with the rear ring parallel. They were riveted in their construction, with the case being welded. Whatever were the subsequent complaints about Bulleid's Pacifics, there was no doubt that the boiler was a truly prodigious steamraiser – 'generally recognised as the best of all Pacific boilers' as H.A.V. Bulleid puts it.

Bulleid felt the copper firebox, with its burden of maintenance, had had its day; welded steel fireboxes after all had been commonplace in the USA for years. The techniques and material (a suitable mild steel amenable to welding) were well tried and copper fireboxes both weighed and cost more than their steel counterparts. (A welded steel firebox saved 1½ tons over a riveted copper box.) X-ray inspection provided a safety insurance.

The fireboxes had two thermic syphons. These improved circulation but Bulleid's main concern, it seems, was a greater safety margin when water was low. Pressure, at 280lb/sq.in. was, after all, very high. (It was this high in order to limit the cylinder size and reciprocating weight in that restricted space below, while keeping the required high tractive effort).

When the news came that the second batch of ten NBL boilers ordered in November 1940 could not be made because of Government requirements, construction was transferred to Eastleigh where, as noted above, suitable equipment had now been made available. Beyer-Peacock once again provided the thermic syphons, work commencing on the ten new boilers in February 1944. Lack of staff and the job of familiarising them with the complicated new techniques delayed completion until the autumn.

The first NBL boilers with the front ring tapering on the underside and the rear ring parallel (again, as noted above) were numbered 1090-1099. Eastleigh's version (1100-1124) had a parallel front and tapered rear ring – representing a further weight saving without reducing the steam surface heating area.

There were in total thirty-five boilers for the class, ten from NBL, thirteen from Eastleigh (1100-1112) with the remainder (1113-1124) built at Brighton.

The original NBL fireboxes all suffered severe cracking in the throatplate, around the thermic syphon connections and around the stay holes in the backplate by the firehole door. It was here that scale tended to build up. Heat was at its fiercest at these points – precisely where the firebox body needed water to circulate the most freely, and it was here, unfortunately, that water circulation was impaired by scale the most. Changing the stays to monel metal (a robust alloy) alleviated the leaking, while the syphons were modified by a separate 'diaphragm', welded around each of the syphon holes.

Untreated feed water, as was comprehensively used with the steel boxes in America, was a principal culprit in the firebox damage and the problems faded when new Eastleigh boxes were substituted, with TIA treatment. Just as deleterious, as had been found in America much earlier, was the washing

---

" Merchant Navy " Class Locomotives
Beyer, Peacock & Co. Ltd.,
Abbey House, Westminster, S.W.1.,
December 28

TO THE EDITOR OF THE RAILWAY GAZETTE

SIR,—With reference to the interesting editorial in your December 21 issue on Mr. Bulleid's " Merchant Navy " class locomotives, there is a small point which we suggest should be corrected in the interests of accuracy.

In the third paragraph the Nicholson thermic syphons with which the engines are fitted are mentioned. These, however (two syphons in each firebox), were made not at Eastleigh, but by Beyer Peacock & Co. Ltd. at Manchester, where X-ray examination was also carried out as a normal routine. Mr. Bulleid mentioned this in his reply to the discussion at the recent meeting of the Institution of Mechanical Engineers.

Incidentally, it might be mentioned that we have manufactured over 400 thermic syphons during the last 15 years and no complaints have ever been received from the overseas railways to which they were supplied.

Yours faithfully,
W. CYRIL WILLIAMS,
Sales Director

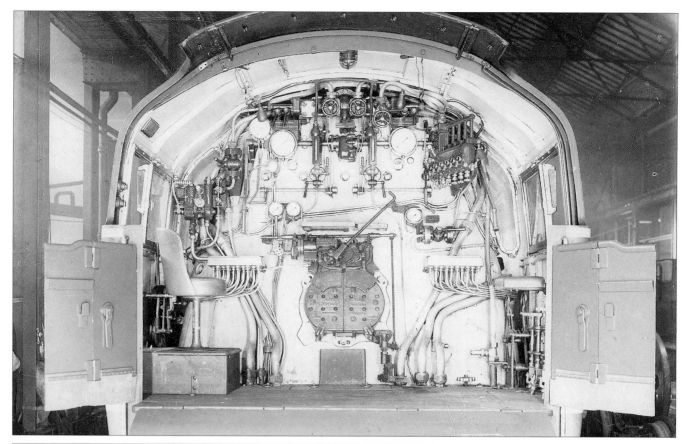

Above. The original cab of CHANNEL PACKET; it was a minor miracle of ergonomics to get all those controls in such an orderly fashion but the view frontwards was never exactly panoramic, even when the modified cabs were adopted. The diesel loco-type drivers seat (left) gave way to a conventional tip-up one; extraordinary features are the commemorative plaque (for the naming ceremony) high up on the left-hand side and light bulbs the glass of which, apparently, only showed ultra violet light. Photograph Collection John Fry.

Left. Main frames laid out at Eastleigh. Photograph Collection John Fry.

Above. Main frames for a Merchant Navy set up at Eastleigh. After the first two were completed, weight reduction was the order of the day, hence the profusion of lightening holes. Note many temporary nuts and bolts as the whole thing is lined up; jig at front as part of the lining up process. The front of the inside steam chest is marked 'No5' which suggests we are looking at the birth of 21C5. This notion is bolstered by the presence of King Arthur 754 – its number is visible through one of the holes. THE GREEN KNIGHT was in Eastleigh for general overhaul from July to October 1941 and CANADIAN PACIFIC was 'to work' on 31 December that year, after several weeks under construction. Photograph John Fry Collection.

Left. Left-hand cylinder of a new Merchant Navy. The flat sided pipe above the steam chest takes exhaust steam to the blastpipe and the round pipework behind carries live steam to the outer ends of the steamchest. The one-piece piston rod and crosshead favoured by Bulleid is clearly seen. Also visible through the frame opening is the rocker arm drive to the piston valve of the inside cylinder. All the cylinders for all the Bulleid Pacifics, Merchant Navy, West Country and Battle of Britain, were cast by Kitsons in Leeds but machined at Eastleigh/Brighton. Photograph John Fry Collection.

Trailing truck of the original locos. It was a large casting which later gave way to a fabricated version. Photograph Collection John Fry.

Stripped to its fibre-glass lagging 21C5 is a thing of monstrous incongruity... This is the driver's side, showing the usually hidden sandboxes. Note too, that splashers *do* exist on an original Bulleid Pacific... Photograph Collection John Fry.

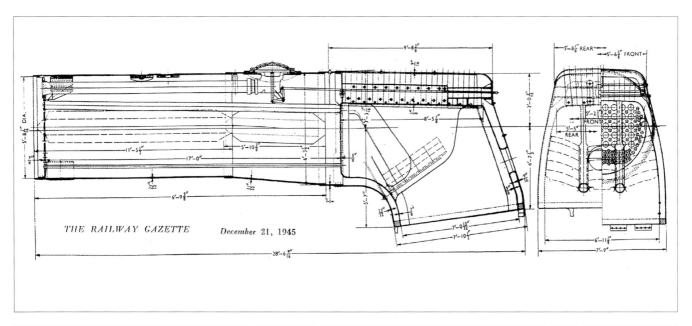

THE RAILWAY GAZETTE   December 21, 1945

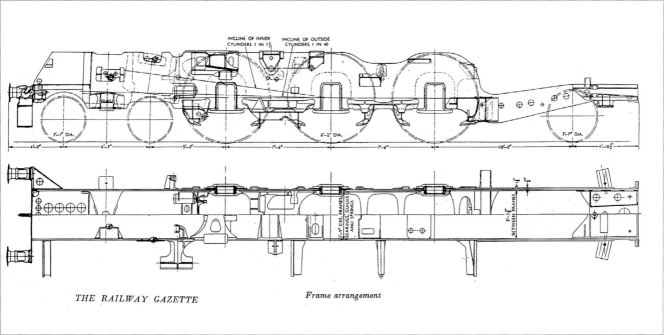

THE RAILWAY GAZETTE   Frame arrangement

out of hot boilers and fireboxes with cold water and the consequent rapid contraction. This, too, without allowing for a proper 'cooling-off period' would also encourage cracking and leaks. Instructions were issued that all locos were to stand for twelve hours before commencing a cold water washout. Firebox life was greatly extended thereafter. Hot water washout, presumably, was the ultimate (American) solution and Bulleid would have been familiar with it from a number of installations on the LNER. He would certainly have thought of it, but no plants seem to have been installed. A couple of elderly locos, a 4-4-0 and an 0-4-2 at Salisbury and Exmouth Junction were provided to supply steam after washouts but these were abandoned after a while as effectively useless.

Bulleid recounted his firebox experiences in *The Railway Gazette* of 21 December 1945 (by which time twenty Merchant Navys were in service): '*Steel fireboxes were said to be unsatisfactory, because of the plates cracking. Copper*

fireboxes, however, are not immune from this trouble. There has been no experience of steel fireboxes in England in recent years, although it was known that firebox steel plate had improved in quality.

'*A special firebox plate manufactured by one steelmaker has been found to be better than anything available previously ... and this new plate is almost free from creep – a great merit. It is readily weldable; and a completely welded inner and outer firebox was a practical possibility, in view of electric welding developments. As riveted joints would be suppressed, there would be no double thickness of metal to cause trouble through overheating and burning away. Moreover, should cracks develop, there would be no difficulty in cutting out the defective piece of plate and welding in a new piece in situ.*

'*The use of steel instead of copper would greatly reduce weight – at least 1½ tons in the present case.*

'*The boilers of the first ten locomotives were built by the North British Locomotive Co. Ltd.;* [here Bulleid acknowledged his

indebtedness to Mr Lorimer and Mr Black of that firm for help in their design and manufacture]. *Subsequent boilers have been produced at Eastleigh. The boiler and firebox are illustrated in Fig 1.* [This is reproduced here.] *All the plates of the outer firebox, comprising back plates, wrapper, throat plate, and tube plate, are also welded together, the top flanges of both syphons being welded to the firebox roof. The inner and outer fireboxes are welded together at the firehole.*

'*For practical reasons the inner firebox has to be inserted through the foundation ring opening, and the shape of the inner firebox has to be checked to ensure that this is possible. All holes in the pressed plates are drilled before assembly. Wrappers are drilled on the flat before bending, as are barrel plates before rolling – an advance in technique which has quickened production considerably. The foundation ring, double-riveted throughout, is welded from four pieces.*'

THE RAILWAY GAZETTE   *July 11, 1941*

Internal and External Transport Link

The introduction of the second of the " Merchant Navy " class of locomotives, the *Union Castle*, which was named by Mr. Robertson F. Gibb at Victoria station on Friday, gave Mr. R. Holland-Martin an opportunity of saying what this new development of the Southern Railway meant in these days of war stress. He was explaining, by way of introducing Mr. Gibb, that some people wondered why his company should spend time on research and the manufacture and introduction of a new type of locomotive in war; but he believed that it was just in such times that every ounce of productive effort should be put forward. After all, as he suggested, Hitler was not abating any of the energies of his productive machines, so why should we? Probably what the Chairman of the Southern Railway Company had at the back of his mind was, not the use to which these new engines could be put in hauling the ocean expresses which cater for the vast Southampton passenger traffic, but their great advantage today when they can be turned to profitable employment as mixed traffic engines for hauling express goods trains whether for imperative war requirements or urgent civilian needs. Thus, again, the policy of long term research for the commerce of peace has been turned to the advantage of a national emergency. It was also a happy augury that—apart from the initial trial engine which, being the Southern Railway's own as it were, the *Channel Packet*, introduced the first of the commercial series—the *Union Castle* links up the railways with the merchant service just as Lord Leathers, who was represented on that occasion by Sir Cyril Hurcomb, has done in the newly co-ordinated Ministry of War Transport.

* * * *

The first ten NBL fireboxes were all condemned at between four and six years' life during 1946 47, at somewhere around 200,000 miles, but with water treatment and washout care the second steel fireboxes fitted to the early boilers and those carried by 1110-1124 lasted the remaining life of the class. After that, boiler or firebox problems hardly ever caused a Merchant Navy to come out of service for repairs. After Nationalisation, the reduction in

working pressure from 280 to 250lb/sq.in. was probably a contributory factor in prolonging their life. 35005, it could be noted, still carries NBL (1095) in preservation.

A 'Packet' Launched
21C1 was first steamed, at Eastleigh, on 17 February 1941, running to Winchester and back the following day. A few days later it worked a ten coach test train to Bournemouth and back. None of this revealed any serious shortcomings it would appear and all was duly ready for its naming ceremony on 10 March 1941. Over the following weeks it worked on various trains but the *Southern Railway Magazine's* comments on its first official outing bearing the name ('it cut through the breeze with superlative ease') proved somewhat hyperbolic. Various faults manifested themselves, including the early embarrassment of the leaking tender tanks. War shortages meant that three sixteenth plate was used and this split when the water surged. The tender ran hot, too, and Bradley records that it was temporarily swapped with the one intended for 21C2, then being built – though this does not show on the record card.

The second Merchant, 21C2 UNION CASTLE, joined 21C1 at Salisbury shed, with the pair employed on heavy goods from there to Eastleigh and Exeter, the traffic having increased to such an extent 'as to demand greater power than was available hitherto'. The 'Packets' were taking heavy 800 ton goods over Honiton bank unaided but passenger traffic had not yet required the use of

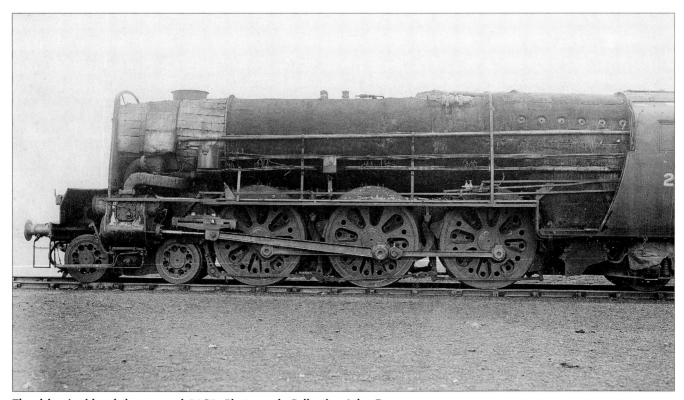
The driver's side of the uncased 21C5. Photograph Collection John Fry.

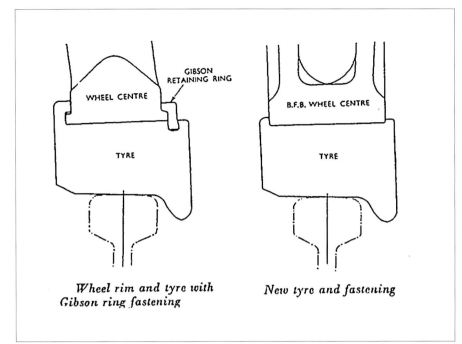

GIBSON RETAINING RING

WHEEL CENTRE

TYRE

B.F.B. WHEEL CENTRE

TYRE

Wheel rim and tyre with Gibson ring fastening

New tyre and fastening

The rest of the 'first batch' of Merchant Navys followed through 1941 and the following year, ending with 21C10 BLUE STAR in July 1942.

Left. **Bulleid found that his new wheels could not be heated up properly on existing equipment and instead of the tyre sitting stationary inside heating shoes it was revolved on a face plate inside stationary gas-fired heating shoes. These diagrams give some idea of the differences.**

the new Pacifics. The cloak was coming off this 'general-service' business, however, and a trial was accordingly devised to demonstrate their ability to handle heavy express trains, a chance for which Bulleid was doubtless itching. Though the War was at its height, incredibly ROYAL MAIL with sixteen *empty* coaches left Waterloo briskly on 9 November 1941 easily attaining maximum permissible speeds everywhere. 21C2 UNION CASTLE took over at Salisbury and put up a similar show, cresting Honiton bank at over 25mph. It was a significant moment: *'This run amply demonstrated the ability of Mr O.V. Bulleid's new engines to handle any traffic likely to be assigned to them. Express trains of so great a weight have not hitherto been worked by one locomotive over the heavily-graded Salisbury-Exeter main line'.*

Below. The first two boilers on their way from North British Hyde Park works at Glasgow to Eastleigh for completion and fixing. They have regulator handles for both driver's and fireman's side – so the latter could close it promptly in an emergency. The fireman's side regulator (it seems only to have gone on the first boiler or two) was later removed. Photograph Collection John Fry.

CHANNEL PACKET taking shape – note the splashers, invisible hereafter and rumoured to be (largely) dispensed with on 21C3-21C10. Photograph Collection John Fry.

21C8, not named as yet, on a train from the West of England at Surbiton in 1942, with LSW stock on the front. Engine is 'as built', with large 'C'; an indifferent photograph but one of exceptional rarity. Photograph Collection E.S. Youldon.

21C8 again, at Salisbury – some onlookers might have thought the Martians had landed. The date is unknown but the period is obviously between its introduction (in black) in June and naming in November 1942 – large 'C' in number.

21C5 CANADIAN PACIFIC in March 1942 as built, in malachite with yellow stripes and, for reasons of good luck, or avoiding bad luck, the 'completed' horseshoe. It was soon in black livery for its naming ceremony.

21C9 SHAW SAVILL with the down Devon Belle at Semley, 30 August 1948. Photograph Reverend Cawston Bequest; Canon B.C. Bailey.

21C8 ORIENT LINE somehow contriving a ship-like look, approaching Surbiton with 'either the 10.50 or 13.00' to Exeter, in the summer of 1946. Photograph Reverend Cawston Bequest; Canon B.C. Bailey.

In its final months of Southern ownership, 20 September 1947, 21C9 SHAW SAVILL is at Salisbury on duty no.473, a down West of England train. 21C9 was based here and would have taken over the train; it did not move shed until after it was rebuilt in 1957. Repainting in malachite green had taken place the year before; it carries the standard smoke deflectors and the tender no.3119 is still in original form. It was modified when 35009 was rebuilt and stayed with the loco all its working life. The central band on the casing reveals that it is composed of the 'limpet' board compressed asbestos material rather than sheet steel – this was a feature of 21C3-21C10 and its purpose was to reduce weight, which it did by about four tons (the cab was made of it too – see 'Losing Weight' at the beginning of Chapter 2). Photo H.C. Casserley courtesy Richard Casserley.

21C1 in awful external condition in Eastleigh works yard on 27 August 1947. It has the first version of the little 'flared out' smoke deflectors and did not lose the giant gun metal plates (barely noticeable under the layered grime) until renumbering by BR. It was about to receive standard size smoke deflectors.

Publicity postcard of the first of the final batch, after running in unfinished livery.

2. The Curate's Egg

Losing Weight

The first two of the class turned out to be heavier than the Civil Engineer liked. This was of course often the case with new locomotives but the two Merchant Navys were too far over to be ignored – they weighed 99½ tons when they should have come out at 92½. Weight saving had to be embarked upon and until the matter was resolved the others of the ten, still in Eastleigh Works, could not be proceeded with. This was a serious situation, and could only be accomplished at great expense. The most rewarding target were the cast steel frame stretchers which could lose

an eighth of an inch without deleterious effect, saving more than a ton in the process. Bulleid was stuck with the stretchers on the first two and could only have a further pattern of lightening holes drilled out, but the castings were refashioned for the next engines in the batch. Enlarging the lightening holes in the frames gained more, or rather less, weight and thinner plating was employed on the casing top, cab sides and smokebox. Lighter frames altogether were made for subsequent engines but the building of 21C3-21C5 was too advanced and these were modified by further holes being cut out.

The king-size number plates were retained on 21C1 and 21C2 until BR renumbering in 1949 and 1950 respectively. The plates for 21C3 had already been cast in fact, and could be found hanging about in Eastleigh Works for twenty years or more. The chimney cover and the top part of the casing around the chimney and in front of it was done away with which had the added advantage of further lifting the exhaust somewhat. It was even said that the wheel splashers under the casing were not fitted but as Winkworth (*Bulleid's Pacifics*) points out, at least one of the batch did in fact have the

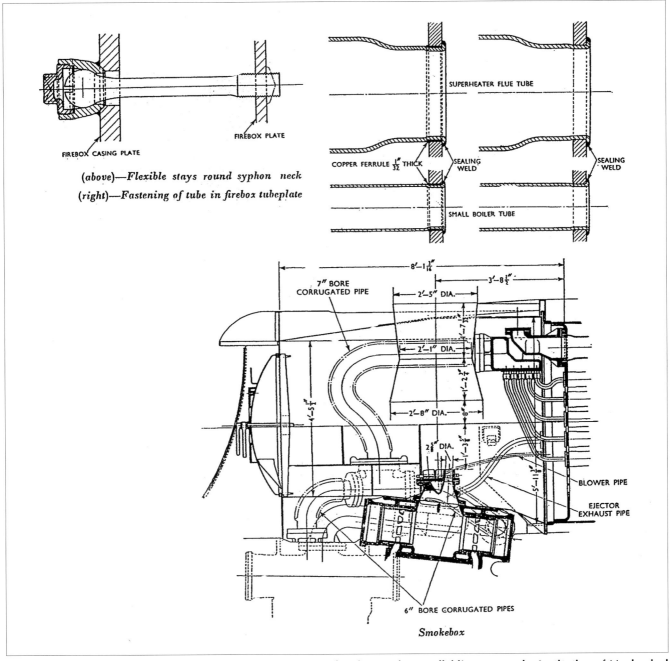

(above)—*Flexible stays round syphon neck*
(right)—*Fastening of tube in firebox tubeplate*

Smokebox

Drawings, from *The Railway Gazette* of 28 December 1945 (taken in turn from Bulleid's paper to the Institution of Mechanical Engineers a fortnight or so before) to show stay and tube details and the smokebox configuration by that time. The smokebox diagram is of interest in showing the new corrugated (and thereby flexible) steampipes adopted by now. Originally they had been cast but were prone to cracking; this new arrangement solved the problem.

The first of the third batch, 35021, under construction in 1948. The fabricated smokebox certainly had 'an irregular shape', as the BR Report into the proposed modification of the class pointed out, in January 1955. Note six washout plugs, clack valves, steam dome, whistle, boiler lagging and the sandbox openings, high up on the side above the lubrication pipe runs. Photograph Collection John Fry.

Later cabs differed from the first efforts; the piping was tidier and these end screens with windows were added.

splashers. Perhaps the most extraordinary outcome (surely unique in British – maybe world – practice) was the resort to a non-metal board for the casing and cab. This 'limpet' board was a pressed asbestos fibre material and was used on the rest of the batch under construction, 21C3-21C10. The cab too was fashioned of the stuff (in all it saved some four tons) and the engines were easily distinguished by a prominent horizontal rib (often covered by the middle yellow line) along the 'waist' of the casing.

Smoke Deflection 1
The air-smoothed casing was supposed to lift air, and with it the exhaust smoke, high and away from the cab but in this function, unfortunately, it failed. On 21C1 the casing was taken up above the level of the chimney rim with an 'air slot' in the smokebox front. It was between the top of the smokebox door and the 'widow's peak' of the casing, making a rectangular cut-out. Aerodynamics have a way of confounding expectations and the 'air slot' and the column of air it was supposed to force through, failed to lift the smoke. 21C2 under construction was accordingly altered with more of the area above the smokebox cut away and

Bogie of 35011.

21C12 UNITED STATES LINES in 1947 near Vauxhall with down West of England express. Note disc code seen throughout this book – one under the chimney with second disc centred over the buffer beam for West of England. The Bournemouth code was one disc over right buffer and second disc on left-hand side of smokebox door. Photograph Reverend Cawston Bequest; Canon B.C. Bailey.

That futuristic cab. A black garbed 21C6 shows the cabside at close quarters to be a panoply of rivet work. Note that the 'C' is slightly larger than the numerals; later it was made standard height. Photograph www.transporttreasury.co.uk

a square hole cut round the chimney. These changes were incorporated in the subsequent eight engines of 1941.

The Curate's Eggs

The 'Ten New Main Line Locomotives' the Southern now had were not proving an immediate success. They were largely used on freights because they were too unreliable for passenger work and the burden of maintenance and servicing was looking ominous. Bradley records that extra fitters had to be drafted in to Salisbury and Exmouth Junction. While work on say, a King Arthur might take an hour, comparable jobs on a Merchant Navy might demand double or treble that. It was as well that the men were available, from sheds in the Kentish Front Line largely closed down.

The engines were new and complicated, parts were sometimes difficult to get and staff and crews were often asked to do too much. Many small failures thus hit the engines' availability. On the road slipping was a problem but then again, this could (in part at least) be attributed to unfamiliarity of handling – as well as on-road oil leaks. There were not that many of the new engines and crews did not get them day in day out. Coal consumption was also high, yet they steamed away 'fit to bust' with the worst wartime dross. They rode beautifully, the cab was a palace (though they were almost *too* comfy in hot weather while working hard) and they were powerful enough to run away with almost anything they were given. This was always the footplate crews' no.1 concern – for plenty of power they

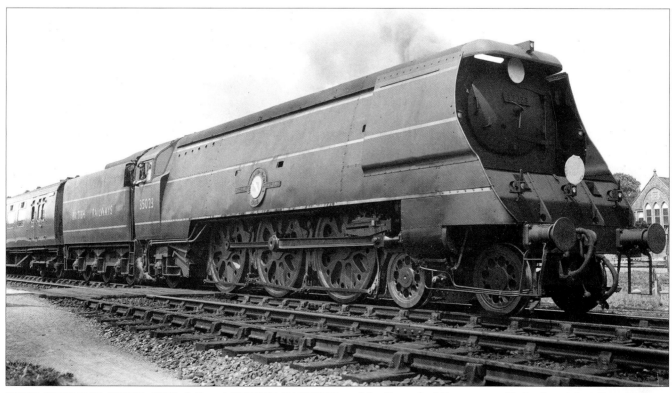

35023 HOLLAND-AFRIKA LINE, lettered BRITISH RAILWAYS and in its malachite green with horizontal yellow lines, at Templecombe about 1949. It went to Exmouth Junction shed and was there until 1960; accordingly it was a familiar engine on the Devon Belle – witness the batten on the smoke deflector for the side wing. Faring in front of cylinder later removed. Photograph W. Hermiston, The Transport Treasury.

The difference a curve makes. 21C10 BLUE STAR had been one of the 'mobile test beds' for smoke clearance trials in 1942-43 and had emerged from Eastleigh with a disastrous arrangement which included a shortened chimney. It was then that recourse was made to the men in white coats at Southampton and the 'cowl' later so familiar on all the Bulleid Pacifics came into being. BLUE STAR was thus the first to get the arrangement; here it is in black livery running into Basingstoke with a down West of England express. The short deflectors are 'flared out' from the casing and not 'bolted on', to use a somewhat laboured vocabulary. The point is, the sweep of the leading edge is as yet uninterrupted.

The difference a curve makes. 21C9 SHAW SAVILL at Semley with 9 a.m. London-West of England in August 1948 now has the 'standard' smoke deflectors fitted to the first ten up to about 1947; the break in curve at the front and the marked difference it makes to the appearance, can be readily appreciated. Photograph Reverend Cawston Bequest; Canon B.C. Bailey.

21C1 CHANNEL PACKET and its small 'flared out' deflectors at Salisbury shed on 26 September 1946. The locos somehow seemed slimmer with the first cab, the curved sided tender and the front end in this 'tight' configuration. Tender no.3111 stayed with 21C1 save for a short period in 1941 when it required axlebox repairs. Cover prominent on trailing truck. Photograph R.C. Riley, www.transporttreasury.co.uk

would forgive a lot. The new engines *were* out of traffic rather too often, it is true, but matters did improve somewhat. By the autumn of 1943 the engines were regularly working expresses out of Waterloo and had entered on a high mileage pattern of passenger trains in-filled with fast freights. They were truly, like the Curate's Egg, 'good in parts', and getting better.

The changed situation had several reasons. Staff grew more adept at fixing things of course and growing familiarity all round meant conditions were less often allowed to become catastrophic. The infamous oil baths had been a thorn in the sheds' flesh from the beginning but little progress was made until a new pattern bath was fitted to 21C6 in 1944. This made for greatly reduced leakage but oil still got out and, worse, water still got in, causing corrosion. Bulleid called it 'continuous flood lubrication'; his idea was that, though the parts were inaccessible the reduced wear and freedom from heating meant that no attention would be needed between General repairs. In this he was wrong.

The practical difficulties of making a leak-proof bath enclosing three sets of valve motion as well as the middle connecting rod slide bar and crankpin, all inside the frames with the complication of relative movement, were immense. Two reversible gear pumps chain driven from the valve crankshaft drew oil from the sump and forced it through discharging pipes over the moving parts. These tended to become clogged with bits of cleaning rag and so on but this too was overcome and in his paper to the Institution of Mechanical Engineers in December 1945, Bulleid claimed: 'Leakage of oil from the sump was considerable at first but this loss has been reduced, and the consumption is now reasonable'. Special (expensive) emulsifying oil also had to be used. Bulleid also claimed that the chain drive 'behaved well' and that none had broken so far. Bradley, however, attributes the mishap and subsequent self-immolation experienced by 21C6 in December 1942 (near Honiton) to a chain parting. Six inch elongations in the chains were said to cause problems later but Bulleid claimed to have more or less 'designed in' a three inch 'sag', and could see no problems in it.

Smoke Deflection 2

Bulleid would have known of the Southampton University wind tunnel laboratory from his LNER days when P2 2 8 2's front end architecture was investigated there. The first modifications to the front ends, in 1941

(*Smoke Deflection 1*) had involved some brief tests with a 1:10 model. These 1941 modifications were not a lasting solution, however, and complaints had continued – 21C6, 21C7 and 21C10 for instance got experimental and apparently valueless deflectors for a while in 1943. So, after drawing up various solutions (reminiscent of A4s and the P2 COCK O' THE NORTH) which never materialised, in 1942-43 Bulleid turned again to the boffins at Southampton. More or less conventional smoke deflectors were found to be the answer but the great departure, which came to characterise the Merchant Navys and the light Pacifics after them, was the making of a cowl, brought forward beyond the smokebox front, to augment the deflectors. The proper lab-approved plates with cowl were applied thus:

21C1	12/43
21C2	6/44
21C3	9/44
21C4	1/44
21C5	3/44
21C6	4/44
21C7	8/44
21C8	6/43
21C9	6/43
21C10	4/43

The deflectors were inconsequential things, 'flared out' from the casing

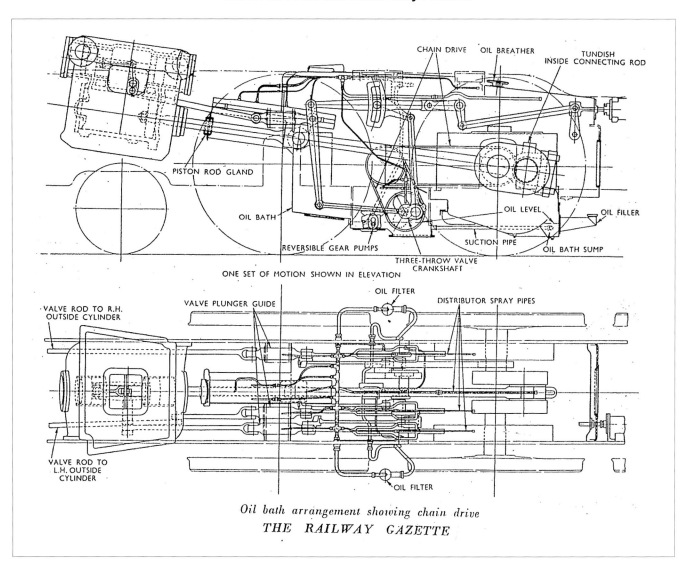

Oil bath arrangement showing chain drive
THE RAILWAY GAZETTE

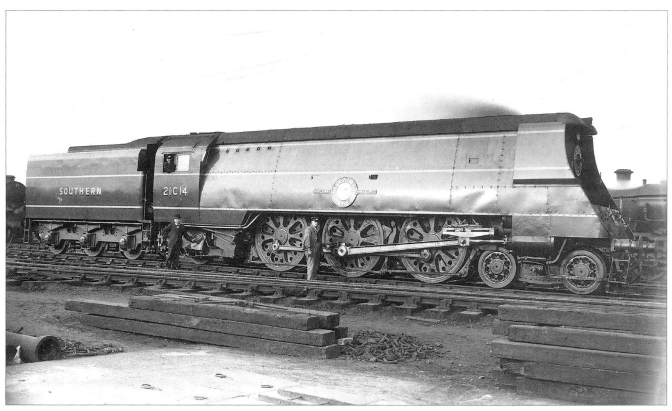

21C14 NEDERLAND LINE in malachite green with short deflectors, with trailing truck cover. The cause of contamination was the ashpan. Photograph Collection E.S. Youldon.

35014 NEDERLAND LINE in SR livery with BR number and smokebox plate. Smoke deflectors lengthened to extend beyond the rear of the cylinders, above the slidebar. The slidebar has one of the ill-fated covers, fitted to combat the sand that inevitably spilled from buckets. These had to be humped up a ladder but the job was not especially more difficult than on 'conventional' engines. It had always been a crude affair in Britain, loading sand but on an original Bulleid it was probably easier than most, in fact. You had to go up the footsteps for most engines, after all, and at least you were spared the hazards of an oily, slippery platform. 'Half' front faring painted black, something that was not common on a malachite green Merchant Navy; the tender is blank. NEDERLAND LINE is as it emerged ex-works from Eastleigh in May 1949, though weathered a bit by now. NEDERLAND LINE is ready, obviously, for the Devon Belle; a Nine Elms engine it is standing at the very end of Salisbury shed yard. This would make it the engine off the down leg, going back to shed for turning and then off again light to Wilton. Strictly speaking, whether it went back to Wilton depended on the day of the week. In 1950 the Devon Belle ran down only on Thursdays, both ways Friday, Saturday, Sunday and Monday and up only on Tuesdays. Photograph W. Hermiston, www.transporttreasury.co.uk.

rather than honest-goodness separate bolted-on plates.

Cabs 1

The Merchant Navys involved a lot of extra work in their operation and maintenance, not least at the sheds. It was ironic, therefore, that labour *saving* was paramount in the designer's mind. The casing too, had labour saving, if not at its heart, then at least it was in the equation, for Bulleid intended (so it is said) that his Pacifics should be able to run through carriage washing plants – no cleaning gangs needed! This was one reason why the first cabs followed the profile of the casing so intimately. They were streets ahead of anything else in comfort, except that at times in summer when the fireman was hard at it they could feel over-warm. Ultra violet lamps provided a glimmer for certain controls during night-time.

Cabs 2

Cabs on the second batch were similar in appearance though the curve and the window edge at the front was slightly different, the layout of rivets varied and back sheets were provided to make the seats either side cosier, shielding them from cross draughts. Yet the sliver of cab front that was possible within the

loading profile was just that, a sliver, and the space available for the window was desperately small. The outlook from the cab, or rather lack of it, was accordingly a perennial cause of complaint. To give a broader window within the profile a 'wedge' or 'V' cab provided an answer; these were appearing on some light Pacifics in August 1947 so one was put on a Merchant Navy, 21C8 ORIENT LINE at the same time – it was unique, in a 'V' shape, and led the way to the final style. It was this type of cab, with three side windows, that afterwards became familiar on all the Bulleid Pacifics. The third batch, 35021-35030, got these cabs from new. The dates are as follows, taken from Winkworth's *Bulleid's Pacifics* (21C8 had got two windows at first; three were provided from 7/49):

21C1-35001	12/50
21C2-35002	1/54
21C3-35003	5/50
21C4-35004	10/50
21C5-35005	2/50
21C6-35006	3/51
21C7-35007	3/50
21C8-35008	8/47
21C9-35009	2/53
21C10-35010	11/49
21C11-35011	9/50
21C12-35012	3/49
21C13-35013	12/52
21C14-35014	5/49
21C15-35015	6/49
21C16-35016	6/49
21C17-35017	4/48
21C18-35018	5/48
21C19-35019	4/48
21C20-35020	5/48

Windows

The Merchant Navys, of course, couldn't even have the same windows. Put briefly, the first two and the last ten had gun metal frames, the other eighteen had wooden ones. There was nearly uniformity in the number of windows, however – all had three apart from one exception (naturally) which had only two. This was 21C8 – and the feature is clear in photographs taken before July 1949.

Valancing

Associated with changes in the curvature of the fronts, the smoke deflectors and so on, and the general passage of time, the curved (distinctly bulbous on 21C1 and 21C11) valancing between the front of the cylinders and the buffer beam gradually disappeared, as on the LNER A4s. They didn't really do much and were a nuisance to get off when work had to be done. This area, between

Sand and sides on different engines. Note all the differences just in this small area of casing; it was always on and off and probably rarely went back *exactly* the same. Hence the wide range of edging, rivets, cuts, dents, patches and plates, not to say the precise position of the plate with respect to the principal joins. The sand filler rectangular slides indicate which side of the loco we are looking at – the rearmost one is above/beyond the NAVY CLASS of the plate on the left-hand side and above/beyond the MERCHANT part on the right-hand side. The Merchant Navys had steam sanding but on 21C1-21C10 at first it was only available to the front of the middle coupled wheels. The sand boxes were filled from these points high on the side, with the fireman clambering up a ladder. The inevitable spillage was the reason the slidebar covers were eventually tried out. On 21C1-21C10 the single sand hole was forward of the nameplate. Later, sanding had to be applied to all coupled wheels and a second sanding hole was made, as here to the rear of the plate, and a third for the front wheels even higher and close up by the smokebox. Sanding thereafter was to the front of each coupled wheel. The second batch and the final series had the same arrangement. The sliding covers jammed and were often left open but there was a further lid (visible for once on BLUE STAR) inside on the delivery pipe, a hinged cover which fell forward (partly visible on HOLLAND-AFRIKA LINE) when opened to project through the sliding outer cover. This sliding cover by the way doesn't slide in the same direction on all engines, or even on the same engine! One oddity was the sanding to the leading tender wheel. Gravity sanding on the front of the tender prevented tender wheels from 'picking up' in poor adhesion conditions. 'Picking up' occurred when braking caused wheels to lock up and skid. This could happen when rails were wet and the tender relatively light, with coal and water low perhaps. One thing the arrangement was not, whatever has been written, was a method of sand delivery for rearward running. When rebuilt, the engines got three conventional sandboxes, overcoming the problem of tender first running by having delivery pipes to the front of the leading coupled wheel and to either side of the middle coupled wheel. Look again at BLUE FUNNEL *LINE*... The plate was thus when the locomotive was named at Waterloo on 17 April 1945. It was soon replaced by a plate where CERTUM PETE FINEM took the place of LINE. See the section on the loco itself.

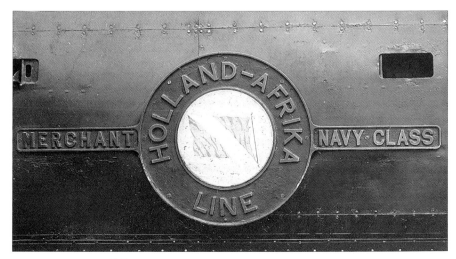

The traditional view from the down platform at Bournemouth Central, looking across the running lines to the shed. Black 21C17 is in the year of its building, 1945, with the small smoke deflectors. Later that year, on 22 October, it will be named BELGIAN MARINE, by which time it will carry malachite green.

There was no better way of picking out the break of curve as the smoke deflectors met the sweep of the casing than to paint it white. This has conveniently been done for us on blue-liveried Royal engine 35019 FRENCH LINE CGT, working to Sherborne and passing Vauxhall on 1 June 1950. According to *The Railway Observer*, this was the visit of the King and Queen to Sherborne School, 'probably the longest non-stop ever recorded on Southern metals … 118.2 miles between Waterloo and Sherborne'. Photograph K.G. Carr.

The short deflectors still on 21C12 UNITED STATES LINE, the first Southern engine to get a coat of malachite green, near the end of the War in April 1945. It still has the original cab, and two side windows. The two feed pipes run from the injectors forward and under the casing to the clack valves. On the rebuilt engines of course, these pipe runs and the clacks were visible at their extremities, though they remained hidden by the footplating in between. It's interesting to note the flexible linkages to the injector, running straight up to the controls under the fireman's seat – see next. From mid-1942, in fact, all Southern repaints were in black, until 1945. That year, malachite green was applied to the Merchant Navys beginning with 21C12, West Countrys from new, a solitary H2 Atlantic 2423 for a special boat train promotion and a handful of Island O2 0-4-4Ts. From early 1946 a whole range of Southern locos started to appear in malachite – but that's another story... Photograph Collection E.S. Youldon.

And there are the injector controls, under the Spartan seat provided for the fireman – in this case on 35028 CLAN LINE. Photograph collection John Fry

35007 ABERDEEN COMMONWEALTH, always a great favourite for the Devon Belle down to Exeter, at Exmouth Junction shed (there was an eyesight testing signal on that water tower – surely the tallest at any shed) in June 1949, after working down from Wilton with the train. It is in early post-Nationalisation garb and the three sand filling holes are shown to good effect – also the similar opening (there was another the other side) which was a 'mudhole door' for washing out, at the base of the firebox. The tender is 3114, an original 5,000 gallon one with the high 'rave' and still with blackout slides on the front. Photograph W. Hermiston, www.transporttreasury.co.uk.

21C10 BLUE STAR in open country somewhere near Semley, 24 August 1948, on the down Devon Belle; no indication yet of any change of ownership. Notice the peek-a-boo hole for the centre lamp under THE in the front board, commented upon elsewhere; this in fact was a bit of a puzzle, for the Devon Belle rosters never involved running after dark! Photograph Reverend Cawston Bequest; Canon B.C. Bailey.

The curious bulbous front end faring as applied to 21C11 GENERAL STEAM NAVIGATION. It had been cut back by half (by 1948) and then disappeared entirely. It is still in its original wartime black; cover prominent on trailing truck.

21C2 with its cowl and smoke deflector arrangement, climbing Honiton bank. Very dirty post-war condition, with faded malachite and stripes and gunmetal plates still on front, cab and tender. In fact it kept the metal plates until January 1950 by which time its livery was truly deplorable. Eastleigh was touchingly reluctant to dispose of the plates – the engine even survived a works visit in September 1949 without getting renumbered! Photograph W. Hermiston, www.transport treasury.co.uk

of the cylinders and the buffer beam, was fully enclosed on the first one and more or less enclosed on the subsequent nine of the first batch. The second batch were somewhat similar except for 21C11 which was a kind of throwback, cursed with a hideously bulbous arrangement which looked like an early experiment in fibre glass moulding gone wrong. The third batch were somewhat similar to the previous engines, 21C12-21C20. The bulbous lower casing on 21C1 and 21C11 were removed in late SR days. All 140 Pacifics commencing in 1952 had the fairing removed between cylinder and buffer beam. All these had been removed by 1954. Their good looks suffered because of it but the reasons were sound; it was for access as well as considerations of safety, for it was found that when a man stepped down from the smokebox the curved part of the fairing immediately above the buffer beam could trap a boot heel.

Ten More – The Second Batch

Whatever the problems, the sheds were getting on top of them by 1944 and it was clear that when working well, the Merchant Navys were capable of anything. The order for ten more boilers, additional to the original ten had been in at North British since 1940 but by now the new machinery was installed at Eastleigh (see the previous section) so that production could be done there instead of Glasgow. There were some difficulties at first, for some of the techniques were new but 21C11, the first of the second batch, was ready at the very end of 1944, on 31 December that year. Thinner frames than those on 21C1 21C10 were used, to lessen weight, along with a thinner (this time metal – the 'limpet' board could be devastated by the slightest shed yard collision) casing. Further weight was saved by altering the disposition of the boiler barrel; this time the front ring was parallel where before it had been tapered. The taper from now on was taken up on the rear ring, at the bottom – see the first section, *Ten New Main Line Locomotives*.

Smoke Deflection 3

The second ten engines, 21C11-21C20 had the cowl and smoke deflectors which had been so painfully arrived at for the first ten, though naturally they varied somewhat. The first ten, as described, 'flared out' from the casing as it were leaving the leading edge of the casing uninterrupted. On the second ten the plates were more obviously bolted on, as distinct attachments and from the front this was evident from the break of curve. The deflector plates on 21C11-21C20 were short at first, extending no farther back than the rear of the cylinders.

The Last Ten – The Third and Final 'BR' Batch

The concentration of work at Eastleigh, which had occurred for the building of the second batch was now reversed, due to the post-war dislocation of staff and equipment. The cylinders and frames were to be built at Ashford, boilers and tenders at Brighton and the rest of the bits provided by Eastleigh, which would assemble the locomotives. The orders were put in place in 1947, before Nationalisation, but the first engine was not ready for a year or more, such were the difficulties with materials and parts. So it was that the last ten bore BR numbers from the first, 35021 to 35030, going out from September 1948 to April 1949.

Smoke Deflection 4

In May 1946 21C18 received a short extension rearwards to its smoke deflectors but the real solution was a much larger deflector, both in length and depth. The curious super-elongation of the plates on 35020 BIBBY LINE* aside, the existing twenty locos got the new, better proportioned bolted-on plates between October 1946 and August 1947. There was a degree of urgency here because the large deflectors were required in any case for the Devon Belle wingplates (the Pullman was to be introduced for the summer of 1947). To hasten the programme of fitting, some deflectors were sent to sheds for attachment, resulting in some engines running for a few days with their plates in undercoat. The last batch, 35021-35030, got the final design of smoke deflector from new; it was this version that came to characterise the class until they were rebuilt.

*35020 BIBBY LINE was standby engine for the 1948 trials, and the long deflectors were related to its possible 'foreign' employment, although 35017 and 35019 on the trials retained normal deflectors. The light Pacifics that went far and wide (34004, 34005 and 34006) were, however, all given long deflectors.

The last Merchant Navy emerged from Eastleigh in 1949. The next year 35030 ELDER DEMPSTER LINES, in sparkling blue, was back at Eastleigh with nameplate covered up in readiness for the ceremony at Southampton Docks three days later, on 5 June 1950.

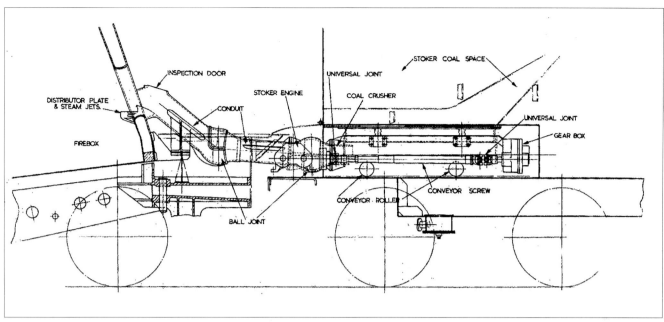

21C5 (it was actually s21C5 by now) CANADIAN PACIFIC as newly fitted (right) with the Berkeley stoker; the drawing above shows the various connections. See also 'Locomotive Test Report' page 44. Photograph collection John Fry.

Mechanical Stoker

Bulleid wanted to try out a mechanical stoker on one of the Merchant Navys almost from the first, announcing in *The Railway Gazette* that 'adequate steam raising in a locomotive boiler under all conditions can be assured *only* [authors emphasis] by fitting a mechanical stoker'. War conditions prevented him acquiring the necessary equipment and it was not until October 1947 that the Southern Railway took delivery of a reconditioned Berkley mechanical stoker – the firm was the one that later provided stokers for the BR 9Fs. 'It was not one of the best-known American stokers' writes Reed in the *Loco Profile* 'but it happened to have a representative in England'. On taking delivery the chosen recipient was 21C17 but when Eastleigh Works attempted assembly of the reconditioned stoker, parts were found to be missing so work was postponed a few months. It was March 1948 before it could be fitted, to 21C5 (S prefix added the same month and renumbered 35005 the next month) at Eastleigh Works. The equipment involved minor rearrangements on the tender for a coal pusher; this got the coal forward to the screw and up to a distributor plate. From here was put about the firebox by steam jets. Coal of a fairly uniform size was necessary and the front of the screw was effectively a coal crusher. One is inclined to suspect that the dust and effort, curses and sometimes danger associated with the thing, together with its 'new-fangled' character (crews after all only came into contact with it intermittently) probably doomed it whatever happened. Before

35013 BLUE FUNNEL after its BR renumbering of 1948; BRITISH RAILWAYS on tender. Photograph Reverend Cawston Bequest; Canon B.C. Bailey.

LOCOMOTIVE TEST REPORT.
The Railway Executive, Locomotive Testing Committee.
Report on SR MN class locomotive no.35005, fitted with a 'Berkley' Mechanical Stoker.
Much-condensed Report no.M3 issued 25 August, 1950.

The 'Berkley' mechanical stoker has 16 steam jets, each three sixteenths of an inch in diameter, six feeding the right hand side and six the left-hand side of the grate working at 8-20lb psi. Two feed each back corner at 60-80lb psi, the pressure being regulated by hand valves. The stoker engine has two cylinders, 5in. diameter X 5in. stroke working normally at 15-40lb psi.

   Prior to the test 35005 was in Eastleigh Works and then in service for about two weeks. Two types of coal were used, Barnboro No.6 and Langwith Cobbles. The Mobile Testing Plant consisted of the Dynamometer Car and two or three braking units as required. The tender was temporarily fitted with coal partitions, a water meter, telephone etc and the locomotive had pyrometer or resistance thermometer elements in the firebox combustion chamber.

        Tests were carried out between Wimbledon and Salisbury with the engine and train working out of Stewarts Lane engine shed.

Conclusion.

From these results it is concluded that for normal English conditions of firing with typical grades of coal the mechanical stoker is less efficient in working than hand firing though the difference is less marked when using poor quality coal. No difficulty was experienced in maintaining with hand firing the maximum supply of steam demanded by the engine in normal circumstances. While the boiler efficiency was good, the efficiency of the engine was found to be variable and its working during the tests was irregular which has been traced to irregularity of motion of the valve mechanism.

that, a surprisingly extensive series of trials were made from Eastleigh shed, conveniently close to the works. It certainly sounded more or less perfect when described in the press: '*A particular advantage of the stoker is that it can adequately deal with varying types of fuel; it crushes the coal, without producing an undesirable amount of dust, to a size easily dispersed by the steam jets over the whole length and width of the grate. It is capable of handling slack coal in wet or dry condition, as well as the hardest run of mine coal*'.

After some further works attention 35005 went to Nine Elms, running nearly 60,000 miles with the mechanical stoker before finding itself back at Eastleigh for a Heavy Intermediate. It then went to Rugby for evaluation on the Testing Plant, running road trips on the LMR with the mobile test unit. This was also taken on to the Southern, running trips between Stewarts Lane and Salisbury. These tests finished on 4 April 1950.

   The stoker was taken out at Eastleigh to compare conditions with the engine fired conventionally – *Trains Illustrated* of July 1950 pointing out that it might be more appreciated on an LMR or the ER Garratt where 'its robot activity would be vastly appreciated by the engine crews'. The SR would not give up and after further modification the

stoker was installed yet again on 35005, in June 1950. Once again 35005 worked from Nine Elms, mainly on the Bournemouth line but a more than usually destructive chain gear failure three months later saw it hauled back dead to Eastleigh, in October 1950. Undeterred, the SR added LMR-style self cleaning equipment in the smokebox and prepared the engine for yet more stoker trials. These finally petered out in April 1951, 35005 having run 77,738 miles with

the stoker in place. Apart from the vast quantities of coal burnt and the inordinate volumes of smoke belched out nothing about the episode was especially notable. Leaving Eastleigh on 27 April 1951 35005 was at last free of the equipment and returned to Exmouth Junction. The tender (3115) was converted back to the standard first series form though when 35005 was rebuilt in May 1959 it was rebodied with a 5,250 gallon tank.

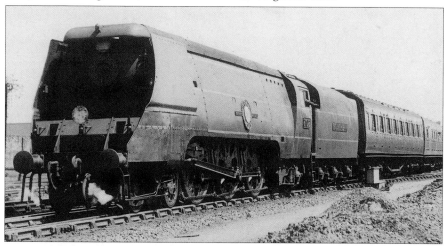

21C2 UNION CASTLE leaving Salisbury for Exeter with the 12.50pm from Waterloo on 21 May 1947. The smoke deflectors are in unlined undercoat and almost certainly were sent out from Eastleigh to Exmouth Junction for fitting. The Pacific had to be back in traffic as soon as possible and painting could wait a few days until it was in for washout or otherwise stopped.

Front fairing now standard. 35011 GENERAL STEAM NAVIGATION with the Bournemouth Belle on 20 May 1949, at Byfleet. Photograph Reverend Cawston Bequest; Canon B.C. Bailey.

Smoke deflectors taken to the limit. These uniquely lengthy plates, fitted (to 35020 only) in 1948 in connection with the forthcoming Exchange Trials, certainly lifted smoke even more effectively than previous plates, but they obstructed forward vision, and were not proceeded with on other Merchant Navys. They covered up, of course, the forward sander and though a sliding hatch was made in the plates themselves, these were eventually abandoned as too awkward and were simply removed and the access plated over so they could not be used again. The position can just be discerned by that rectangular outline in this photograph. BIBBY LINE (at Nine Elms in July 1953) was thus the only Merchant Navy so fitted and kept them until rebuilding. The tender was modified as shown after the Crewkerne accident. Cab lining has been modified to suit the panelled tender. Photograph www.transporttreasury.co.uk

Study in injectors on BROCKLEBANK LINE, Nine Elms, 1952. Note linkages to injector controls in the cab. The two feed pipes run from the injectors forward and under the casing to the clack valves. On the rebuilt engines of course, these pipe runs and the clacks were visible at their extremities, though they remained hidden by the footplating in between. Photograph Collection Alec Swain, www.transporttreasury.co.uk

The first twenty Merchant Navys had this cast steel form of trailing truck with its characteristic arched casting, covered at first by asbestos cloth (some say canvas or leather, some Rexene!) sheeting which was generally abandoned as useless after the War. Ash, ominously, has been trickling onto the main casting... Photograph www.transporttreasury.co.uk

21C11 GENERAL STEAM NAVIGATION in black at Nine Elms in 1946. One-piece crosshead and piston rod, later developed into two separate, cottered components. Mechanical linkage for drain cocks is clear to see, along with part of the bulbous extra casing ahead of the cylinders. Note also forward sand filler hole and front sand pipes. Photograph Collection Alec Swain, The Transport Treasury.

Above and below. On the last series, for reasons of weight saving, this fabricated version of the cast trailing truck was substituted – the most obvious change in appearance was the loss of the 'arched' look. Subsequently the two types were mixed willy-nilly at Eastleigh, the early cast versions appearing randomly on 35021-35030, and the later fabricated ones on the earlier twenty, 35001-35020. The ashpan was in three sections, one between the frames, the other two outside; note the dampers either side, fitted from new on the third series and opened from the cab, on 35025 BROCKLEBANK LINE, at Nine Elms in 1952. At the bottom of the ashpan is the curved 'self cleaning' hopper door operated from rail level, using a handle a bit like a hefty broomstick – accidents sometimes occurred resulting in this door welding itself to the third rail! 'Small additional cleaning doors at the back' (according to Bulleid's paper to the Institution of Mechanical Engineers in 1946) 'enabled any ash accumulation at the rear to be dislodged'. That's the dynamo behind the trailing truck under the cab rear, a 24V Stone's generator. Photographs transporttreasury.co.uk

35019 FRENCH LINE CGT with LMS tender 10219 sweeps past the Great Western engine shed at Reading with an up test train from the west of England on one of the Plymouth workings at the end of April 1948, GW dynamometer car in tow. The SR engines involved in the trials got Flaman speed recorders – indicated by the bracket by the rear driving wheel.

3. Testing Times

Locomotive Exchanges 1948

These Exchanges have been exhaustively 'gone over' down through the years but, hoping not to repeat too much, they remain very much part of the Merchant Navy story. Their purpose was to determine 'the most desirable features to incorporate in the design of future steam locomotives' though it is doubtful whether the times and place of the trials could ever really have provided for this. Ordinary service trains on lines often badly affected by post-war deficiencies, driven to no discernible common pattern hardly provided incontestable data.

The steam locomotives used came direct from traffic, normally having run between 15-20,000 miles since their last General Repair and besides this 'on the road' testing it was intended that they should be run at the Swindon and Rugby Testing Plants too – which took some years and became increasingly irrelevant as the BR Standard series was established.

The Merchant Navys involved in the trials were 35017, 35018 and 35019 with 35020 as a spare engine, running on test (there was a week's preliminary running before each week of tests) with dynamometer car as follows:-

35019 on the 1.30pm Paddington-Plymouth North Road on 27 and 29 April; balanced workings were the 8.30am Plymouth North Road-Paddington, 28 and 30. 35017 on the 1.10pm Kings Cross-Leeds on 25 and 27 May; balanced workings were the 7.50am Leeds-Kings Cross on 26 and 28 May. This engine also worked the 10am Euston-Carlisle on 11 and 13 May; balanced workings were the 12.55pm Carlisle-Euston on 12 and 14 May.

35018 was used on its home Region, on the 10.50am Waterloo-Exeter Central on 1 and 3 June; balanced workings were the 12.37pm Exeter Central to Waterloo on 2 and 4 June – both trains, in fact, were the 'Atlantic Coast Express'.

Predictably, at several times with good rail conditions, partial slipping for considerable distances was recorded with the Merchant Navys and, in one instance with a light Pacific. 35019 in one incident slipped for 2¼ miles on Rattery Bank between Totnes and Wrangaton in Devon. They worked with somewhat different cut-offs and so on while on the various main lines and, characteristically, steamed freely and well. On the Paddington-Plymouth run for instance 35019 ran away with itself, the safety valves lifting on Hemerdon Bank at 270lb. And of course they rode well, as would be expected.

There were minor faults experienced, of precisely the niggling type which kept their availability low at home on the Southern. On 27 April 35019 had three fusible plugs leaking at the threads at Plymouth and on 28 April firebox stays below the firehole door were blowing badly. On 25 May 35017 had to have attention to the non-return valves; the cylinder lubrication was

35019 FRENCH LINE CGT at Wakefield on a pre-test run (no dynamometer car, note). It worked on Whit Monday 17 May 1948 and returned from Leeds the next day, failing, according to *The Railway Observer* 'with a blowhole in a thermic syphon'.

35019 with its incongruous black Stanier tender at Eastleigh; there is no date but it looks a bit careworn, so presumably it is after arrival back on home ground. Modified cab and a Flaman speed recorder.

35019 at Paddington waiting with the 1.30pm to Plymouth North Road on 19 April 1948. Various bemused observers gaze at the strange apparition. Photograph J.C. Flemons, www.transporttreasury.co.uk

'playing up' and (an old one this) the steam reversing gear was causing trouble, owing to the cut-off position not being held.

The SR crews could hardly expect to be expert in the use of water scoops (but what was the Inspector doing?) and on 11 May the pick up gear on the LMR tender attached to 35017 took a whack, which meant an extra water stop at Lancaster. Two days later, after the Euston-Carlisle run, four stays were found leaking in the firebox, two of them blowing badly and repairs were effected. There were other minor ailments, particularly to do with lubrication and, however much the Exchange Trials fell short of a stern analysis upon which to build a Standard fleet, they did, almost perfectly, show up the strengths and weaknesses of the Merchant Navy design. Strong, free steaming, beautifully riding and at times brilliant engines, brought low by too many elementary defects and a high coal/water consumption.

The Southern engines (the Merchant Navys and the light Pacifics) in fact did rather better than the framework of the Exchange Trials allowed. Winkworth (*Bulleid's Pacifics*) makes the telling point for instance, that the SR engines were among the best in keeping to the timetables, which is arguably a more desirable state of affairs (for the passenger) than arriving twenty

minutes late having saved a bit of coal on the way. The Southern engines seemed to have been run 'flat out' to give good times and high power outputs, and coal and water per mile would necessarily have been on the high side; moreover, SR engines figured in the highest power output figures out of all proportion to their numbers. Other Pacifics were quite capable of reaching these levels and the significance of the figures is their indication of differing ways of driving. If the others had ran 'flat out' the consumption figures might have been more comparable.

BR Performance and Efficiency Tests March 1952-January 1954

No one was really happy with the outcome of the 1948 Exchanges and in the ensuing years the availability of the new Rugby Test Plant meant that a more studied and objective appreciation could be made of the capabilities of the various types. The value of all this work had to be doubted at least slightly, given that by now the future course of the BR Standard fleet was more or less set. However, 35022 HOLLAND AMERICA LINE was selected for a number of tests, both stationary and on the road, which took place between March 1952 and January 1954; the results were published in British Transport Commission British Railways

Bulletin No.10, *Performance & Efficiency Tests of Southern Region 'Merchant Navy' class 3 cylinder 4-6-2 mixed traffic locomotive*. The Bulletin was prepared by the Rugby and Derby testing staff and was published in January 1954 at the splendid price of ten shillings. HOLLAND AMERICA LINE was a high mileage loco which was unusual for this programme of tests. Maybe the SR thought the results would have no tangible effect whatever the outcome and pragmatism dictated that an engine was sent that would be missed least; re-building, even scrapping was in the air and maybe it was not in the Region's interest for the engine to do well at all… The Test Bulletin preferred to put it another way: 'The engine was prepared for testing during a classified repair and ran 1,115 miles in traffic before commencement of the tests. During the first series of plant tests it ran 10,300 miles and 3,840 miles on the road'.

There were three main elements to the testing, all using 35022 HOLLAND AMERICA LINE, as follows.

The first (main) set of tests, running the locomotive 'on the rollers' and out on the road between March and October-November 1952.

A second set examining a configuration of single blastpipe on the SR.

35017 BELGIAN MARINE heads up Holloway Bank on test in the Exchange Trials – destination Leeds. Cecil J. Allen wrote of one climb with the SR engine from Grantham to Stoke Summit in *The Locomotive Exchanges 1870-1948* (Ian Allan 1949) declaring that he could not find any record of a start with a comparably loaded LNER Pacific 'quite as fast as this'. Photograph Collection E.S. Youldon.

35019 FRENCH LINE CGT shows its paces with the Western Region dynamometer car at Bruton, the gangers more taken with the cameraman than this other stranger in their midst. Photograph Collection E.S. Youldon.

BIBBY LINE was the spare for the Locomotive Exchanges and though it stayed at home had to be fitted out for work in the event of failure among the other three (35018 on the home Region, 35017 on the East and West coast routes and 35019 on the WR). It thus ran like this equipped with speed recorder and Stanier tender. In the event it was not needed. These enormous smoke deflectors were also fitted for the Exchanges; BIBBY LINE was the only one so equipped so it was slightly odd that it was the only one not in fact used. As is obvious, the deflectors obscured the leading sand filler, so another 'sliding hatch' had to be cut in the new plates; it wasn't a particularly perfectionist job and the join of the new plate with the old is quite clear!

BIBBY LINE, of course, more than made up for the anonymity of the Locomotive Exchanges by fracturing its axle at Crewkerne, as these familiar pictures record. Quite what left the engine (it was doing 70-80mph) to half demolish the canopy of Crewkerne station does not seem to be recorded, though it was almost certainly chunks of brake gear, and this was the scene afterwards. To this day, the steel uprights that replaced the demolished cast iron round columns can be identified. It was the felling of the columns that brought the roof down. The centre driving wheel, leaning drunkenly when the loco came to rest, had been held more or less in line by the motion which, though it buckled and bent, thankfully held at the last.

A third set running the engine with a firebox without thermic syphons.

First Set of Tests – Rugby Stationary Plant and on the Road

The first part of the tests, on the plant rollers, took place from March 1952 with the engine deemed to be in its 'as designed' state. Tests, it was hoped, would 'define the relationship between coal as fired and water as drawn from the tender, tractive effort and horsepower, both as available at the tender drawbar'. This saw the use of three different coals – South Kirkby, a grade 1A hard coal from South Yorkshire, Blidworth, a grade 2B hard from the East Midlands and Bedwas, a grade 2A soft coal from South Wales. This last was friable with a lot of dust and regarded as more closely similar to that normally used for the Bulleid Pacifics.

Working of the locomotive was in two distinctive ways:
1) with relatively short cut-offs and fully or nearly fully open regulator and
2) at relatively long cut-off and partially open regulator.

The Merchant Navy was not going to give up its secrets easily; the locomotive proved difficult to test owing to inconsistent performances and it was thus impossible to obtain reasonable accuracy or repetition on different occasions, for performance would sometimes change appreciably over quite short periods of time. 'Accurate measurement was exceptionally difficult, especially on the stationary test plant'. 'Phenomena of a kind known to be characteristic of this class' were found which 'may vary from one engine to another and from time to time'. The reason was the valve gear and its unfathomable behaviour inside that bath.

Cut-off relationships could not be definitely established for reversing gear and cylinders and results were downgraded to 'general representations'. On one day tests made a recorded pull at 15mph that was double that of the day before and at 20mph more than half as large again! The cut-off changed apparently of its own volition and in some cases the indicated cut-off could not be relied upon to be correct, for power outputs that were theoretically impossible for particular cut-offs were recorded. The steam reversing gear 'crept' slightly when the engine was working so special 'distance' pieces were made to hold it in a definite fixed position. These of course could only be changed when the engine was stopped on the rollers. Slipping was alarming. The old bugbear, leaking lubrication oil, reached the wheel treads and the Test Plant Rollers had to be wiped at regular intervals. It even led 'to buckling coupling rods which happened a number of times in the stationary plant and on the line.' In the confines of the Test Plant, this must have been truly terrifying. Steps, it was noted, 'were already in hand to redesign the ... coupling rods'. At the stationary plant the period of the tests varied between 60 and 150 minutes and there were a number of shorter ones on the determination of power outputs and steaming rates only. Failures on the Test Plant included heated coupled axleboxes, heating of inside big ends, heated coupling rod bushes and so on. It was damage to the rollers themselves, however, and the catastrophic consequences that might flow from such an unwelcome event, that was uppermost in the testers' minds. Fearing for their lives they shrank, understandably, from pursuing 35022's

The aftermath at Crewkerne. Trains/locomotives have mounted platforms and demolished canopies before and since, but seldom has this level of damage been done by an errant part flying off – though Norman McKillop in *Enginemen Elite* (Ian Allan, 1958) tells the story of a section of a V2 tyre slicing a telegraph pole in half!

35022 under test at Rugby in March 1953.

maximum boiler capacity. Maximum steaming rates on the plant were found to be 33,300lb/hr with Blidworth, 37,000lb/hr with Bedwas and (briefly) a peak of 42,000lb/hr with South Kirkby (this would be true 'collar work').

The Controlled Road Testing that followed took place over the Skipton-Carlisle route October-November 1952 and there was, inevitably 'some discrepancy between the results of the plant tests and those on the line'. On the line the duration of the journeys were between 65 to 75 minutes though some were shorter. Sustained rates of firing of over 3,000lb/hr were attained, employing two firemen 'to avoid undue fatigue'. This sort of rate was greater than anything normally required from the Merchant Navys.

Out on the road the 'Swindon Type Steam Flow Indicator' was used and the ranges of speed, nominal cut-off and steaming rate were all appreciably less in the 'real world' than on the stationary plant: *'The maximum steaming rate was limited to about 29,000lb/hr, which sufficed to work a train of 20 bogie coaches of 594 tons at the scheduled speed involved … [this was] the largest number of bogie coaches ever operated over this route'.* On line slipping was again the great shortcoming, the engine experiencing buckled coupling rods.

On conclusion of the first set of investigations the Test Committee felt that 'as designed' the Merchant Navy was *'a most effective and capable engine but one that is relatively uneconomical. If operating, as they frequently are in service, with the reversing gear in a relatively long cut-off and with the regulator very little*

opened [they] *will be still less economical though their performance will then be more reliable from the mechanical point of view and from that of power output'* Combustion was 'never very good, especially with the lower grade coal'.

Some improvement suggested were:-
Wider spacing of the grate bars.
Provision of a deflector plate.
Admission of more air through the firehole door with the doors closed.
New chimney design – *see next set of tests.*

Second Set of Tests – Modified Chimney with Single Blastpipe
All the Merchant Navys were built with a single large diameter chimney employing multiple jet blastpipes and the 'new chimney design' involved a smaller diameter one with a single blastpipe. As it happened, the Merchant Navy chimney had been occupying minds on the Southern for a year or more and 35019 FRENCH LINE C.G.T. had been so equipped in June 1951. It reacted indifferently despite alterations running into the following year, 1952. Time was lost, crews complained and the multiple blastpipe went back on in September 1954. Despite this, the Rugby test engine, 35022 HOLLAND-AMERICA LINE was also fitted with single blastpipe, in February 1953 but results do not appear to have been much different than with FRENCH LINE C.G.T.. It was run on the Test Plant again during March-May 1953. With the modified chimney it ran 2,460 miles at the test plant and then returned to traffic.

The essence of the problem was the height available between the top of the inside valve chest and the top of the chimney, with the latter of course dictated by the loading gauge. The main reasons for the 'high' position of the inside steam chest were:
a) the inclination of the inside cylinder in order for the connecting rod to clear the leading coupled axle and
b) the position of the inside steamchest directly above its cylinder.

The distance to the top of the chimney was very restricted for so large a locomotive and a larger blastpipe was desirable to direct the exhaust better. (Remember how the design had been shoe-horned with marvellous skill into the restrictive Eastern Section profile.) None of the combinations of blast pipe and chimney gave results up to the standard set by the multiple jet arrangement normally fitted to the class: *'use of the multiple jet arrangement is practically unavoidable if anything like full use is to be made of the steaming capacity of the boiler when inferior coal is used'.* The work ended in May 1953.

Third Set of Tests – Boiler without Thermic Syphons
The jury had long been 'out' on the efficacy of thermic syphons in British conditions, where boilers were relatively small. The fourth and final element of the test series therefore examined an engine without this equipment. The boiler, No.1107, had been fitted with a non-thermic syphon firebox more than a year before and was running on 35014 NEDERLAND

LINE. Steaming had not been as good, despite alterations to the brick arch, though it was deemed satisfactory by the spring of 1952. The boiler and firebox were afterwards put on to 35022 HOLLAND AMERICA LINE and after running in it duly made its way back to Rugby in December 1953, returning in the January of the following year.

Without thermic syphons 35022 ran 2,820 miles on the stationary test plant. Despite the full panoply of modern test equipment there was little that could usefully be said and the Test Committee could never really be sure whether such differences as were discerned were due to the absence of thermic syphons or the rearranged brick arch: 'such differences as were observed may have been due to as much to the different arch as to the absence of the syphons.' Other imponderables concerned the quality of the coal ('it left something to be desired resulting in bad clinkering of the grate and 'birdnesting' of the tubeplate') 35022 was more difficult to fire correctly than on the previous test and combustion was not improved nor was smoke emission reduced. 'Removal of the thermic syphons had virtually no effect on the maximum output of the boiler' though their removal and a different brick arch saw an increase in the inlet steam temperature of some 40 to 60 degrees Fahrenheit. It was not worthwhile, concluded the Report, 'on boiler performance grounds alone', to remove the thermic syphons; moreover it was not worthwhile to fit them in any British coal-fired locomotive of similar or smaller size especially if hand firing was required. 'An advantage' would be expected, however, in improved steam consumption from the higher superheat resulting from the removal of the syphons.

This was all becoming increasingly academic of course, for re-building – or even scrapping – of the class was now very much in the air.

BIBBY LINE and the Axle Emergency
On 24 April 1953 35020 BIBBY LINE, working the 2.15pm Plymouth-Waterloo train, suffered a broken middle driving axle, approaching Crewkerne at an estimated speed of 70-80mph. The crank axle fractured through 'the sprocket seating of the left-hand axle piece'.

35020 had run 353,256 miles since it was new in July 1947, 154,322 miles since its last General Repair in May 1950 and 49,273 miles since its last Intermediate in June 1952. The offending crank axle was No.E4237, manufactured at Eastleigh to Drawing No.E31968, and had run with the locomotive all its life. Crank axle pieces had been made from steel to Southern Railway specification No.324; they were normally visually examined at shop repairs and the crank pins tested magnetically.

On 27 April 1953, a week after the mishap, instructions were sent out for magnetic crack detection test to be carried out on the crank axles on all the Bulleid Pacifics.

Practical investigation using supersonic flaw detector equipment commenced at Eastleigh on 10 May and the very next day, 11 May instructions went out that all Merchant Navys would be withdrawn from service 'that night' until all crank axles had been tested on a magnetic flaw detector at Eastleigh. The work was complete on all but two of the class by 18 May; 35022 HOLLAND AMERICA LINE was still on its interminable tests at the Rugby plant and would be examined in due course.

Flaws were found in the sprocket seating of crank axles on fourteen Merchant Navys; the other fourteen were returned to traffic. However, during the stripping down of one of the faulty crank axles (in order to investigate the problem further) more damage was detected, in the axle pieces under the web seats. It was then decided that the fourteen 'returnees' should be further tested by the ultrasonic flaw detector. The fourteen that *were* showing flaws on the sprocket seating should be completely stripped down and examined for flaws on the axle pieces under the webs. As a result nineteen crank axles (and their engines of course) had to be withdrawn from service – 35022 turned out to free of the affliction – either from flaws in the sprocket seating (14) or in the crank web seats (5).

Analysis
35020 had suffered a complete fracture of the cross section of that portion of the axle on which the sprocket was clamped. It was ascribed to 'progressive fatigue' which extended to six inches of the diameter. The remaining two and a half inches represented the sudden, disastrous failure. Microscopic examination and even looking with a hand lens betrayed bands of corrosion and fatigue cracking, though chemical and mechanical tests on the fractured axle found the steel to be of acceptable quality.

For detailed technical reasons the cause of failure was deemed to be 'fretting corrosion fatigue', a phenomenon which occurred at the contact between two highly loaded metals. The solution (the reader will

FLAW RESULTS IN MERCHANT NAVY PACIFICS

Engine No	Crank axle number	Mileage of crank axle at date of examination	Shed	Initial reason for locomotive being withdrawn from traffic		Result of subsequent examination of crank axle when stripped		
				Sprocket seat (magnetic test)	Web seat (supersonic test)	Sprocket seat (RH axle piece)	Web seat	
							LH	RH
35001	4072	524,794	EXJ	-	flawed	clear	flawed	flawed
35005	4090	383,729	EXJ	flawed	#	flawed	flawed	flawed
35007	4063	393,130	SAL	flawed	#	flawed	flawed	flawed
35008	4117	545,057	SAL	flawed	#	flawed	flawed	flawed
35009	4642	278,222	SAL	flawed	#	flawed	flawed	clear
35011	4156	372,659	NEL	flawed	#	flawed	flawed	flawed
35012	5233	208,927	NEL	-	flawed	clear	flawed	flawed
35013	4201	369,124	NEL	flawed	#	flawed	flawed	flawed
35014	4108	432,393	NEL	flawed	#	flawed	flawed	flawed
35015	4192	379,797	NEL	-	flawed	clear	flawed	flawed
35017	4210	389,273	NEL	flawed	#	flawed	flawed	flawed
35018	3848	188,201	NEL	-	flawed	clear	flawed	clear
35019	4228	247,678	NEL	flawed	#	flawed	flawed	flawed
35020	4237	353,256	NEL	BROKEN	#	BROKEN	flawed	flawed
35023	4174	386,033	EXJ	flawed	#	flawed	flawed	flawed
35024	4183	397,182	EXJ	flawed	#	flawed	flawed	flawed
35025	5251	220,831	EXJ	flawed	#	flawed	clear	flawed
35026	5260	190,857	STL	-	flawed	NOT CONFIRMED		
35028	5278	166,151	STL	flawed	#	flawed	flawed	flawed
35030	5296	151,982	DOV	flawed	#	flawed	flawed	clear

Supersonic test on the web seat not necessary, as the axle was withdrawn due to flaw under sprocket
EXJ Exmouth Junction
SAL Salisbury
NEL Nine Elms
STL Stewarts Lane
DOV Dover

When, on 11 May it became clear that the Merchant Navys would have to come out of service 'that night' the other Regions were alerted and were rallying round, drumming up locos almost within hours. Less than two days later WR Britannias were at work and a day after that V2s of all things were also on Southern trains. And popular enough they were too – or at least they were not deeply unpopular – some SR men had trouble with the regulator apparently. They seemed to have done the job well enough, but were not really considered the equal of the Merchant Navy. On 21 May 1953 Doncaster's 60896 had charge of the Belle at Waterloo, alongside Urie Arthur 30744 MAID OF ASTOLAT. Photograph R.C. Riley, www.transporttreasury.co.uk

The miscreant crank axle of BIBBY LINE, showing the site of the catastrophic failure.

Ultrasonic testing underway on one of the Merchant Navys.

On 29 May 1953 60916, still bearing its New England shedplate, waits at Waterloo with the 5.30pm to Bournemouth, alongside Exmouth Junction Merchant Navy 35023 HOLLAND-AFRIKA LINE, by now tested and certified free of axle flaws. Photograph John Aylard.

appreciate that extreme para-phrasing is being employed here) was a re-design – temporarily at least – of the crank axle. Increasing the diameter of the axle portions between the crank webs and the journals by just three eighths of an inch reduced the stress at 80mph sufficiently to render the metal free of the damaging consequences. Modified cranks would be fitted to all the locomotives as soon as the sprockets were ready, 'to alleviate the position'. After that new balanced cranks would be fitted but in the meantime, as there was no reliable guide to how cracking might have advanced (it was independent of mileage for instance) regular nine-monthly supersonic tests would be carried out at the sheds 'until such time' as the supply of material permitted balanced cranks to be fitted, or until further information warranted an alteration in the period between examinations. With that, the emergency was fading.

Fun All Round
During the temporary withdrawal of the MERCHANT NAVY Pacifics replacements were loaned by other

Regions and for a short while observers on both the Western and Eastern Sections of the SR had an enjoyable time recording these visitors to their part of England. *The Railway Observer* for June 1953 gives an excellent account of these movements – on 13 May 1953 for instance, the WR sent Britannias 70017, 70023, 70024, 70028 and 70029 to Nine Elms while the LMR sent 70030 and 70034 to Stewarts Lane shed and, later, some Black Fives to Nine Elms. The ER came up with a number of V2s which needed minor amendments to the cab steps and live steam injector pipe so they could work Waterloo-Exeter and via Sway to Bournemouth. These were 60893, 60896, 60908, 60916, 60917 and 60928. With some of the light Pacifics needing attention as well some more replacements were in order – three BR Standard class 5 4 6 0s and fifteen B1s from the ER. The work of these loaned engines involved Waterloo-Bournemouth duties including the Bournemouth Belle; Waterloo-Exeter; Waterloo-Basingstoke semi-fasts; goods work; Victoria to Ramsgate and Ashford with 70030 and

70034 noted on Boat Train duties. The temporary allocations were:-
Nine Elms: 45051, 45061, 45130, 45216, 45222, 45223, 45350, 60893, 60896, 60908, 60916, 60917, 60928, 73003, 73015, 73017.
Exmouth Jct: 70024, 70028, 70029.
Salisbury: 70017, 70023.
Stewarts Lane: 61015, 61041, 61050, 61109, 61133, 61138, 61148, 61188, 61192, 61219, 61273, 61274, 61329, 61338, 61354, 70034.
Dover: 70030.

The first Merchant Navy to be rebuilt was 35018 BRITISH INDIA LINE, coming into traffic in February 1956 – here it is taking shape in Eastleigh Works on 18 January 1956. Unlike other famous classes, such as the Royal Scots, these were genuine rebuilds, and not new locomotives under some accounting cloak. The *Report on Proposed Modifications* to the engines (see text) listed the features to be replaced – principally the valve gear/oil bath, smokebox and the casing, with the tender to be severely modified. The tender modification of course had seen the light of day as early as 1952 with three so treated and one more in 1953. The rest of the tenders were done from 1956, except where they were re-bodied. The most obvious way in which the engines changed was of course in the removal of the casing and the remaking into a locomotive of conventional outline. The boiler and firebox, the excellent fundamentals of the design, were kept, along with the outside cylinders; the old fabricated smokebox with all its odd angles was done away with and replaced by a firmly conventional cylindrical one. The oval door kept the look of the original, and helped among many other things to make the new design distinctive, even though it was being made 'more conventional'. Photograph Les Elsey.

4. Flight of the Pheonix

Once Bulleid had gone from the Southern, in September 1949, there would be no more serious development of his Pacifics – in anything like their original form that is. The work of further testing (as described earlier) was done with the Rugby engine, 35022 HOLLAND AMERICA LINE with single blastpipe and then without thermic syphons, and haulage trials were done on the Eastern Section, comparing a Merchant Navy with a light Pacific and a Britannia. No obviously lasting consequences seemed to derive from this and by 1954, though reliability had increased markedly since the early days, the unthinkable was being thought; would it be easier just to scrap the engines? This feeling had in fact been around since before the last of the Merchant Navys had been built (!) for a programme announced in 1946 predicted the end of all steam on the

Southern by the middle 1950s. By 1954 it was clear that this would not be attained so rebuilding into a more conventional form figured increasingly in the Region's councils.

If the engines were to be scrapped, something would have to be built new to replace them, and this, logically, could only be another thirty Britannia Pacifics. With the boiler and firebox condition of the Merchant Navys specially checked and found to be rather good, the equation swung very much in favour of rebuilding. Much of the argument is contained in the report reproduced here (which of course considers the light Pacifics too) made at Brighton in January 1955. Some of the details are alarming – there were no less than *thirty-eight* fires recorded for 1953 alone for instance – see under PERFORMANCE (ii) (c) Air Smoothed Casing below. Curiously the fires do not

feature as a 'cause' in the 'Availability' section.

****

REPORT ON THE PROPOSED MODIFICATIONS TO THE 'MERCHANT NAVY' AND 'WEST COUNTRY' CLASSES OF LOCOMOTIVES

INTRODUCTION
The 'Merchant Navy' class of locomotive was introduced on the former Southern Railway in 1941 and 30 of this class were built in three batches between the years 1941 and 1949.

The 'West Country' class of locomotive, which includes the 'Battle of Britain' class, was brought out in 1945 and is similar, in all major respects to the 'Merchant Navy' class but is of less weight so as to be available for use on routes where the restrictions are more

BRITISH INDIA LINE close to completion 1956. Three sets of Walschaerts valve gear to replace Bulleid's chain driven motion necessitated a new inside admission middle cylinder. For economy the two outside cylinders were retained with their outside admission. This is why the rebuilds could often be found with steam escaping from around these cylinders. A rocking grate was provided, with six moveable sections each side of the centre line. Each section was operated manually. Plain section coupling rods instead of the I section ones were fitted to combat buckling when slipping. The mechanical lubricators for cylinder valve chests were moved from their awkward and ash-prone site below the smokebox frontplate up on to the running plate above the front drivers, two on the left and one on the right. A fourth was added on the right-hand side to supply oil to the cylinders and leading axleboxes. This superseded the multifeed boxes (or 'trays') in the cab. Other modifications included reverse sanding on the middle driver (see elsewhere) and different intermediate drawgear between engine and tender. The drawbar was now pin jointed to the tender by means of a plunger sliding freely in guides and controlled by the intermediate drawbar rubber spring, which cushioned the pull. When Bulleid was shown photographs of the rebuilt 35018 and asked his opinion he replied, characteristically, that if he thought them better that way, he'd have done them like that himself! Photograph Collection John Fry.

severe. Between 1945 and 1951 110 of this class of locomotive were built.

DESIGN
Although the locomotives follow the normal modern design tendencies for a Pacific type with three-cylinders and a wide firebox boiler, there are a number of features which are not usually employed in British locomotive practice, among which are:-

(i) Special valve gear, having a chain drive to a three-throw crank shaft, which drives valve gear for each of the three cylinders. Each gear is connected to the piston valve through a rocking arrangement having a 3:8 ratio, which in practice has proved to be unsatisfactory.

(ii) An oil bath enclosing the three sets of special valve gear and the inside motion. This is intended to give continuous lubrication to the working parts.

(iii) A smokebox, of irregular shape, as opposed to the more usual one of cylindrical form.

(iv) Special casing over the whole of the upper part of the locomotive described by the designer as 'air smoothing'.

PERFORMANCE
The locomotives, when hauling the principal express trains of the Region have demonstrated their ability to run to time with an ample margin of power, due to their excellent steaming properties, and free running characteristics. From availability and maintenance points of view, however, the locomotives are less satisfactory, whilst their consumption of coal, water and oil is high in relation to other modern locomotives.

The unsatisfactory features can be covered under four headings:- (i) running costs, (ii) reliability, (iii) availability, (iv) cost of repairs and maintenance.

(i) Running Costs
(a) Thermal Efficiency
Tests were conducted in 1951 and 1952 at Rugby and on the road between Carlisle and Skipton, with 'Merchant Navy' Class locomotive No.35022 and one of the BR Class 7 Pacifics. These tests have demonstrated that whereas there is no substantial difference in the boiler efficiency between the two classes, (actual average boiler efficiency of the 'Merchant Navy' in standard condition is only 1½% less than that of the Class 7) the cylinder thermal efficiency shows to disadvantage over a wide range of working as indicated by the Table 1:-

The lower thermal efficiency of the 'Merchant Navy' as compared with the BR class 7 4 6 2 (and with practically all other classes which have been tested) is due primarily to the inefficient utilisation of the steam in the cylinders. The fact that the superheat temperature of the 'Merchant Navy' is about 50°F lower than that of the Class 7 4 6 2 locomotive will have some effect, but in the main the lower thermal efficiency must be attributed to the faulty distribution of the steam by the valves.

Indicator cards taken during the Rugby tests have been examined and very erratic results are shown. In some cases the indicator card may consist of a diagram of large area in one end of the cylinder whilst the other end may enclose practically no area at all. In other cases, diagrams of appreciably different shapes are obtained and different results are observed simultaneously in the three cylinders.

(b) Coal
In the road tests, results generally corroborative of those given above were obtained and for a direct comparison of operating economy, the comparable figures of coal consumed are as follows (Table 2):-

TABLE 2. Pounds of coal (Blidworth) per drawbar horsepower hour

Speed mph	60			40		
Drawbar horsepower	800	1200	1600	800	1200	1600
BR C1 7 4-6-2	2.40	2.22	2.40	2.15	2.00	2.20
Merchant Navy	2.77	2.47	2.40	2.46	2.35	2.39
Increase %	15.4	11.3	0	14.4	17.5	8.6

The high consumptions of coal by these locomotives is also apparent from a comparison with other Regional classes. In the Interchange Trials of 1948 the following average figures were obtained running over all the routes (Table 3):-

TABLE 3. Pounds of coal per drawbar horsepower hour

Express Passenger Types	lb.coal/DB HP per hour
ER A4	3.06
LMR Duchess	3.12
LMR Royal Scot	3.38
Average	3.19
SR Merchant Navy'	3.60
Mixed Traffic Types	lb.coal/DB HP per hour
ER B1	3.59
LM Class 5	3.54
Average	3.57
SR West Country	4.11

These figures show an increased consumption of 13% and 15% in the case of the 'Merchant Navy' and 'West Country' class locomotives respectively compared with similar class locomotives operating in other regions.

One other factor in high coal consumption of the 'West Country' class in ordinary service is the absence of damper doors on the ashpan, on all but

the last twenty locomotives and three others which have been subsequently modified experimentally. Very skilful handling on the part of the fireman is necessary in order to avoid blowing off under these conditions and considering the youth and inexperience of many firemen who have to work on these locomotives today, it is unquestionable that unnecessary blowing off occurs, with consequent waste of coal and water.

(c) Water
The water consumption of a locomotive gives a measure of the cylinder efficiency and for any similar degree of superheat it is approximately true that the cylinder efficiency and the water per indicated horsepower hour are inversely proportional. The Rugby trials showed that the water consumption of the 'Merchant Navy' was high in relation to that of the BR Standard Class 7 Pacific. The following figures were obtained in the road tests between Carlisle and Skipton (Table 4):-

TABLE 4. Pounds of water per drawbar horsepower hour

Speed mph	60			40		
Drawbar horsepower	800	1200	1600	800	1200	1600
BR C1 7 4-6-2	20.2	17.4	17.2	18.3	16.2	16.2
Merchant Navy	23.2	19.6	17.9	21.0	18.9	17.8
Increase %	14.9	12.6	4.1	14.8	16.7	9.9

These figures are in reasonable agreement with the results of the 1948 Interchange Trials in which the average water consumption of the 'Merchant Navy' class was approximately 18% higher than that of the average of the Eastern & North Eastern and LM regional classes.

(d) Oil
The oil consumption of the 'Merchant Navy' and 'West Country' locomotives is influenced principally by the provision of the oil bath for the valve gears and inside motion. It was intended that this arrangement would function as an oil circulating system which would require occasional topping up, instead of the system normally used on locomotives. In practice it has been found virtually impossible to make the oil bath oil tight. The net result of leakage from the oil baths is that, over a typical period of 18 months, the average consumption of high quality lubricating oil amounted to just over 2 gallons per 100 miles for the 140 locomotives, making a total annual use of 120,000 gallons. This is in addition to the 15 pints of engine and cylinder oil per 100 miles which is issued to enginemen and artisan staff. The comparable issue for a 'Lord Nelson' class locomotive is 9½ pints per 100 miles, which is the total required for the locomotive.

TABLE 1. Cylinder Thermal Efficiency %

Steam rate lb/hour	14,000 (light working)			20,000 (Normal working)			28,000 (very heavy working)		
Speed mph	20	40	60	20	40	60	20	40	60
Efficiency % BR CI 7 4-6-2	11.9	13.0	13.4	11.6	13.5	14.0	10.2	12.6	13.25
Efficiency% Merchant Navy	9.7	11.0	-	10.3	11.6	11.85	10.2	11.5	11.95
Reduction %	18.5	15.4	-	11.2	14.1	15.3	0	8.7	9.8

Pacifics were in and out of Eastleigh throughout the rest of the 1950s after BRITISH INDIA LINE at the beginning of 1956. This is 35017 BELGIAN MARINE nearly complete as 'a rebuild' in March 1957. The work depended to a great extent on the humble wooden ladder and all the ones around, like that on the cab floor, are carefully painted with its owner's name – *L. ROBERTS ERECTING SHOP* – to stop them being 'borrowed'. Mr Roberts was one of the three Erecting Shop chargehands involved with the rebuilding. Photograph Collection John Fry.

(ii) Reliability

As a result of investigations into the troubles and failures which have occurred with these locomotives, modifications have tended to be introduced which have tended to improve their reliability. The principal features which have caused unreliability are:-

(a)   valve gear
(b)   oil bath
(c)   air-smoothed casing
(d)   smokebox and leading end of locomotive
(e)   rocking grate on 'West Country' class.

These features have been unreliable throughout the whole life of the locomotives to date; some of the troubles have been lessened by modification, but the main sources of unreliability are inherent in the design.

(a) Valve Gear

In service, failure of the valve gear is a not infrequent occurrence, the principal causes being fracture of the rocker shafts, fracture of driving chains, and damage to valves due to over-travel. These failures give rise to loss of availability and high cost of repairs at the depots and in outstation material.

(b) Oil Bath

The oil bath, apart from requiring constant attention in the form of topping up, makes maintenance at the depots more difficult as the big end and valve gear parts cannot be so readily examined. It has, moreover, proved very difficult to exclude water from the oil bath and when this gains access appreciable corrosion occurs on the motion parts.

(c) Air-smoothed Casing

Fires on orthodox locomotives are practically unknown, but are a frequent occurrence in the 'Merchant Navy' and 'West Country' classes, 38 cases being reported in 1953.

Most of these fires commence in the vicinity of the ashpan hopper doors, due to accumulation of oil-soaked inflammable matter and frequently spread to the boiler lagging plates and clothing. The latter tend to become soaked in oil which presumably condenses from vapour escaping from the oil-bath. The shape of the air-smoothed casing tends to trap heat from the engine and set up temperature conditions approximately of the same order as the flash-point of the oil, so that once a fire starts, combustion can proceed readily under the casing, which forms a furnace. In cases where fires have gained a firm hold not only have the casing and paintwork been badly scorched, but the 'Yorkshire' joints in the lubricator pipes have been melted out, necessitating the withdrawal of the locomotive from traffic for repairs. Modifications have been made in the hope of reducing the tendency for the fires to spread to the boiler lagging. Clothing plates have been fitted to the underside of the boiler barrel, but nevertheless it has not been possible to prevent the occurrence of fires.

The air-smoothed casing is troublesome to maintain and great care is required to prevent parts from becoming detached. It has proved particularly difficult to fix the doors which are needed to allow of access to sanding fillers, whistle valve etc. The 'air smoothed' casing unquestionably makes more work at motive power depots as parts requiring attention are generally hidden and removal of part of the casing is often necessary, or the work can only be carried out under difficulties.

(d) Smokebox and leading end of locomotive

The frames of the locomotives have behaved very well, the only trouble experienced being at the leading end of the 'West Country' class at the front of the inside cylinder where there is a common line of bolts with the back flange of the outside cylinders. To combat this trouble a stronger stretcher and additional horizontal and vertical plate stretchers between the outside cylinders, have been fitted. In spite of this alteration, however, there is still a measurable amount of frame torsion which gives rise to trouble with the main steam pipes in the smokebox. Leakage at this point and at the stuffing box, where the steam pipe enters the smokebox, has a very detrimental effect upon the steaming.

The safety valves on a rebuilt Merchant Navy – moved to the firebox crown from their original site halfway along the boiler. Photograph Collection John Fry.

(e) Rocking grate on 'West Country' class locomotive

The design of the grate on the 'West Country' class gives rise to a great deal of trouble. The grate is of the rocking type, with a 'drop' section, the latter having rocking bars mounted in it. In consequence of its unreliability, the grate is little used in the manner intended, since experience of the grates collapsing, following use either for rocking or firedropping, has produced a feeling of lack of confidence in it.

(iii) Availability

The number of weekdays out of service for running repairs and examinations in 1952 for the 'Merchant Navy', 'West Country' and 'Lord Nelson' Classes are given below. These figures are extracted from the return rendered by the Locomotive Accountant, headed 'Costing of Locomotive Repairs, Annual Mileage & Weekdays out of Service.'

Merchant Navy	61.69 weekdays out of service
West Country	53.95 weekdays out of service
Lord Nelson	49.38 weekdays out of service

Specially kept records show that the number of weekdays lost to service on account of engine defects at sheds in 1953 for the 140 locomotives, from all causes was 5,501 or 39.3 days per engine. Of these the following totals were attributable to individual causes:-

Valve gear	1,021 days
Valves and Pistons	251 days
Steam and Exhaust pipes	423 days
Grates and Ashpans	215 days
Steam reversing gear	50 days

(iv) Cost of Repair and Maintenance
The cost of maintenance of these locomotives is materially influenced by the considerations set out under (ii) and (iii) - Reliability and Availability.

The following is taken from Individual costing of locomotive repairs returns for the three years 1950-1952, headed 'Classified repairs to selected locomotives at Workshops and Motive Power depots'. The cost of repair in pence per engine mile is shown (Table 5) for three classes of Southern Region

locomotives and also for comparable 'Pacific' classes from other Regions.

Boiler costs per mile for MN and WC are wildly in excess of those shown for other classes and take some believing. If the figures were true, why were the boilers retained in the rebuilding? The word 'fiddle' comes to mind!

In the Works, considerably more man-hours are required for intermediate and general repairs to the Merchant Navy and West Country class locomotives than for other locomotives of approximately comparable size and power. The cost of general and intermediate repairs to engines and

tenders (excluding work on the boilers) to 'Merchant Navy' and 'West Country' class locomotives is 20% more than comparable repairs of 'Lord Nelson' class locomotives, as shown by the following figures taken from the individual costing of locomotive returns:*(see table opposite)*

The differences are accounted for largely by (1) the work involved in removing the air-smoothed casing before the essential parts of the

REGION	CLASS	PENCE PER ENGINE MILE			
		Engines (between general repairs)	Boilers	Tenders(between repairs)	Total Engines, boilers and tenders
SR	Merchant Navy	10.692	2.145	0.870	13.707
	West Country	10.571	2.579	0.861	14.011
	Lord Nelson	7.107	0.516	1.021	8.644
ER, NER	A1	5.623	0.587	0.797	7.007
	A4	7.967	0.936	0.673	9.576
	A2/3	7.101	0.990	0.797	8.888
LM	Coronation	7.967	0.936	0.673	9.576

locomotive can be stripped and its replacement after repairs have been carried out and (2) the complexity of the valve gear and its associated parts including the oil bath and the extent of wear and tear on those and the need for much renovation and renewal.

PROPOSAL TO MODIFY THE LOCOMOTIVES
Three 'Merchant Navy' and three 'West Country' class locomotives have recently been modified in a number of respects, in an endeavour to eliminate as many as possible of the troublesome features of the locomotives short of a major

Total Cost of 41 General and Heavy Intermediate repairs to Merchant Navy and West Country class locomotives (Period 5/50 to 12/53)	£132,812
Average per repair	£3,239

Total Cost of 12 General or Heavy Intermediate repairs to Lord Nelson class locomotives (Period 5/50 to 12/53)	£32,370
Average per repair	£2,697

Increased cost of repair of Merchant Navy and West Country class locomotives compared with the Lord Nelson class locomotives (These costs have been equated to 1954 price levels)	£542 (=20%)

modification. Some improvement has been shown in the case of the parts actually modified. In addition, various modifications have been made to individual components, when it has been necessary to replace them.

The proposal now put forward will virtually eliminate the principal troublesome features and will bring the running costs into line with those of the other principal express passenger locomotives without impairing their performance in any way and increase the availability, while reducing the maintenance in Shops and Motive Power Depots.

The proposal involves the retention of the boiler, frames, outside cylinders, wheels, axleboxes etc and the replacement or removal of the following existing components:

(i)   Special valve gear and rocker shafts.
(ii)   Inside cylinder.
(iii)   Smokebox, superheater header, steampipes etc.
(iv)   Reversing gear.
(v)   Piston heads and rods.
(vi)   Oil bath.
(vii)   Air-smoothed casing.
(viii) Mechanical lubricators.
(ix)   Regulator.
(x)   Ashpan and grate.
(xi)   Cylinder Cocks
(xii)   Sandboxes.
(xiii) Tender. (a) raves and provision of tunnel for fire irons.
(b)   tank sieves.
(c)   water level gauge.
(d)   intermediate drawbar.

Account has been taken in the financial statement of those components on the above list, which would require replacement or repair during the shop overhauls at which the modified components will be fitted.

The main points in the design of the components which will replace the twelve components (i)-(xii) listed above are given below:-

(i) Valve Gear
The main purpose of the modifications is to provide the locomotive with three independent sets of Walschaerts valve gear of a type which has been well proved and which is known to give a very good steam distribution. The cylinder efficiency will then be brought into line with other modern steam locomotives. The two outside sets of valve gear will be similar to those of the standard Class 4 2-6-4 tank locomotives and the inside valve gear will follow the design of the Southern Region 'Schools' class. Two new driving crank pins will be provided to take the return cranks. An eccentric will be placed on the crank axle in place of the existing chain-driving sprocket. Provision was made for this latter modification when the crank axle was re-designed, following upon the failures of the crank axles which were the subject of my report of January 1954.

(ii) Inside Cylinder
Forward of the inside cylinder (which will have a piston valve with inside admission), and bolted to it, will be a saddle. These two components will butt up to the existing stretchers and give a very strong construction, which will eliminate the frame fractures which have been experienced at the leading end of the 'West Country' class.

(iii) Smokebox, Superheater header and Steam pipes
A circular smokebox, fitted to the saddle, will ensure a robust construction, which will remove the troubles experienced with the present design of steam pipes and stuffing boxes. The latter will be similar to those on the standard locomotives. A new header will be required to suit the circular smokebox, but the existing smokebox door will be retained.

(iv) Reversing gear
The reversing gear will consist of one shaft for both inside and outside valve gears, operated by means of a screw. This type of gear will enable fine adjustments of the cut-off to be made and will result in the locomotives being worked at an early cut off with a degree of certainty not possible with the steam reversing gear.

(v) Piston heads and rods
It is proposed to replace the existing type of piston heads, having a coned attachment to the piston rod, by parallel fastened heads of the type used on the BR Standard locomotives. A good deal of trouble has been experienced in the past due to the piston heads becoming loose and the BR type of attachment will eliminate this trouble. The new piston rods will be fitted to separate crossheads and this will enable the piston heads and rods to be removed out of the front of the cylinders as one unit in the normal manner.

(vi) Oil bath
The elimination of the oil bath will make the examination of the inside big end and motion much easier and the trouble which has been experienced of rusting of pins and gear will cease. This will be beneficial from the point of view of cleanliness of the underside of the locomotive and also in regard to slipping, as with the present arrangement a lot of oil finds its way on to the driving wheel treads. The Civil Engineer will also be relieved of certain maintenance since at the present time the loss of oil to the ballast is a source of embarrassment to him.

(vii) Boiler Clothing
The normal type of clothing will be fitted to the boiler which, together with the removal of the oil bath, will eliminate the trouble which has been experienced of fires occurring in oil saturated boiler clothing mattresses. Many details, particularly pipework, will be far more accessible than heretofore. Opportunity will be taken to provide footplating along the side of the engine.

(viii) Mechanical Lubricators
Two new mechanical lubricators will be used for the lubrication of the cylinders and axleboxes, and will be mounted at suitable positions on the motion brackets and driven in the usual manner. If the three existing mechanical lubricators which lubricate the cylinders and which are mounted in front of the smokebox were used, it would be necessary to increase this number to four in order to include the axleboxes; experience shows that with a number of lubricators to fill, one is very liable to be missed. The existing mechanical lubricators will be fitted to other classes of locomotives.

The use of a mechanical lubricator for the axleboxes will considerably reduce the length of copper piping, which must, of necessity, be used with the existing method of lubrication by a large trimming fed oilbox mounted on the cab.

(ix) Regulator
The existing regulator will be replaced by one of the horizontal grid type, arranged in such a way as to give a well graduated opening, in order to reduce the tendency of the locomotives to slip.

(x) Ashpan and Grate
Both classes of locomotive will be fitted with new ashpans with hopper bottom doors and front and rear damper doors. The fitting of dampers will improve, as far as the 'West Country' class is concerned, the control which can be exercised on the fire in order to prevent blowing off. The ashpans will be self-discharging to a greater extent than those now fitted and will therefore assist in the disposal of the locomotives.

(xi) Cylinder Cocks
The existing coned plug type of cylinder

The 'original' if that is what we can call 35001 with its vastly altered outline, climbing up out of Blackboy tunnel with the London-bound ACE, with Exmouth Junction marshalling yard on the right, 13 August 1954. CHANNEL PACKET itself was among the last of the 'Packets' to be rebuilt, late in 1959 but it is interesting to observe how far it has come to resemble, in small doses, the 'final state' of the original engines. The faring is gone in front of the cylinders, it carries the larger smoke deflectors and it has the wedge cab, though the tender has yet to be 'modified' – that is, cut down; the curves on the casing at the lower edge mark it out as a first series loco. Photograph J. Robertson, www.transporttreasury.co.uk

cock has proved expensive to maintain in a proper state of repair and the poppet type will be fitted in its place.

(xii) Sandboxes
New sandboxes will be provided and fitted, where possible, between the frames.

(xiii) Tender
(a) Raves and provision of tunnels for fire irons
Reference has been made in paragraph 1 of the section above headed 'PROPOSAL TO MODIFY THE LOCOMOTIVES' to the modifications which have been made to three locomotives of each class. Included in these modifications were the removal of the raves and the provision of tunnels for fire irons and covers over vacuum brake reservoirs.

The Motive Power Superintendent is satisfied that there is an improvement in the coaling and taking of water of these modified tenders. He also states that previous to the provision of the tunnel for the fire irons, it was necessary periodically for shed staff to clear the coal from the side troughs in order that the fire irons could be safely retained on the pegs provided. These modifications will be carried out on the remainder of

the tenders of these two classes of locomotives.

(b) Tank Sieves
The strainers as originally fitted on these tenders did not provide a positive means of preventing foreign matter, principally particles of coal, from passing from the tender tank along the feed pipes. This resulted in the failure of the injectors. An improvement has been made to the existing strainers, but they are not entirely satisfactory and must be cleaned at regular intervals. The cleaning involves the emptying of the tank, since it is necessary for staff to enter the tank for this purpose.

Sieves located in boxes mounted external to the tank will now be fitted, following the design on BR locomotives. The boxes can be shut off from the tank, enabling the strainers to be cleaned without the necessity of emptying the water from the tank.

(c) Water level gauge
The existing water level indicator is of primitive design, consisting of a vertical tube with small holes located at intervals throughout its height. The indicator has been generally unsatisfactory either due to the water valve being difficult to operate or to the small holes becoming blocked.

The BR type of water level indicator will be fitted.

(d) Intermediate drawbar
Over 90% of the drawbars on the locomotives of these classes entering the works are found to be flawed when magnetically tested and are replaced. The trouble has been traced to two features of the drawgear which tend to induce very high stresses in the components:-

(i) The use of a curved rubbing block on the tender, which rubs against a flat block on the engine drag beam. On a reverse curve this arrangement produces a large stroke of the drawbar spring with the consequent high loading of the drawbar. Tests have shown that where both rubbing blocks are suitably curved this effect can be eliminated.

(ii) The use of a spherical bearing surface at the point where the load in the drawbar is transmitted to the tender underframe, in front of the drawbar spring. Experience of spherical surfaces generally has shown them to be unsatisfactory as there is a high resistance to movement with consequent imposition of bending stresses in the drawbar.

In order to prevent the possibility of engine and tender parting in service, all the locomotives have now been fitted with safety links.

The drawgear will be modified to include curved rubbing blocks and the replacement of the spherical bearing surface by a pin joint, similar in principle to the design in use on the Eastern and Northern Eastern regional locomotives.

PROGRAMME FOR THE CONVERSION OF THE LOCOMOTIVES

It is proposed that the 30 'Merchant Navy' class locomotives should first be modified, followed by the 110 'West Country' class. Drawings can be prepared in such time as will enable six 'Merchant Navy' class locomotives to be modified during 1955, the remainder of the locomotives being covered at the rate of 24 per year during 1956 and the following years, until the completion of the work in 1961.

FINANCIAL ASPECT OF PROPOSED MODIFICATIONS

The gross outlay involved in the proposed modifications is £5,615 per locomotive.

Operating Savings
The operative savings that can be expected from the proposed modifications have been discussed with the Motive Power Superintendent and he has agreed that the following annual savings will accrue (Table 6):-

The annual mileage per locomotive on which these savings are based are

number of locomotives required on the region, provided that the workings remain the same as at present. The class and number of the locomotives will be decided when the modification to the 'Merchant Navy' and 'West Country' class locomotives has been completed.

Savings at Main Workshops
The repair savings at General and Intermediate repairs at the Main Workshops are estimated at £445 per repair.

Summary
The Regional Accountant has been consulted and a copy of his memorandum setting out the financial aspect of the scheme is attached. This shows that the total estimated net saving up to the assumed date of scrapping of the locomotives, before taking account of the interest factor is £2,051,402. Bringing interest into the calculations produces an equivalent capital sum as at 1955 of approximately £850,000.

Authority is required for an amount of £760,400 made up as under:-

	£
Gross outlay	786,100
Less: estimated recoveries	25,700
	£760,400
	======

Chief Mechanical & Electrical Engineer's Office
BRIGHTON
January 1955
Thus was the case made, though there remain causes for suspicion. Take the

TABLE 6 COAL, WATER AND OIL

	30 Merchant Navy	110 Light Pacifics
Coal @ 3lb per mile		
2,010 tons @ 78/6d per ton	£7,889	-
6,350 tons @ 78/6d per ton	-	£24,924
Water @ 3 gallons per mile		
4,500,000 galls @ 2/3d per 1,000 (treated)	£506	-
14,200,000 galls @ 2/3d per 1,000 (treated)	-	£1,598
Oil @ 2 gallons per 100 miles		
30,000 galls @ 2/3d	£3,375	-
94,000 galls @ 2/3d	-	£10,642
	£11,770	£37,164

50,000 and 43,000 for the 'Merchant Navy' and 'West Country' classes respectively. These figures are taken from the return 'Locomotives - Annual Mileage and Analysis of Weekdays for Year 1952' which is compiled by the Locomotive Accountant.

Staff
When all 140 locomotives have been modified there will be a saving of ten Grade 1 fitters and seventeen fitters' assistants Group 4, with a financial saving of £13,650 per annum in the Motive Power Superintendent's department.
Availability
The increased availability of the modified locomotives will no doubt make possible a small reduction in the

savings claimed in fitting staff. The fact was that in practice motive power depots were so woefully short of such staff that it is highly unlikely that any would have gone 'down the road' just because a few rebuilt Pacifics arrived! In due course, in February 1956, a very different Merchant Navy indeed emerged from Eastleigh Works, 35018 BRITISH INDIA LINE. Its first days turned out to be slightly less auspicious than the authorities would have liked... It was in the Works Yard for official inspection on 9 February 1956 and the following day ran a trial trip to Botley and back. On 12 February it set off for Nine Elms and inspection at Waterloo by Sir Brian Robertson the next day. BRITISH INDIA LINE returned to Eastleigh on 14 February and on the 17th was rostered

for its first passenger work proper, Eastleigh shed duty 253, taking over the 9.54am train from Waterloo and the 1.29pm Fareham-Bournemouth West at Southampton Central. A glorious debut it was not to be, however, and it was afterwards noted dead at St Denys, being hauled tender first by M7 0 4 4T 30376. BR Class 5 73052, itself bound for shopping at Eastleigh, took over 35018's train. The failure, recorded *The Railway Observer* (here a rueful smile might have appeared in some quarters) was 'believed to be due to a lubrication fault'...

BRITISH INDIA LINE was soon back in action, running a trial to Botley and back on 20 February and then resuming work on duty 253 until the 27th, when it failed, immobilised at Farnborough with radius rod trouble. It was dragged to Eastleigh Works again and once the clearances were opened out 35018 worked away happily, with only a short one day works check-up – these visits were not noted on the Record Card. It was telling, and indicative of the contradictions in the class, that at the same time, while 35018 was feeling its way (including a few turns on the Bournemouth Belle) some of its fellows in original condition were putting up perfectly exhilarating performances. On 14 April for instance, as *The Railway Observer* recorded, 35021 rolled into Salisbury with the down Atlantic Coast Express six minutes early with a train seventy tons over the 'norm' – '*to the astonishment of the station staff and relief engine crew*'. By 8 May 1956 the second rebuild, 35020 BIBBY LINE was limbering up on its running in turns. What follows is the 'Financial Memorandum' mentioned in the *Summary* of the Report above, setting out in more detail some of the financial figures (look at some of the projected dates for the demise of the Pacifics...)

***

FINANCIAL MEMORANDUM
'Merchant Navy' and 'West Country' and 'Battle of Britain' class locomotives: proposed modifications to Valve Gear and other parts on engines and modifications to tenders.
The scheme provides for an estimated net expenditure of £687,850 in the years 1955 to 1961 on the alterations to the engines and tenders and will result in estimated savings in maintenance and operating costs, up to the assumed date of scrapping, of £2,739,252 in years 1955 to 1987, i.e. a net estimated ultimate saving of £2,051,402, ignoring the factor of interest, which is considered in the conclusion. The figures for the separate schemes are set out in Table A.
(see overleaf)

SAVINGS
In order to assess these, it has been

35009 was ex-works after rebuilding in March 1957; it was an Exmouth Junction engine and here it is in the shed yard there a few months later, on 15 August 1957. Tender has the second crest introduced in March 1957. Photograph W. Hermiston, www.transporttreasury.co.uk

TABLE A

140 Locomotives	30 MN Locomotives and Tenders	110 WC/BB Locomotives and Tenders	Total
Anticipated net expenditure on alterations	£146,600	£541,250	£687,850
Anticipated savings in maintenance and operating costs	£455,383	£2,283,869	£2,739,252
Anticipated net savings	£308,783	£1,742,619	£2,051,402

General - all expenditure is at 1954 price levels

Anticipated net expenditure on alteration is made up of:-

	30 MN Locomotives and Tenders	110 'WC/BB' Locomotives and Tenders	Total 140 Locomotives
Gross outlay @ £5,615 each	£168,450	£617,650	£786,100
Less recoveries during alterations	£ 5,500	£20,200	£25,700
Amount for which authority is sought	£162,950	£597,450	£760,400
Less cost of repairs avoided	£16,350	£56,200	£72,550
Net additional outlay	£146,600	£541,250	£687,850

TABLE B

	30 MN	110 WC/BB
Coal @ 3lb per mile		
2,010 tons @ 78/6d per ton	£7,889	£24,924
6,350 tons @ 78/6d per ton	-	
Water @ 3 gallons per mile		
4,500,000 gallons 2/3d per 1,000 (treated)	£506	
14,200,000 gallons @ 2/3d per 1,000 (treated)		£1,598
Oil @ 2 gallons per 100 miles		
30,000 galls @ 2/3d	£3,375	£10,642
94,600 galls @ 2/3d	£11,770	£37,164

1962. The repair savings have been assessed firstly on the basis of prime costs factors supplied by the Works Manager at Eastleigh, at £445 per repair (for variable costs only). It has been assumed that these savings will commence in 1957 and attain maximum in 1962.

Secondly, the Motive Power Superintendent estimates that, as a result of rebuilding of these Locomotives, he will save ten fitters, grade 1 and seventeen fitters assistants, grade 4, with a total saving of £13,650 per annum, which includes overtime and Sunday working. This has been apportioned £2,925 against 'Merchant Navy' and £10,725 against the 'West Country' and 'Battle of Britain'; the saving being deemed to commence in 1955 and reach a maximum in 1962.

The maximum annual operating savings have been made up as shown in Table B.

CONCLUSION
From the appendices it will be seen that, on the basis of the figures as they stand, the whole cost will be recovered by the year 1962 for 'Merchant Navy' locomotives and by the year 1966 for 'West Country' and 'Battle of Britain' locomotives.

As shown in the first two paragraphs the total estimated net saving up to the assumed date of scrapping of the locomotives, before taking account of the interest factor, is £2,051,402. Bringing interest into the calculations produces

necessary to make assumptions as to when the expenditure will be incurred and when the resulting savings will fructify.

It has been assumed that the output of converted locomotives will be equally spread from October 1955 to July 1961 inclusive; that certain preparatory expenditure will be incurred in 1955; and that the last 12 months (1960/61) expenditure will be correspondingly reduced. On this basis and a periodicity between repairs (general and intermediate) of eighteen months, it has been assumed that partial repair economies will result in the second half of 1955, and continue until the locomotives are withdrawn from service, but will not reach their maximum until 1962.

Similarly, on the above basis of output it has been assumed that operating savings will begin to accrue in 1955 (for three months) in respect of 50% of the output of that period and again reach their maximum and continuing figure in

TABLE C (WAS 'APPENDIX 'A' PAGE 40 IN ORIGINAL *BOOK OF THE MERCHANT NAVY PACIFICS*)
ESTIMATED SAVINGS ON THIRTY 'MERCHANT NAVY' LOCOMOTIVES

Expenditure on Alterations			Savings in maintenance and operating costs up to assumed date of scrapping				
Year	Current Expenditure	Aggregate Expenditure	Year	Maintenance	Operating	Total	Aggregate Saving
1955	£72,992	£72,992	1955	£284	£294	£578	£578
	£73,608	£146,600	1956	£1,706	£7,062	£8,768	£9,346
			1957	£9,557	£11,770	£21,327	£30,673
			1958	£11,825	£11,770	£23,595	£54,268
			1959	£11,825	£11,770	£23,595	£77,863
			1960	£11,825	£11,770	£23,595	£101,458
			1961	£11,825	£11,770	£23,595	£125,053
			1962	£11,825	£11,770	£23,595	£148,648*
			1963	£11,825	£11,770	£23,595	£172,243
			1964	£11,825	£11,770	£23,595	£195,838
			1965	£11,825	£11,770	£23,595	£219,433
			1966	£11,825	£11,770	£23,595	£243,028
			1967	£11,825	£11,770	£23,595	£266,623
			1968	£11,825	£11,770	£23,595	£290,218
			1969	£11,825	£11,770	£23,595	£313,813
			1970	£11,825	£11,770	£23,595	£337,408
			1971	£11,825	£11,770	£23,595	£361,003
			1972	£11,825	£11,770	£23,595	£384,598
			1973	£11,825	£11,770	£23,595	£408,193
			1974	£11,825	£11,770	£23,595	£431,788
			1975	£11,825	£11,770	£23,595	£455,383
		£146,600		£224,397	£230,986	£455,383	

Point where saving overtakes expenditure ignoring interest.

MILEAGE, UTILISATION
Improvement in Utilisation by Rebuilding, overall = 15%
Table prepared by E.S. Youldon and first published in the journal of the Bulleid Society, *The Leader*.

MN	ORIGINAL FORM			REBUILT FORM			Best Utilisation when
	Years/ Months	Mileage	Yearly average	Years/ Months	Mileage	Yearly Average	
35001	18 6	807318	43639	5 3	288566	54965	Rebuilt
35002	16 11	776797	45919	5 9	325117	56542	Rebuilt
35003	17 11	859784	47988	7 11	272009	34359	Original
35004	16 9	750880	44829	7 3	378537	52212	Rebuilt
35005	17 5	632322	36306	7 5	344484	46447	Rebuilt
35006	17 10	862757	48379	4 10	271562	56185	Rebuilt
35007	15 11	799299	50218	9 2	519466	56690	Rebuilt
35008	14 11	730712	48986	10 2	555706	54660	Rebuilt
35009	14 9	684482	46406	7 2	442970	61810	Rebuilt
35010	14 6	663174	45736	9 8	578775	59873	Rebuilt
35011	14 7	670782	45996	6 7	398346	60508	Rebuilt
35012	12 1	564821	46744	10 2	570015	56067	Rebuilt
35013	11 3	517915	46037	11 2	596743	53440	Rebuilt
35014	11 5	516811	45268	10 8	545583	51148	Rebuilt
35015	13 3	549700	41487	5 8	264250	46630	Rebuilt
35016	12 1	467091	38656	8 4	433456	52026	Rebuilt
35017	11 11	594522	49890	9 4	423232	45346	Original
35018	10 9	504900	46967	8 6	451644	53135	Rebuilt
35019	13 11	617368	44362	6 4	329976	52101	Rebuilt
35020	10 10	507958	46888	8 10	473521	53606	Rebuilt
35021	10 9	575993	53581	6 2	283669	46000	Original
35022	7 8	329083	42924	9 11	574459	57929	Rebuilt
35023	8 3	433833	52586	10 5	507493	48719	Original
35024	10 5	552053	52162	5 9	287362	49976	Original
35025	8 1	419374	51881	7 9	420041	54199	Rebuilt
35026	8 1	311063	38482	10 2	547721	53874	Rebuilt
35027	8 5	363351	43170	9 4	508939	54529	Rebuilt
35028	10 10	401005	37016	7 9	393386	50759	Rebuilt
35029	10 7	428621	42862	7 0	319722	45675	Rebuilt
35030	9 0	351234	39026	9 3	499642	54015	Rebuilt
Averages	12 8	574833	45480	8 1	426883	52447	Rebuilt

an equivalent capital sum as at 1955 of approximately £850,000.

It will be understood that if the cost of the work increases by price level or other causes and the savings do not increase pro rata, the period of complete recovery of outlay will be delayed and the total savings will be reduced.

For J W J Webb
(Intld) RWK
Regional Accountant's Office
Deepdene House
DORKING
10 January 1955

A Cautionary Note
While these reports and estimates throw much valuable light on the thinking of the time, they are, in reality, 'archaeological' fragments only, illuminating in the way fossils are illuminating – they allow a fairly convincing picture to be drawn but they fall far short of revealing everything, and new evidence might always be around the next corner. And again some aspects of these reports prompt doubts; the 'Financial memorandum' for instance projects a scrapping year of 1987, which is unrealistically late because as early as 1958 it was known that precious little steam operation would survive on the Southern beyond the summer of 1967. Small wonder that the Southern's Administration and Accounts man W.

Marsh (see below) couldn't agree with the savings claimed!

There were other (protracted) suggestions as to what to do with the Bulleids, for instance, envisaging replacement of the valve gear only (with Walschaerts) and leaving the engines otherwise unchanged. Even in the 'might have been' stakes the Merchant Navys out-complicate other classes!

Regarding the reports above, it must be said that while it is all very well producing estimates to show savings, the only truly worthwhile figures are those based on what *really* ensued. The rebuilt engines certainly had some very good strong features but it would be wrong to suggest they were a bed of roses. There was a design fault with the outside piston valve spindles for instance on the first fifty (Merchant Navys and light Pacifics) that called for some re-design work. Even so, as maintenance standards declined the high pressure glands at both ends of the outside steamchests caused problems. Steam leakage then took place on a massive scale. Roughness could also develop more rapidly, some of the 'converteds' seeming to knock themselves to pieces after a few years. In the rough and tumble of ordinary service coal saving turned out to be minimal – when driven with gusto the rebuilds could throw fires out of the chimney with the best of 'em. Crews, certainly, did not find the rebuilt engines an obvious 'leap forward', far from it. And don't forget the introductory note of the 1955 Report; the original engines *'have demonstrated their ability to run to time with an ample margin of power, due to their excellent steaming properties, and free running characteristics'*. Now *that* was what crews were interested in.

It is perhaps useful to quote Bulleid himself, when contemplating the projected savings from the rebuilding episode. He remarked that, while every defect that could be levied against his engines was taken into account when costing their limitations, for the rebuilds the savings were based on hoped-for achievements only. It is also useful to recall W. Marsh, the Southern's Assistant for Administration and Accounts, who studied the Reports on savings expected by the Regional Accountant in accordance with the BR (ex-LMS) standard method. Marsh did not wholly agree with the LMR methods and submitted his own calculations which were less favourable to the project. This was (inevitably?) overruled.

Rebuilding Dates
35001	8/59
35002	5/58
35003	8/59
35004	7/58
35005	5/59
35006	10/59
35007	5/58
35008	5/57
35009	3/57

Rebuilt CHANNEL PACKET at Bournemouth shed. Photograph J. Davenport/B.K.B. Green Collection, Initial Photographics.

35010	1/57
35011	7/59
35012	2/57
35013	5/56
35014	7/56
35015	6/58
35016	4/57
35017	3/57
35018	2/56
35019	5/59
35020	4/56
35021	6/59
35022	6/56
35023	2/57
35024	4/59
35025	12/56
35026	1/57
35027	5/57
35028	10/59
35029	9/59
35030	4/58

ATC/AWS

Along with other BR classes, from H 0-4-4Ts upwards, the Merchant Navys began to get the Automatic Train Control, later designated Automatic Warning System; this was started on the Southern in 1959 and the first Merchant Navy so fitted, appropriately, was 35001 CHANNEL PACKET, in August 1959. The others followed at intervals thereafter. The battery box was sited prominently at the front above the buffer beam. Other equipment was inside, out of sight between the frames.

Liveries

Given their pedigree in all other respects, it might be assumed that the Merchant Navy liveries would be hideously complicated. This, fortunately, proves not to be the case; well, not much...

Coming out new in wartime did not help but the first engines, 21C1-21C6, carried the malachite green livery with three horizontal yellow bands. Economic constraints meant they were soon in black, along with the final ones of the first series, 21C8-21C10. 21C2 had emerged new in unlined malachite for trials but returned to Eastleigh to get the full lined livery. 21C7 too came out briefly with unlined malachite green, for works trials only before returning to works to emerge, in its turn, in black, which had just been introduced as the standard livery for all SR engines. The second batch too came out in wartime and 21C11-21C20 were accordingly garbed in black.

To black livery:-
21C1 1/44; 21C2 5/44; 21C3 5/43; 21C4 7/43; 21C5 3/42; 21C6 5/42; 21C7 6/42.
Black from new:-
21C8 6/42; 21C9 6/42; 21C10 7/42.
21C11 12/44; 21C12 1/45; 21C13 2/45; 21C14 2/45; 21C15 3/45; 21C16 3/45; 21C17 4/45; 21C18 5/45; 21C19 6/45; 21C20 6/45.

After the War the restoration of malachite green livery was the first step back to normality for the class, though Nationalisation made for further alterations.

From black to malachite green livery at the War's end and after:-
21C1 12/45; 21C2 7/46; 21C3 11/45; 21C4 4/46; 21C5 1/46; 21C6 9/46; 21C7 7/47; 21C8 8/47; 21C9 11/46; 21C10 6/47; 21C11 1/47; 21C12 4/45 (repainted grey from 2/45); 21C13 11/46; 21C14 11/45; 21C15 11/45; 21C16 1/47; 21C17 10/45; 21C18 8/45; 21C19 8/45; 21C20 9/45.

The third series, 35021-35030, had the following liveries from new:-
unlined malachite green (the malachite, incidentally, wore rather badly): 35021 9/48 (lining added 11/48); 35022 10/48; 35024 11/48; 35026 12/48; 35027 12/48.
lined malachite green: 35023 11/48; 35025 11/48; 35028 12/48; 35029 2/49; 35030 4/49.

The reason for 35021, 35022, 35024, 35026 and 35027 coming out in unfinished (i.e. unlined) malachite was because they were the ones attached to light Pacific tenders. When, one by one, they got their proper 6,000 gallon tenders, they received full liveries as follows:
35021 to full malachite 11/48 (6,000 gallon tender attached)
35022 to full malachite 1/49 (6,000 gallon

tender attached)
35024 to experimental blue 2/49 (6,000 gallon tender attached)
35026 to standard blue 7/49 (6,000 gallon tender attached)
35027 to full malachite 4/49 (6,000 gallon tender attached)

35024 had quite a history of its own so far as early liveries were concerned:
13/11/48 New in unlined green (as above)
12/2/49 Experimental blue with three crimson lines. The blue encompassed wheels and skirting. Hand painted lion on wheel emblem.
29/3/49 Three crimson lines replaced by two black lines edged in white. Front skirting black together with cylinders.
30/4/49 Black skirting now continued throughout length of engine and tender. Wheels black. This now became the standard blue livery for the class.

With the formation of British Railways there were various experiments as to which liveries would suit which type of locomotive. For a while the majority of the Merchant Navys were painted dark blue; this appeared in February 1949 with horizontal red bands on 35024 EAST ASIATIC COMPANY*. These bands were promptly replaced by two lines in black with a fine white lining and later black wheels and a '...narrow black splash skirt'. Next for this treatment was 35026 LAMPORT & HOLT LINE in July 1949 when blue became the 'standard'. 35011, 35014 and 35023 were never painted blue, however, while 35001, 35017, 35024, 35026, and 35029 got blue twice each.

Dates repainted in the standard BR blue:-
35001 10/49; 35002 1/50; 35003 6/50; 35004 10/50; 35005 2/50; 35006 3/51; 35007 3/50; 35008 7/49; 35009 8/49; 35010 11/49; 35012 2/51; 35013 8/50; 35015 2/51; 35016 5/50; 35017 7/49; 35018 9/49; 35019 1/50; 35020 5/50; 35021 9/50; 35022 6/50; 35024 2/49; 35025 9/49; 35026 7/49; 35027 4/50; 35028 1/51; 35029 2/51; 35030 5/50.

Blue unfortunately proved a poor second to the malachite green both in appearance and expense – blue cannot wear like other colours it seems, which was proved all over again when BR repainted its diesels less than twenty years later. In June 1951 instructions were issued that all blue locomotives were to be painted dark green with black and orange lining. Eventually all thirty were repainted BR standard dark green and once again 35024 was the first one dealt with.

Dates to BR standard dark green:-
35001 5/52; 35002 6/51; 35003 8/53; 35004 3/53; 35005 2/54; 35006 9/53; 35007 12/52; 35008 5/52; 35009 2/53; 35010 11/52; 35011 11/51; 35012 7/52; 35013 12/52; 35014 8/51; 35015 6/53; 35016 3/53; 35017 3/53; 35018 7/51; 35019 6/53; 35020 6/52; 35021 2/52; 35022 1/52; 35023 3/52; 35024 5/51; 35025 6/52; 35026 6/52; 35027 11/53; 35028 6/53; 35029 7/52; 35030 5/53.
Upon rebuilding, the BR standard dark green was kept, though the black skirt on the bottom of the cab and tender was left out and rectangular panels appeared instead. These panels also appeared before rebuilding where the engine was paired with a cut-down tender.

*35024 was the only one with red bands – it was, at the time, an experimental livery.

Dimensions, as built.
'The three sets of valve gear...and the inside connecting rod are completely enclosed in an oil bath...lubricated by a circulating oil system, driven by two gear pumps, connected by a chain to the crankshaft.'
Three cylinders: 18in. diameter X 24in. stroke.
Piston valves = 11in..
Bogie wheels = 3ft. 1in. diameter.
Driving wheels = 6ft. 2in. diameter.
Trailing wheels = 3ft. 7in. diameter.
Wheelbase = 6ft. 3in. + 5ft. 6in. + 7ft. 6in. + 7ft. 6in. + 10ft. = 36ft. 9in..

Boiler diameter = 5ft. 9¾in. to 6ft. 3½in.
Boiler length = 16ft. 9½in.
Tube length = 17ft..
Firebox length = 7ft. 10½in..

Heating surfaces
Tubes 124 X 2¼in. = 1,241.6 sq ft.
Flues 40 X 5¼in. = 934.3 sq ft.
Firebox and thermic syphons = 275 sq ft.
Total evaporative surface = 2,450.9 sq ft.
Superheater = 665 sq ft.
Total = 3,115.9 sq ft.

Grate area = 48½ sq ft.
Working pressure = 280 lb per sq in.

Tractive effort = 37,500 lb.

Tender = 5 tons of coal and 5,000 gallons of water.
Estimated weight in working order* = Engine 92 tons 10 cwt.
Tender 50 tons 0 cwt.
Total 142 tons 10 cwt.
*As published both by the Railway Magazine and Railway Observer in 1941. They also published different heating surface figures:-
Tubes = 1241.6 sq ft.
Flues = 934.3 sq ft.
Firebox = 275 sq ft.
Total = 2450.9 sq ft.
Supheat.= 822 sq ft
Total 3272.9 sq ft (Railway Magazine gives it as 3,273 sq. ft.)

Rebuilt Dimensions
First one was 35018 BRITISH INDIA LINE. Dealt with at Eastleigh Works between Wednesday 16 November 1955 and Wednesday 14 February 1956.
The two main differences were the removal of the air smooth casing and the replacement of the valve gear by conventional Walschaerts arrangement.
Three cylinders = 18in. diameter X 24in. stroke.
Bogie wheels = 3ft. 1in. diameter.
Driving wheels = 6ft. 2in. diameter.
Trailing wheels = 3ft. 7in.
Wheelbase = 6ft. 3in. + 5ft. 6in. + 7ft. 6in.+ 7ft. 6in. + 10ft. = 36ft. 9in.
Length over buffers: As built = 69ft. 7¾in.
            As rebuilt = 71ft. 7¾in.

Heating surfaces:
Tubes and Flues = 2175.9 sq ft.
Firebox = 275sq ft.
Superheater = 612sq ft.
Total = 3062.9sq ft.

Tube length = 17.ft.
Grate area = 48½ sq ft.
Boiler pressure = 250lb.
Tractive Effort = 33,495lb.
NB. Work on reducing the boiler pressure had started in 1952.
Modernisation of the tenders had also started in 1952.

For M1173/58

COPY

YOUR REF. M.1173/37

DATED

BRITISH TRANSPORT COMMISSION
BRITISH RAILWAYS
SOUTHERN REGION

OUR REF. TL.1/37/J.
DATE 2-7-58

B.R. 4/3

Locomotive Works Manager,
Eastleigh.

FROM Mechanical Engineering Asst.,
C.M. & E.E.'S Dept.,
Southern Region,
Ext. Brighton 1.

Modified "Merchant Navy" & "West Country" Class Locomotives

You will recall that when Locomotive No. 35022 passed through your Works for Intermediate Repairs, it was fitted with an altered arrangement of valve spindle for the outside cylinders, incorporating U.K. packings at both the front and back ends.

The purpose of this alteration was to remove the unbalance of the valve, caused by the greater area under pressure at the front end of the valve, which has given rise to excessive wear of die blocks and motion pins. By allowing the spindle to pass through glands at both ends of the steam chest the areas become equal, and the loading of the valve gear should, consequently, be reduced.

The modification to No. 35022 appears to be very satisfactory, but owing to the amount of wear which had already occurred in the expansion link die paths, it is somewhat difficult to judge the amount of improvement being obtained in respect of the wear between the die blocks and the links.

I am now considering the application of this feature to further locomotives as they are converted, but before coming to a decision, I am anxious to know the approximate additional cost. Apart from the longer valve spindles (in the case of No. 35022 these were lengthened by sleeving, but if the feature is adopted, the spindles would be redesigned) you will have to supply front covers, bushes and U.K. packing the same as those at present used only as the rear covers, etc. In addition, there are the two split feed units on the mechanical lubricators, and the appropria[te] piping, as well as a small cover in the sloping part of the platform. The displaced articles which will no longer be requir[ed] are the existing front covers, bushes and tail rod cover.

Will you please ascertain the cost of the new and displace[d] details, and let me know the additional cost involved if balan[ced] piston valves are fitted.

for
(Signed) A.E. HOARE

* Being dealt with — file M/1173/

DP

YOUR REF. M1173.58

DATED

BRITISH TRANSPORT COMMISSION
BRITISH RAILWAYS

ocomotive Works Manager,
STLEICH.

OUR REF. TL.1/130/La.

B.R. 9203/5

DATE 23rd May 1958

FROM

MECHANICAL ENGINEERING ASSISTANT
CHIEF MECHANICAL & ELECTRICAL ENGINEER'S DEPT.
SOUTHERN REGION
BRIGHTON 1

Telephone : BRIGHTON 26261 Ext. 106

Modified "Merchant Navy" Class Locomotives.

     Confirming Mr. Haile's telephone conversation with Mr. Bolton this morning, the rough riding experienced on Engine No. 35002 is similar to that which occurred on Engine No. 35022 but is not quite so severe. It would appear that something of the same trouble is developing between the manganese steel liners on the coupled axleboxes and guides and the locomotive is being returned to you for examination of these details. Will you please advise me when it comes to hand so that my representative can be present when the engine is lifted.

     Whilst the locomotive is in the Works, I shall also be glad if you will give attention to the following defects:-

1)   Tender tank leaking at a weld in the vicinity of the water level indicator, and also at a joint between the indicator sector plate.

2)   Ashpan side doors - refitting.

3)   Platform plates to be welded and refitted where existing bolt holes have been drilled incorrectly.

4)   Trailing truck to be examined for a very severe squeak.

        for A. E. HOARE.

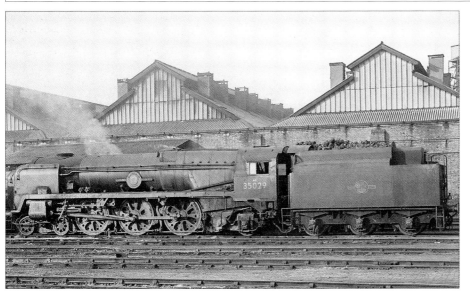

How it would end. The 'American' look of the rebuilds encapsulated by 35029 ELLERMAN LINES at Nine Elms; note the speedometer, fitted to all the Merchant Navys as a general BR policy from about 1959. A sectioned ELLERMAN LINES now sadly rotates at the command of children, a giant version of those old Science Museum models, at the NRM. Photograph Paul Cotterell.

The tender off 21C1 at Eastleigh, no.3111 awaiting attention, 22 September 1945. The tattered canvas sheet has obviously had its day and a length of chain is dumped on the bulkhead. The mysterious lettering reads: TO BE PUT IN TENDER BEFORE LEAVING SARUM, a reminder to insert water treatment briquettes. The front end filler looks very securely battened down indeed, and hardly likely to give way to a water surge during braking. These first, rather streamlined tenders looked a bit cumbersome on their own but it couldn't have been an easy job to get all those curves right (in such thin metal) and keep them like that. The rear of the cabs curved in to match this curve at the tender's leading edge. (Post-War, the combination of an early Merchant Navy plus Bulleid coaches made for an impressive assembly.) Those long spring hangers went out of use and were not employed on the second batch, though the holes for the brackets that held them were drilled in the frame. Just visible above the notice is a bracket for a wartime 'tin hat'. Photograph H.C. Casserley, courtesy R.M. Casserley.

Both looking completely ghastly, 21C2 and tender no.3112, at Salisbury on 20 July 1947. Fire damage might explain the marks on the casing, but the tender just seems to be suffering from extreme weathering, of the sort the blue diesels got in the 1970s. There is a longitudinal patch, recalling the problems when weld lines split under the weight of surging water. Photograph H.C. Casserley, courtesy R.M. Casserley.

5. The Tender Trap

The Merchant Navy tenders abounded in detail variation, a veritable trap for the engine picker. It is possible to outline the principal changes but in a description the host of minor changes, when and where and how they were effected, will inevitably get blurred or lost, even where one is truly confident of the precise events. With luck, some of these photographs, and others elsewhere in the book, will illustrate most of the points. As you'd expect, the tenders were built in three batches of ten to match the engines, so we have three separate generations, all with their own differences and all sporting the modifications (or not) which might then be applied to pre-existing ones. Or not. BR carried on the changes and while doubtless all steam locomotive tenders were effectively re-tanked (and thereby 'rebuilt') over the years the Merchant Navys have to be one of the few classes where all the tenders had to be *systematically* rebuilt. It is a complex bundle of changes; what follows is a summary of the principal differences at least, enough to set the reader (or perhaps more especially the modeller) on the right path for a particular engine at a particular time. As ever, the right photographs are the best way of avoiding the tender trap...

First Series

The first tenders, for the initial batch of ten engines, 21C1-21C10, were built at Ashford, where apparently the necessary welding techniques and equipment were available. They carried five tons of coal and bore 5,000 gallons of water. These tenders were high at the sides and uncomplicated, the curve at the front of the 'self-trimming' bunker running in line with the cab roof; at the front the sides ran up and joined to give an arch matching the profile of the cab roof.

The curves at the top of the tender sides, incidentally, are given the curious name 'raves', which apparently dates from the fifteenth century ('origin unknown' according to the *Concise Oxford Dictionary*) and for most of the 600 years or so since has quite innocently referred to the permanent or removable framework added to the sides of carts to increase capacity. The art of engine picking has brought about a modest revival in the fortunes of this otherwise surely doomed word.

On the first two, 21C1 and 21C2, the 'rave' (that word just has to go in inverted commas) ran across the back of the tender to hide the vacuum cylinders and so on that were placed up there. Hidden away inside the tank was a strainer to stop particles (rust flakes, coal fragments, bird feathers and anything else known to man) reaching the injectors. It was an American idea to place this essential item in an accessible place outside, something taken up enthusiastically in the BR Standards where it certainly saved time and labour. Bulleid, like his contemporaries, put the strainers *inside* the tank (there was nothing perverse in this – Stanier's 8Fs were the same for instance) where every inevitable blockage required half a day's stoppage while the tank was drained and a cleaner lad bullied into climbing inside and clearing the wretched thing. Elsewhere, on post-War LMS locos and on the BR Standards, the strainer was in a box carried on the tender framing, outside. It froze every now and then, true, but blockages and routine maintenance could be settled in minutes. A new strainer later replaced the inside one on the Merchant Navys but even so it was in a sump, behind the framing and still pretty awkward to use.

On the first three tenders the fireman climbed up the back like a monkey, using a complicated arrangement of footsteps and handrails and doubtless lamp irons too. Like all the tenders, there was a pattern of electric lights for night-time when running backwards – though, as on the LNER, plenty of photographs show traditional lamps stuck on the irons above the electric lights. In any case, locos always had to have a conventional red tail lamp – even

A tender piled-up high at Nine Elms, on 35008 ORIENT LINE backing into Waterloo on 21 February 1951. Photograph Stephen Gradidge.

The evolution of the Merchant Navy tenders, if it could be summarised, was one of 'de-streamlining' and the reduction of frills. Thus the 'raves' gradually disappeared, beginning with the bit at the back; on the first two, the rest didn't have the rear 'raves' to start with. This revealed the vacuum reservoir cylinders, as on 35011, backing on to an Exeter-Waterloo express at Salisbury in June 1948. Note that the 'raves' on the sides had supporting brackets, and that the Bulleid tenders (like many SR tenders in fact) did not carry the traditional cast plate on the rear, to give number, capacity, date and so on. In the case of the Pacifics there wasn't really the room! Instead a simple plate giving the number only – 'T3112' or whatever – was attached, barely noticed, to the frames on the left-hand side, under the front steps. The cab curve on the tender front has not yet acquired the typical dents inflicted by years of coaling at Nine Elms, Salisbury and Exmouth Junction. Note uncovered vacuum cylinders; you can see how terribly vulnerable those connecting pipes were with big lumps of coal falling about – let alone a fireman's boots – so the imperatives for shielding them later on are obvious. Water level on the first two series was determined using an upright pipe with holes in it; when a cock was opened water came out of the relevant hole, each being calibrated to a the nearest thousand gallons or so. The more holes dispensing water, the fuller the tender was. Photograph George Heiron, courtesy Mrs Shirley Heiron, www.transporttreasury.co.uk

More 'raves', ladders and liveries, on 35003 ROYAL MAIL at Nine Elms in 1950. The engine is newly in blue, the central rib betraying the asbestos boarding of the casing. First series tender still with long spring hangers, this would be no.3117 originally attached to 21C7 ABERDEEN COMMONWEALTH. Photograph www.transporttreasury.co.uk

Apart from matters of accessibility the tenders had constructional defects – there is after all a lot of stresses set up in tenders as several tons of water sloshes about. Welds/joints move, allowing corrosion – observe the marks at the base of the 'rave' on 35004 CUNARD WHITE STAR at Andover Junction.

First series tender No.3115 (four steps as opposed to the normal three) behind 35005 CANADIAN PACIFIC (with which it ran most of its life) at Clapham Junction on 13 August 1948. This was the tender fitted with Berkley mechanical stoker (see the earlier section *The Curate's Egg*); the 'raves' do not have the 'depth' of other engines because the tender top has been raised, to compensate for loss of capacity when the stoker gear was installed. Photograph H.C. Casserley, courtesy R.M. Casserley.

35021 NEW ZEALAND LINE largely (the boiler was No.1098 which was on 21C9 when it was built in 1942!) brand new, 11 September 1948, in beautiful shiny (partly varnished) unlined malachite green. Delays in building the tenders at Brighton meant NEW ZEALAND LINE had to go into traffic with this light Pacific tender. The name stayed covered up until November when a proper 6,000 gallon one was available and the naming ceremony could proceed after finish painting and lining. Photograph H.C. Casserley, courtesy R.M. Casserley.

Modified first series 5,000 gallon tender on now-rebuilt 35004 CUNARD WHITE STAR at Yeovil shed on 15 June 1964, keeping unlikely company in the shape of a 64XX pannier tank. The tender would be 3113, originally on 21C3. After 35004 was withdrawn towards the end of 1965 following a furious wheelspin and buckled rods, the tender went to 35029. Photograph www.transporttreasury.co.uk

the diesels didn't escape this, for some years! Discs were supposed to serve in place of the electric lamps during daylight hours. The familiar tubular steel ladders made their appearance with the fourth tender, fitted to 21C4 CUNARD WHITE STAR. The previous tenders got ladders after a short while. As with many tender attachments, the shape and disposition of the ladders changed over the years.

As a weight saving measure, or possibly because the right material just wasn't to be found in wartime, these first ten tenders had inadequate shells. The metal of the sides was thin (only three sixteenths of an inch) and poorly braced and sometimes just the surging of the full weight of water, let alone a minor yard collision or argument with a fire iron, caused splits or rents in the sheeting. Patches and welds were, literally, 'fingers in the dyke' until some internal rearrangement could be done.

In an attempt to counteract all this, tender 3114 from 21C4 CUNARD WHITE STAR was fitted in January 1944 with additional wash-plates and in April returned to traffic behind 21C7 ABERDEEN & COMMONWEALTH, with noticeable improvement. When 21C2 UNION CASTLE was in works for its first General Repair (March-June 1944) its tender 3112 in turn had the wash-plates rearranged, together with strengthened side bracing. Many of the welds were redone at the same time, relieving some of the inordinate stresses. This turned out to be the cure, and by December 1945 all ten first series tenders had been similarly modified. The 'rave' at the rear of the first two

tenders was cut away almost to nothing and new ladders with the conspicuous swan necks were fitted, replacing the steps. There were further modifications, rearranging the bulkhead at the front with new lockers and forming fire iron tunnels between the 'rave' and the bunker. Windows made for more comfortable tender-first running, though coal debris accumulating in the channel between 'rave' and coal bunker often cancelled out this advantage.

One peculiar feature was a set of two water filling caps at the *front* of the tender. The conventional rear filler remained where it was supposed to be, at the back, and these two front ones were apparently put there for the convenience of the fireman, who wouldn't then have to climb up on the tender back. Unfortunately they could overflow – as any filler could – but into the cab! Or they could burst open as the tender filled from the rear, or merely as water surged forward upon braking. They were, accordingly, deeply unloved and secured more or less permanently, so far as was possible. It is doubtful if they were used much before being quietly done away with after a few years – see their fate later under *Second Series*.

Six of the 5,000-gallon tenders (3113, 3114, 3116, 3118, 3119 and 3120) were partially renewed in 1945-47 but water capacity was not increased or the design modified to that of the second series 5,100 gallon ones. Externally there was no difference, the changes being entirely concerned with the strengthening of the coal space and tank plating, in order to combat rust and rough treatment.

The 'raves' were further reduced under BR, the tenders beginning to acquire the general form with which we all became familiar in the 1950s and 1960s; eight were so dealt with but five were so bad they were rebodied using yet another tank version, 5,250 gallon examples built at Ashford.

****

They rode well and in the later two series offered an unobstructed view rearwards, but the Bulleid tenders were not the lap of luxury; the high sides made watering and coaling hard work. 'Modification' beckoned...

'Modification'

All the Merchant Navy tenders were 'modified' – 'cut down' that is, with the 'raves' finally done away with to give those rather pleasingly minimalist edges and slopes with which the engines saw out most of their BR lives and all of their rebuilt lives. 'Modified' is in a way an inappropriate term because it is not that specific, for the Merchant Navy tenders, above all others, perhaps, never stopped getting modified in one way or another. 'Cut down' would be far better in the case of the Merchant Navys but the term 'modified' has, through repeated usage come to mean *only* that – the cutting down of the tenders by BR. So, 'modified' it is.

All thirty Merchant Navy tenders were either cut down (mainly when the locos were rebuilt) or were rebodied – this latter outcome limited to a few rebuilt locos). Cutting down – 'modification' – commenced in 1952 but the programme didn't really get under

35021 NEW ZEALAND LINE restarts after a signal check at Basingstoke, 4 August 1964. The modified third series 6,000 gallon tender, no.3342 now running with CLAN LINE, is of course subtly (or not so subtly) different from its sisters; cab curve cut back (probably damaged), different vacuum pipework, prominent 'spout' and different site for briquette hatch. The 'spout' is an air vent (not all tenders had them and the position varied when they did – naturally!) and was not the 'breather' pipe desirable on tenders which took water from troughs, there being of course, no troughs on the SR. Photograph Alec Swain, www.transporttreasury.co.uk

Tender 3115 again, still with 35005 CANADIAN PACIFIC (running into Waterloo with a late afternoon train, 14 May 1965) and still with the frames seen earlier at Nine Elms but now with the first of the Ashford-fabricated 5,250 gallon bodies to go to a Merchant Navy (some had gone to light Pacifics), fitted in May 1959. It has a single, 'central' (actually offset) ladder, covered vacuum tanks and rectangular filler lids (one each side) with the BR briquette chute between them. The water filler caps (various types, size and number), BR briquette chute/holder, TIA tank, vacuum cylinders and ladders together have, potentially, an almost limitless variety of combinations. It doesn't make it easy... In the background, incidentally, is the old Waterloo training school. Photograph Peter Groom.

way until rebuilding of engines started in 1956. To complicate matters a few tenders were first cut down and later still rebodied. The story is best revealed in the individual engine and tender pairings

Vacuum Cylinders

If the ladders, steps and fillers and just about everything else on a Merchant Navy tender changed and migrated during the working lives of the locomotives, the most prominent feature to change was the vacuum cylinder arrangement. They could be found in almost every possible configuration over the years, whether covered or uncovered. Strictly speaking, they were the vacuum reservoir cylinders; interconnected by piping, there were three of them, set atop the tender and slightly off centre, held together by metal bands. They were set differently (of course) on other tenders – on some 6,000 gallon ones for instance, there were two one side and one on the other. Like this, they proved vulnerable to damage by falling lumps when taking coal. When the BR briquette system of water treatment came in there was more 'room on top' and the vacuum cylinders were repositioned more close in behind the bunker and all were covered over in one way or another.

Second Series

The second series of Merchant Navys, 21C11-21C20, naturally got a separate tender design from the first series. This time they held 5,100 gallons. Ladders were remodelled while the appearance was rather different – this was because the top edge of the sides ran straight all the length of the tender body. They still had the front fillers and the 'tunnels' between the 'raves' and the bunker sides.

The long spring hangers of the earlier first series 5,000 gallon tenders were replaced by brackets on the spring ends; this modification was determined upon after Ashford began assembly and the unplugged holes for the hangers remained as evidence of this late change of mind – see photographs and occasional comments, mainly in the individual photographs in *The Record*. The steam carriage-heating pipe was now visible (very much so – again, prominent in many photographs) below the tank instead of being concealed behind the skirt of the tender side.

Water surges from the front fillers when braking hard remained a problem but the idea of these things had happily lost support at court; the last three, 21C18, 21C19 and 21C20, went into service with the fillers plated over and the others, 21C1-21C17, were so treated fairly quickly, by 1946. Bradley records that much of this work was actually done at the sheds even before authorisation was officially issued. The sheds were obviously anxious, where they could, to do away with this particular mortification as soon as possible!

(Although Second Series capacity was officially given as five tons of coal and 5,100 gallons of water, a test in March 1945 revealed these to be six tons and 5,194 gallons.)

Modification

When the second series tenders were modified the top edge of the bunker was revealed to have an inward curve to it; moreover the vacuum cylinders were fully enclosed, the position of the TIA tank varied and later on a smaller cover for the vacuum cylinders appeared.

Third Series

The last ten 'BR' Merchant Navys, 35021-35030, saw the introduction of a third major tender variant – 6,000 gallon vehicles, six wheeled as before but with an unequal wheelbase of 7ft. 4in. + 7ft. (total wheelbase 14ft. 4in.); this compared with 6ft. 6in. + 6ft. 6in. (13ft. total) on the first twenty. The increase in capacity was reportedly to alleviate crews' fears of running dry on non-stop Waterloo-Bournemouth jobs. The new tenders looked similar to their predecessors but by now of course the front filler holes had gone. The ladders were different again, so were the vacuum cylinders; the important variation was TIA.

Traitement Integral Armand represented the sort of water treatment that the steel fireboxes should have got from the first (upon which the success of such boxes in America was predicated) and it was extended to all the other twenty Merchant Navys by 1951. It had been standard fare on the SNCF for years and was far more 'scientific' than most procedures familiar at running sheds, requiring some firm adherence to daily schedules of upkeep. Water in the tender and boiler was tested chemically during an engine's daily

Second series 5,100 gallon tender no.3125, behind 35016 ELDERS FYFFES at Nine Elms about August 1957, shortly after it was modified. The vacuum tanks were entirely enclosed, in two or three ways (naturally) and some covers were bigger than others. A further variation could came into play so far as the TIA tank was concerned – said mixing tank projects out from under the main vacuum cylinder cover. Photograph J. Robertson, www.transporttreasury.co.uk

The coal-weighing tender, looking a bit wrinkled but virtually newly modified behind 35018 at Eastleigh on 12 July 1952; it's useful among other things for an unusual view of the sanding pipe on the tender (the straight narrow pipe pointing at the leading tender wheel). Some of the weighing gear (or more accurately perhaps the gear for fixing it down when running) can be seen 'on top' together with the padlocked control cabinet. It has 'Lord Nelson' vacuum tanks mounted cross-wise, a TIA box and as yet does not have any tender cab roofing. The unions objected to its absence and the tender could not be used until one was fitted. A clash in lining is revealed – the tender is panelled but the cab remains straight lined, to match a high-sided tender. Photograph Les Elsey.

work and water, charged with the treatment solution at appropriate strength, was discharged automatically from a small tank set on the top of the tender behind the bunker. The composition of this solution was supposed to vary according to the volume of water going into the tank, from day to day according to the results of daily examinations. Doubtless in the 'front line' reality of everyday working it was rather less perfectly carried out than this.

The result was that the scale-forming compounds in hard water were precipitated out as a soft mud, eliminating the hardness of the water and stopping corrosion. A blowdown valve operated from the cab every half an hour or so of running blew out the sludge and deposited it on the track to either soak or wash away, or dry out and blow away in the breeze. The system famously increased boiler wash-out periods from seven to *fifty-six* days, happily coinciding with the inspection period for the firebox stays and plates.

A correspondent for *The Railway Observer* was around at Eastleigh when the final batch of Merchant Navys was being built and in the cabs of 35021-35025 he reported, there was *'a gauge and clock combined which is made by ACFI and calibrated in French lettering with the face of the dial marked off in days, Lundi, Mardi etc. 35027 does not appear to have these cab fittings whilst 35026 has not been*

checked. 34033 a 'West Country', now carrying tender No.3286 was ex-works week ending 11.12.48 and also has these cab and tender fittings'.

The simpler and cheaper BR system of briquettes replaced the TIA apparatus from about 1956. A simple tube replaced the tender top mixing tank, its presence indicate only by a small filler cap, looking like a smaller version of the main filler. Briquettes were loaded in the shute below the cap every few days and like the TIA system, adjusted according to the results of regular water analyses. A small yellow circle on the cabside below the number indicated TIA, and later a yellow triangle was applied to show that the BR water treatment was installed instead.

There was a further complication with the third series in that Brighton Works, which this time had got the job of making the tenders, failed to have enough ready in time. This meant that five of the new Merchant Navys came out with spare light Pacific tenders. 35021, 35022 and 35024 came out with 5,500 gallon Battle of Britain tenders and 35026 and 35027 with 4,500 gallon West Country tenders. All got their proper 6,000 gallon tenders within a few months as they became ready; one BB tender, No.3333, was passed from one Merchant Navy, 35021, straight to another, 35024, before going on to its proper 'intended'.

Modification

The third series, 6,000 gallon tenders were modified like the rest; the 6,000 gallon example No.3342, attached to 35021 NEW ZEALAND LINE, was indeed the first. The bunker top edge also had a curve to it. The bunker was not as long as on the two earlier series and there was much more room on top for the various items; the vacuum cylinders were partly covered in.

'New BR Bodies'

Five of the first series 5,000 gallon tenders were rebuilt over the period 1959-1963. 5,250 gallon tanks (they were later found to hold fifty or so gallons more than this) with entirely new tops were made at Ashford and fitted to tenders which had suffered particularly badly from corrosion. These were (as given in Bradley):

3111	(35001)	2/63
3112	(35002)	4/60
3115	(35005)	5/59
3117	(35003)	8/59
3118	(35018)	1/62

No.3343, the ex-coal weighing tender, was also re-bodied, as from February 1962, but its capacity was 6,000 gallons. All rebodied tenders were readily identifiable by their straight profile tops

The Coal Weighing Tender

This was No.3343, a standard third series 6,000 gallon tender modified by

Second series tender 3127 on BELGIAN MARINE at Waterloo. It kept this tender through its working life, interrupted only by the fitting of an LMS tender during the Exchanges. Photograph Paul Chancellor Collection.

35024 at Bournemouth in the early 1960s – it obviously had to be sent off shed before cleaning was finished! The tenders had prominent pipes on the framing immediately below the lower edge of the tanks; the nearest one, on the right-hand side, carried the steam heat (hence the lagging) and that on the left-hand side (far side in this case) was for the vacuum brake. 35024 ran with coal weighing tender no.3343 from May 1958 to December 1961 and with this one, Third Series (3341-3350) no.3346 from then until withdrawal. Photograph P. Hocquard, www.transporttreasury.co.uk

replacing the top parts in 1952. The main apparatus weighed the coal put into the bunker (which became a sort of separate weighing table) and readings were made and set from equipment in a padlocked cabinet at the rear of the bunker. (Even this minor detail, of course, changed over the years.) Like some of those on the other Regions the SR's coal-weighing tender rode around for years serving in a conventional fashion with the weighing bunker firmly secured (as it always was when running) and the equipment probably rusted solid, until the thing was dismantled and the tender rebodied in 1962, as noted above.

Mark Arscott of Markits (*'all your 4mm Bulleid wheel needs'* 01923 249711) writes: 'It entered traffic on 11 June 1952 attached to 35018, regularly rostered by Nine Elms to the 10.30am Waterloo-Bournemouth. It was back in the works 28 September 1952, where it was removed and after adjustments to the drawgear and springing and minor modifications to the weighing equipment, on 8 November 1952 was attached to 35014. This locomotive carried the boiler (No.1107) without the thermic syphons and was of particular interest to the trials staff. It was worked extensively on Bournemouth and West of England expresses and Nine Elms-Southampton fitted freights. After these trials, the tender remained with 35014 until the loco entered Eastleigh for rebuilding on 18 May 1956. The tender reappeared in July 1956 attached to 35015; was removed on 1 May 1958 and from 14 May that year was attached to 35024. The pair entered Eastleigh Works in February 1959 and re-emerged with 35024 now rebuilt, the tender remaining attached until 20 December 1961, when the coal weighing equipment was removed and the tender rebodied with a stretched version of the 5,250 gallon tank – which would have held considerably more than 6,000 gallons. It was then partnered with 35008, in February 1962. In October 1964 it was withdrawn and sent to Woodhams in South Wales for scrap, attached to 35018. Despite this, 3343 is still with us today, with its last partner 35018.'

The Tender Tale

21C1/35001: no.3111 2/41; no.3112 5/41 (while no.3111 received tank welding and axle box repairs), no.3111 5/41 (modified 6/56); rebodied 2/63; no.3349 3/65 (after engine withdrawn).
21C2/35002: no.3112 6/41; no.3115 3/52; no.3112 3/52 (modified 5/58); rebodied 4/60.
21C3/35003: no.3113 9/41; no.3117 2/44 (rebodied 8/59).
21C4/35004: no.3114 10/41(modified 9/56); no.3113 1/44 (modified 6/58), no.3121 10/65 (after engine withdrawn).
21C5/35005: no.3115 12/41 (rebodied 5/59); no.3348 8/65.

35003 ROYAL MAIL at Clapham Junction on 11 November 1959; presumably it had been used to bring some stock out from the terminus and is now proceeding to Nine Elms shed. A good view of its re-bodied tender 3117, one of the First Series 3111-3120. Photograph John Scrace.

21C6/35006: no.3116 12/41 – stayed with 35006 all its working life. Modified 10/59.
21C7/35007: no.3117 6/42; no.3114 5/44 (modified 9/56); no.3127 9/66.
21C8/35008: no.3118 6/42 (modified 5/57); no.3343 2/62; no.3118 10/64.
21C9/35009: no.3119 6/42 – stayed with 35009 all its working life. Modified 3/57.
21C10/35010: no.3120 7/42 (modified 1/57); no.3122 12/64, fitted at Nine Elms.
21C11/35011: no.3121 12/44 (modified 8/57); no.3129 10/65.
21C12/35012: no.3122 1/45 (modified 7/52); no.3343 7/52 for 2 weeks supposedly; may well not be 'real'; no.3122 7/52; no.3120 12/64.
21C13/35013: no.3123 2/45; no.3124 8/50 (modified 12/52).
21C14/35014: no.3124 2/45; no.3123 6/50; no.3343 11/52; no.3126 7/56; no.3345 3/65; no.3115 9/66.
21C15/35015: no.3126; no.3343 7/56; no.3123 (modified 6/58).
21C16/35016: no.3125 3/45 – stayed with 35016 all its working life. Modified 4/57.
21C17/35017: no.3127 4/45; LMS no.10123 4/48; no.3127 6/48 (modified 3/57); no.3114 9/66 (after engine withdrawn.)
21C18/35018: no.3129 5/45; no.3343 7/52; no.3346 10/52 (modified 2/56); no.3118 (rebodied 1/62); no.3343 10/64 (after engine withdrawn).
21C19/35019: no.3128 6/45; LMS no.10219 4/48; no.3128 5/48 (modified 5/59).
21C20/35020: no.3130 7/45; LMS no.10373 5/48; no.3130 6/48; no.3347 6/52 (modified 6/53); no.3345 5/56 (for dynamometer car tests between Waterloo and Exeter); no.3344 7/56.
35021: no.3333 9/48 (BB tender, 5,500

gallons); no.3342 11/48 (modified 2/52); no.3126 10/65 (after engine withdrawn).
35022: no.3335 10/48 (BB tender, 5,500 gallons); no.3345 1/49; no.3347 6/56.
35023: no.3341 11/48 – stayed with 35023 all its working life; modified 2/57.
35024: no.3333 11/48 (BB tender, 5,500 gallons); no.3346 2/49; no.3123 11/52; no.3343 5/58; no.3346 12/61.
35025: no.3343 11/48; no.3350 6/52 (modified 12/56).
35026: no.3260 12/48 (WC tender, 4,500 gallons); no.3350 7/49; no.3130 6/52 (modified 1/57); no.3349 3/65; no.3111 4/65.
35027: no.3288 12/48 (WC tender, 4,500 gallons); no.3349 4/49 (modified 5/57); no.3130 3/65.
35028: no.3344 12/48 (modified 7/56); no.3345 7/56 (modified 10/59); no.3126 3/65; no.3342 10/65.
35029: no.3347 2/49; no.3129 7/52 (modified 9/59); no.3113 10/65.
35030: no.3348 4/49 (modified 4/58); no.3345 10/65.

'Rebodied' indicates the need for a new tank where corrosion had worn the original out – were 5,250 gallons and retained the five tons coal capacity, except that rebodied tender 3343 was 6,000 gallons.

A contrast in tenders if you like. First, 35010 BLUE STAR in almost simply perfect external condition, newly rebuilt in Eastleigh shed yard on 20 January 1957. The tender, no.3120 which it had had from new, was modified at the same time. The trailing truck looks at first to have changed from the original cast unit to one of the later fabricated ones, but it turns out to be an original cast truck with a new cover over the top. The early crest appeared on the first ten rebuilds. Five years later BLUE STAR is as filthy as can be and tender 3120 certainly matches its loco. Framed in that marvellous gantry on 21 July 1962 is Basingstoke shed, alive with steam including at least two WR locos and a Schools 4-4-0. Photographs Les Elsey and Alec Swain/ www.transporttreasury.co.uk

Splendidly, luxuriantly, scintillatingly finished, the first Bulleid Pacific, the original 'Packet', glints in the sun alongside the Eastleigh coal stage on 10 November 1962 with re-bodied tender. Its condition seems to owe nothing to any recent repair, it is just in perfect external nick. This was not the first time it had appeared radiant – for sheer splendour, for instance, its highly polished appearance in April 1946 for the reintroduced 'Golden Arrow' took some beating. Notice the screw reverse set in a recess in the firebox side, replacing the troublesome steam reverser and the BR speedometer and the sloping footplating. The lengthened valve spindles (1959) extended forward and holes were cut ahead of them in the sloping footplating. These holes had to be covered by the said 'pockets' which, inevitably with this class, were of no less than three different types. The covers came to double as footsteps, beginning life (on 35022 only) as cone shapes inside the smoke deflectors, progressing to boxes and finally, as seen here, becoming larger boxes either side of the smoke deflector, which had to be cut round them. Once you get your eye in they are quite plain in views such as these but it takes a while even to believe in them! Follow your eye leftwards from the top edge of the AWS battery box (35001 was the first to get AWS incidentally) and stop after about two feet... The wheel in the firebox 'shoulder', often prominent in photographs of the rebuilt engines, is the steam manifold cock. For a complete account of the pockets see the British Railways Illustrated issue of March 2011. Photograph Les Elsey.

6. The Record

Notes Accompanying Tables

As in the original 'Book of...' the tables are still divided between Works:1 and Works:2 . Since 2001 more information has come to light thanks to further delvings, communications from readers and access to some but not all of the Boiler Record Cards. Thus some of the locos have a good deal of additional information while others have only a little added. Some corrections have been made to the dates of works visits and other dates added.

All works visits were to Eastleigh and others are indicated in each individual table where necessary such as 'At Bricklayers Arms shed'. It would be satisfying to complete the Works entries from building to the early 1950s so if any reader has access to the information please send to the publisher. These are the levels of repair:-

NC Non Classified
LI Light Intermediate
HI Heavy Intermediate
LC Light Casual
HC Heavy Casual
GO General Overhaul

Some were upgraded as the work unfolded which explains such entries as **LI-GO** though very rarely it was downgraded such as **LC-NC**. Mileages listed under Works:2 was normally that run since the previous **GO**.

w/e = week ending and p/e = period ending.

Also added to the works entries are the tenders used; the boiler list has been updated and the liveries entered under the dates they were applied.

'Tests' that individual locos underwent are listed on the back of the BR9215 engine record cards but the BR9637 forms, *British Railways Southern Region Return of locomotives undergoing repair at Eastleigh Works*, kept at the National Archives, Kew lists these in more detail. As in the original book here is a list but this time in numerical rather than year order. No special significance should be attached to the 'Test' listed under each reference number; they seemed to vary over time and their accuracy as entries is not guaranteed. Some items were recorded a 'U' Undisturbed; 'R' Reconditioned or 'O' Overhauled.

T2064 'C.P.' brand tyre (standard)
T2068 Natural or standard rubber jointing
T2081 Regulator valve setting C.I. This usually refers to Cast Iron as a material - in this case, it is assumed, a cast iron valve seating was fitted into the main regulator body casting which was possibly steel - the object would have been to prolong service life
T2133 Casings at safety valve
T2162 Anti-attrition brakes. These were substitute cast iron brake blocks of a different constituency from the norm, to extend life in service
T2195 Self cleaning smokebox gear (revised test)
T2196 Modified steam reverser

T2204 LMR steam heat relief valve
T2207 Drain pipe fitted to tender TIA doser tank. The 'TIA doser tank' was a steam heated tank fitted to tenders to hold a water treatment compound. This was to combat water side corrosion of the steel fireboxes in the variable boiler water conditions found on the Southern. The TIA system developed in France, was displaced by the BR tube feeder system from 1956.
T2219 Single blastpipe and chimney (35019 works visit 18/2/54-27/2/54**LC**)
T2228 Intermediate rubbing blocks
T2231 Tender raves and tool pockets
T2232 Rocking levers and outrigger brackets
T2241 Modified ashpan and damper gear
T2242 Coupling rods MN class (new test)
T2249 Strengthening of trailing truck
T2258 Boiler barrel plates
T2274 Test mudhole door joints, bottom corners of firebox
T2281 Steam chest drain valves
T2282 Boiler water gauge and drain cocks
T2285 Metcalf's steam heating couplings (new test)
T2292 Vacuum ejector cones mild steel, Davies and Metcalf vacuum ejectors
T2296 Bogies and coupled springs (new test)
T2300 Modified whistle valve springs
T2302 Inside big end heat detector
T2304 MN and WC inside big end cotters (new test)
T2305 Driving coupling rod bushes
T2307 Mechanical Lubricator drive
T2310 Eccentric strap bolts and locking plates
T2319 TIA blowdown valve type C
T2321 Sand ejector steam nozzles
T2322 Inside cylinder lubrication
T2326 Vacuum brake piston rods
T2341 New floorboards to drawing E52266 (new)

Perfect pairing at Folkestone Junction, with Boat Train Pacifics coaling for their return to London. The date would be between the summer of 1958 when 35015 ROTTERDAM LLOYD was rebuilt and autumn 1959, when 35028 CLAN LINE was dealt with. Photograph D.W. Winkworth.

21C1 CHANNEL PACKET

Entered service 5 June 1941 part of order No.1068.
Named 10/3/41 in Eastleigh Works Yard by Rt. Hon. J.T.C. Moore-Brabazon, Minister of Transport.
From new fitted with cast gunmetal cabside number plates and sloping number plate above the buffer beam which was later re-affixed on a vertical face. On the tender side were cast SOUTHERN plates, also on the smokebox door in an inverted horseshoe shape – replaced in early 1942 by a full circular type. For a while in May 1942 it was fitted with tender 3112 while the original 3111 received axlebox repairs.
Renumbered 35001 21/10/49; it lost its smokebox door roundel and cast plates but received a smokebox number plate as 35001.

Tenders
3111 4/6/41*
3349 2/1965
* Although it is mentioned 21C1 'borrowed' no.3112 in May for a short while,
Engine Record Card has entry to traffic as 4/6/41

Boilers
1090 from new
1102 23/8/47
1107 21/10/49
1115 22/12/50
1096 9/6/56
1118 8/8/59

Allocations
Salisbury p/e 5/6/41
Exmouth Jct. Autumn 1942
Stewarts Lane 4/46*
Exmouth Jct. 4/46
Stewarts Lane p/e 25/1/57
Nine Elms p/e 14/6/59
Bournemouth p/e 14/9/64
*short term loan to cover reintroduced Golden Arrow

Works: 1

24/6/41	Left works 22/8/41 painted in malachite green livery
18/12/41	Fitted with new valve gear chains and modified oil bath, having covered 11,069 miles since 4/6/41, horseshoe on smokebox converted to roundel
6/1/42-16/2/42**C**	11,069
2/6/42-13/7/42**C**	
4/9/42-10/9/42**C**	New right hand side cylinder
5/10/42-16/10/42**C**	
31/12/42	Mileage run 35,082
11/10/43-10/12/43**C**	65,074 Smokebox hood fitted and flared deflectors
15/1/44-19/1/44**D**	67,164 repainted wartime black
30/1/44-31/1/44**D**	70,732
14/7/44-9/9/44**A**	89,995
9/4/45-22/4/45**C**	27,554 Exmouth Jct shed
4/9/45-30/11/45**B**	50,644 speedometer,repainted Malachite Green, new cylinders and equalising pipes, extension of mileage 50,000
30/3/46-9/4/46**C**	64,856 Fittings for Golden Arrow regalia
16/7/47-23/8/47**A**	123,403 Standard smoke deflectors
9/9/49-21/10/49**A**	106,214 Renumbered, repainted in BR Blue livery, straw coloured Gill sans numerals, large BR crest
22/5/50-16/6/50**LC**	37,372 Attention to tyres on driving wheels, plates fitted, 'Test no.2064. C.P. Brand Tyres on Coupled Wheels' and Test No.2162. Bronze Bushes supplied-Anti Attrition Co
23/10/50-3/11/50**LC**	55,067 Repaint and check over to work special train for the Queen of the Netherlands
29/11/50-22/12/50**HC**	57,209 Modified cab, 600 steel stays riveted over, 124 new tubes, 'Talbot Stead' and 40 new superheaters

Works: 2
(Mileages = *since last General Overhaul*)

15/4/52-17/5/52**HI**	133,984 miles repainted BR Green, sliding covers for whistle and manifold valves, 450 steel stays riveted over, fusible plugs, flaw in syphon neck welded, 15 new tubes 'Howell'
14/5/53-16/5/53**NC**	195,332 miles Axle examined for flaws
4/6/53-11/6/53**LC**	198,985 miles Driving axle replaced
29/9/53-30/10/53**LI**	214,646 miles Front casing removed, 4 monel metal renewed and 520 steel stays riveted over, fusible plugs, 124 new tubes, 'Stewart and Lloyds' 19 second hand welded superheaters Boiler record card: 'Internal examinations extended to 12/56. Ref.M1163. 10/2/55'
7/12/53-10/12/53	219,313'Return' for previous **LI**
11/6/54-12/6/54**NC**	257,240 miles
17/2/55-12/3/55**LI**	292,480 miles three modifications, boiler pressure reduced, 5 monel metal renewed and 320 steel stays riveted over, 2 syphon patches, lead plugs renewed and plug holes reinforced by welding, 23 new tubes Stewart and Lloyds' 12 new superheaters

30/4/56-9/6/56**GO**	361,312 miles eleven modifications, safety valves resited, TIA recorder removed and connections blanked off, plain coupling rods, tender modified, 43 monel metal, 163 steel and 16 roof stays renewed, 6 new plugs, 2 syphon back patches, set of new tubes 'Howell' set of new superheaters, modified crank pin, plain coupling rods
12/11/57-7/12/57**LI**	82,942 miles one modification, 'Test 2207', 'drain pipe and clip for Tender TIA Doser Tank', 304 steel stays riveted over, 6 fusible plugs, 15 new tubes 'Stewart and Lloyds'
27/5/59-8/8/59**GO**	126,394 miles BR type AWS fitted, rebuilt having covered 807,318 miles since new, anti glare shield, 2nd BR tender emblem, PV spindle pockets
8/12/60-14/1/61**LC-HI**	83,669 miles repair upgraded to **HI, s**peedometer fitted and briquette tube feeder added
3/1/63-2/2/63**LI**	198,007 miles new tender tank, 5,250 gallons
27/11/63-28/12/63**LC**	243,516 miles

Experiments listed on BR9215 card: 2296 2305 2307 2326

Withdrawn 22/11/64 with tender 3349 having worked 1,095,884 miles, 288,566 as a rebuild, stored at Eastleigh shed 12/64-2/65.

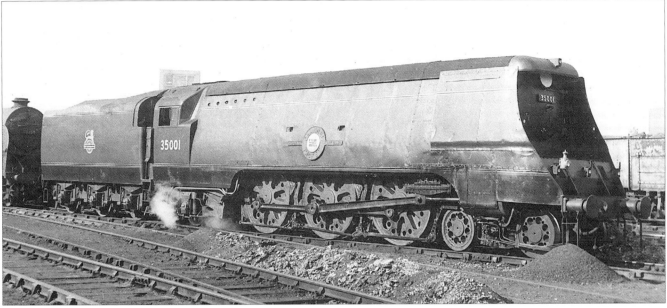

CHANNEL PACKET in blue, after it had its cab modified in December 1950, at its then home shed, Exmouth Junction by the look of it; tender still with black-out slides, slidebars covered. The new smoke deflectors were made in two sections, not always (we note) married together entirely happily – that's apart from the dents from carelessly placed fire irons.

CHANNEL PACKET at Exmouth Junction in August 1956. It had tender 3111 more or less all its life until it was withdrawn at the end of 1964, after which the tender saw a little more service with 35026 LAMPORT & HOLT LINE. Tender 3111 was 'modified' in June 1956, some years before its parent loco was rebuilt and, it must be said, the combination (it occurred several times) looked a little odd. Equally, the opposite combination – a rebuild with an original high-sided tender – was an ill-matched one, though it happened only once, when 35020 was undergoing dynamometer car tests in 1956. It is interesting to recall, as an aside, that in parallel with the cutting down of numerous Bulleid tenders, almost all BR Standard locomotives from around 1955 were built with high-sided tenders, where previously low-sided tenders were the norm! Photograph Peter Groom.

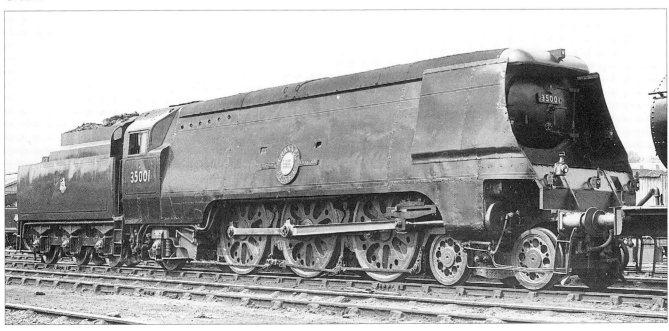

35001 had a couple of brief spells on the Eastern Section; this is during its second stint, passing Shakespeare Halt (the tender was modified in 1956) on 5 August 1957. Traditionally there were three Merchant Navys at Stewarts Lane, supposedly for the boat trains for which they had been so heroically squeezed into the restrictive profile all those years before. Photograph J. Robertsonwww.transporttreasury.co.uk

In the Kentish countryside; near Ashford on 20 October 1957. The Eastern Section ones seemed to have a quieter life than those in the West; Bradley for instance (*Locomotives of the Southern Railway Part Two*, RCTS, 1976) reckoned that, holiday times aside, they 'seldom earned their keep'. Paul Chancellor Collection.

Unmistakably the Western Section; CHANNEL PACKET and high tender with the ACE, passing Vauxhall on 10 July 1952. In BR green, 35001 retains the fairings ahead of the cylinders. Photograph B.K.B. Green, Initial Photographics.

On the first post-war Golden Arrow out of Victoria; first short form of smoke deflector. On 13 April 1946 21C1 made a trial run for the train ('attaining the speed of 98 mph near Paddock Wood') and two days later the public service started with 21C1. A Pullman car was taken out to reduce the load to eight and very soon the Merchant Navy was returned to Exmouth Junction, a light Pacific taking over the working.

A sparkling 35001 CHANNEL PACKET at Eastleigh on 22 August 1959; shedplates were a bit foreign to the Southern and sheds were sometimes a bit remiss when it came to changing them. 35001 had been a Nine Elms engine for some weeks now but still carries its 73A plate. The explanation in this instance would be that 35001 was transferred while still undergoing its rebuilding at Eastleigh (hence the shining condition); it went in as a Stewarts Lane engine and emerged as a Nine Elms one. Photograph Stephen Gradidge.

CHANNEL PACKET with a Nine Elms 70A plate on 29 May 1961, taking water at Basingstoke with the 3pm from Waterloo (through coaches to Plymouth, Ilfracombe and Torrington). Photograph R.S. Greenwood.

Super portrait at Southampton Central with the 11.35am to Waterloo, 27 July 1963. It would later move to Bournemouth as Nine Elms was divested of its express locomotives. Tender has been rebodied by this time. Photograph Nick Nicolson, www.transporttreasury.co.uk

21C2 UNION CASTLE

Entered traffic 16 June 1941, part of order No.1068.
Named on 4/7/41 at Platform 7, Victoria Station by Mr R.F. Gibb, director of the shipping line. From new had cast plates like 21C1.
Worked down Salisbury-Southampton goods trains 5-10/6/41; Salisbury-Eastleigh goods trains 20-23/8/41 and the 'Early morning goods from Salisbury-Southampton 25/8/41'. On 13 August 1945, Stewarts Lane footplate crews worked 21C2 on the 8.55am Victoria-Ramsgate to familarise themselves with the engine, and on 15-17August the engine had test runs Victoria to Dover Marine, two return trips each day with ten Pullmans and two corridor coaches.
Renumbered 35002 4/1/50

Tenders
3112 14/6/41
Engine record card only list above tender, no mention of no.3115

Boilers
1091 14/6/41
1096 13/11/47
1090 6/1/50
1121 27/8/55
1114 10/5/58

Allocations
Salisbury 16/6/41
Exmouth Jct. Autumn 1942
Bournemouth p/e 13/5/54
Exmouth Jct. p/e 22/6/54
Bournemouth 6/6/58
Nine Elms p/e 24/11/60
Bournemouth p/e 17/1/61
Nine Elms p/e 27/1/64

Works: 1

24/6/41	Left 19/8/41 painted Malachite Green
17/11/41-30/12/41**D**	
22/1/42-16/2/42**D**	Attention to main steam pipes having run 15,411miles, piston valve problems saw a balancing pipe fitted between the ends of the steam chests, horsehoe on smokebox converted to roundel
24/6/42-28/7/42**D**	Separate top cowl
31/12/42	39,892
20/3/44-3/6/44**A**	97,212 tender wash plates resited and side bracing strengthened, hood and flared deflectors Repainted wartime black
4/4/45-7/7/45**A**	42,463 fitted with a speed recorder inside the cab and three new cylinders with equalising pipes
13/5/46-25/5/46**C**	38,858
12/6/46-13/7/46**C**	42,954Flaman speed recorder disconnected and the recorder box covered by a plate, repainted Malachite Green
4/1047-13/11/47**A**	98,287Standard smoke deflectors, New steel firebox, internal tubeplate welded and sealed, set of new tub s and new superheaters
17/1/49-25/2/49**B**	67,254 Exmouth Jct shed
23/8/49-30/8/49**D**	89,567
7/11/49-7/1/50**A**	102,322 Repainted BR Blue, straw coloured Gill Sans numerals, renumbered and lost its cast brass number and 'Southern' plates, large BR crest
28/5/51-30//51**HI**	86,252 Repainted BR Green

Works: 2
(Mileages = since last General Overhaul)

3/7/52-22/8/52**I**	150,999 miles Sliding covers on whistle and manifold valves, front casing removed
13/5/53-15/5/53**NC**	192,057 miles Axle examined for flaws only
1/12/53-31/12/53**LI**	217,114 miles Cab modified
1/6/54-5/6/54**NC**	226,358 miles, 'Modification 176, Test 2242'
8/9/54-22/9/54**NC**	249,330 miles, Boiler pressure reduced
8/7/55-27/8/55**GO**	274,531 miles, twelve modifications, 'Tests 2268 2274 and Intermediate type crank axle fitted'; safety valves resited, 136 monel metal renewed and 590 steel stays repaired, 6 fusible plugs renewed, 2 x 1/2 diaphragm patches, 2 syphon pipes patched, set of new tubes 'Stewart and Lloyds', set of new superheaters
7/3/56-21/4/56**LC**	At Bricklayers Arms shed
30/8/56-22/9/56**LI-HI**	60,136 miles, seven modifications, 'Tests 2268 and 2274', TIA recorder not fitted and connections blanked off, 322 steel stays riveted over, 6 fusible plugs renewed, 16 new tubes 'Howell'
1/6/57-29/6/57**NC**	122,816 miles, Tests 2268 and 2274 *
28/3/58-10/5/58**GO**	161,982 miles, ten modifications, 'Tests 2264, 2277, 2081 and 2289; rebuilt having run 776,797 miles, tender modified, Briquette container modified, 2nd BR tender emblem, 142 steel and 16 crown roof stays renewed, 2 diaphragm neck, 2 back end and 2 pipe portions all fitted and welded to syphons, 6 fusible plugs, mudhole seating fitted, 124 new tubes 'Stewart and Lloyds' 40 new superheaters, boiler modified and safety valves resited

30/5/58-20/6/58**NC**	162,850 miles;'Tests 2264, 2277, 2081 and 2289
12/11/59-9/12/59**LC**	At Exmouth Junction shed
8/12/59	Light engine to Newton Abbot for weighing. Returned next day
22/3/60-9/4/60**LI**	117,837 miles, AWS and speedometer fitted, whistle gear, reversing shaft bushes, tender rebodied, 1
monel	metal renewed and 470 steel stays riveted over, 6 fusible plugs, 15 new tubes 'Stewart and Lloyds'
5/9/61-22/11/61**LC**	At Bricklayers Arms shed
27/9/62-3/11/62**LI**	275,140 miles, 1 monel metal renewed and 784 steel riveted over and 26 roof stays repaired, 6 fusible plugs 32 new tubes 'Tube Products' 16 new superheaters, PV spindle pockets
	Boiler record card: Internal examination extended from 5/63-5/64: M1163 10/1/63
	Experiments listed on BR9215 card: 2081 2242 2264 2268 2274 2277 2289 2296 2305 2341 2347

Modified crank pin and plain coupling rods fitted before rebuilding, dates unknown

Withdrawn February 1964 having run 1,101,194 miles, 325,117 as a rebuild, stored at Nine Elms shed January-July 1964.

Festooned in metal plates of various sorts; name, number, roundel, SOUTHERN, black liveried 21C2 UNION CASTLE with the first short smoke deflectors is at Exeter Central on 31 August 1945. Photograph H.C. Casserley, courtesy R.M. Casserley.

21C2 UNION CASTLE at Salisbury shed, 9 July 1949. Three sand filler hatches by now, one for each wheel. It bore the gunmetal plates until renumbered and painted blue in early 1950; the Flaman speed recorder was put on in 1945 for test runs Waterloo-Bournemouth, as mentioned early on. Photograph H.C. Casserley, courtesy R.M. Casserley.

A somewhat down-at-heel 21C2 UNION CASTLE, still with gunmetal plates and speedometer, stands outside Exmouth Junction shed in 1949. The rather home-grown looking ACE board was an early design made from sheet metal, used for several named trains on the SR – note hole for lamp behind. The oblong sheet is the seldom-seen hinged inspection cover (for access to mechanical lubricators as they were then sited) open in front of smokebox. Photograph W. Hermiston, www.transporttreasury.co.uk

35002 UNION CASTLE, at the time an Exmouth Junction engine, arrives at Waterloo on 21 February 1952. Photograph Stephen Gradidge.

35002 UNION CASTLE at Eastleigh on 30 August 1952. By this time the class had all been renumbered and repainting from BR blue to dark green had started, with 35002. Cylinder fairings started to disappear around this time, lending a scrappy look, to the early Merchant Navys in particular. Photograph Stephen Gradidge.

35002 on 2 November 1957, at Andover Junction with the 6.35am Exeter Central-Waterloo.

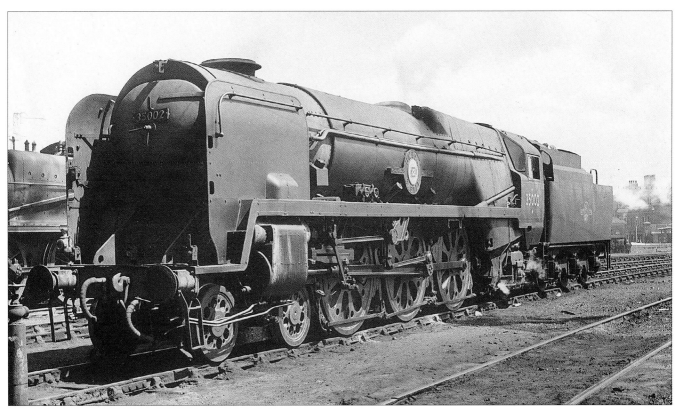

UNION CASTLE unclothed, standing in the yard at Nine Elms in 1962. No speedo, pre-AWS, the three sand filling points replicating the sites in the old casing; sanding on the original engines had (eventually) been to the front of all three coupled wheels but, as we know, the leading one had been blanked off because of the problem of sand getting on the slidebars. In the rebuilds the leading sander was restored; the middle sander served the front of the middle driver as before but the rear one, instead of supplying the rear wheel, was turned round to deliver to the rear of the middle driver, for running in reverse. The rebuilt locomotives are often assumed to have been superior to their predecessors in almost every way but as this book tries to demonstrate, this was not the whole case by any means. Just as Bulleid paid for advantages in disadvantages (as any engineering undertaking does) so it was with the rebuilds. The old oil bath was difficult and dirty to work on but that isn't really the point; it was *intended* to be relatively maintenance free and, for much of the time it was. It's great drawback lay in the fact that when it *did* need attention the job was usually horrible. But look at the successor; in the rebuilt engines there was very little space indeed between the frames; most of the time the originals didn't need a pit but with the new engines one was essential. Getting in there was not fun, by any means. Photograph www.transporttreasury.co.uk

On August Bank Holiday, 4 August 1958 UNION CASTLE, barely run in after rebuilding, on the 1.25pm Weymouth-Waterloo. Photograph Michael Mensing.

Southampton on 27 July 1963. UNION CASTLE had been rebuilt in the spring of 1958; the tender, no.3112, was modified at the same time as the rebuilding and was re-bodied in June 1960 with a 5,250 gallon tank as the earlier version was badly corroded. AWS battery box between frames at front. Photograph Nick Nicolson, www.transporttreasury.co.uk

Arriving at Southampton Central with the 9.22am Bournemouth-Waterloo train, 18 July 1960. Photograph Brian Wadey.

21C3 ROYAL MAIL

Entered traffic 13 September 1941 to order No.1068.
Named on 24/10/41 at Waterloo station by Lord Essendon, Chairman of Royal Mail lines. The engine was now in full malachite green livery. With numbers and lettering in Southern yellow instead of cast brass plates. All letters black lines near the edge. Small window high on cab side, above main window. Glass in side window replaced by plate.
'...cabside windows are of wood and are painted green ...other alterations ...consist chiefly of the use of thinner plates ...reduction of weight of various castings'.
Renumbered 35003 7/6/48.

Tenders
3113 13/9/41
3117 16/2/44

Boilers
1092 13/9/41
1095 17/5/47
1094 19/3/55
1093 29/8/59
1110 25/5/63

Allocations
Salisbury 9/41
Exmouth Jct. autumn 1942
To WR stock, 1/1/63
Nine Elms p/e 20/7/64
Bournemouth p/e 14/9/64
Weymouth p/e 17/10/66
Nine Elms p/e 17/4/67

Works: 1
24/9/41	Malachite Green livery
1/10/41-9/10/41**D**	
6/11/141-8/11/41**D**	
11/11/41-12/12/41**D**	
30/1/42-11/2/42**D**	3,888
26/2/42-31/3/42**D**	
5/6/42-22/6/42**C**	
29/4/43-18/5/43**C**	58,175 Repainted Wartime Black
21/12/43-16/2/44**B**	91,235 fitted with new cylinders and equalising pipes
5/9/44-7/9/44**C**	111,819 Separate top cowl, extension of mileage 10,000
27/11/44-6/12/44**C**	121,789 At Exmouth Junction shed
25/8/45-3/11/45**A**	162,307 new left hand cylinder, repainted Malachite Green and newly painted smokebox door replaced circular doorplate
2/5/46-10/5/46**C**	26,000 At Exmouth Junction shed
21/4/47-17/5/47**B**	71,793 Standard smoke deflectors, new steel firebox, 57 monel metal and 1452 steel stays renewed, new firebox, set ofnew superheaters
19/4/48-5/6/48**A**	109,660
16/6/48-19/6/48**D**	Renumbered, Malachite green livery with yellow lines, 'Sunshine' style numerals, BR lettering, 204 steel stays repaired, 6 drop plugs renewed
12/7/48-17/7/48**D**	35
20/4/49-20/5/49**C**	50,970
13/4/50-9/6/50**A** internal	95,001Cab modified, repainted BR Blue, 520 steel repaired and 2 monel metal stays renewed, tubeplate holes welded, 6 fusible plugs, set new tubes set new superheaters
23/4/5-5/5/51**LC**	41,294
21/3/52-26/4/52**HI**	3 steel renewed and 880 steel stays riveted over, 5 cracks welded, plugs renewed, sliding covers over whistle and manifold valves

Works: 2
(Mileages = since last General Overhaul)
14/5/53-16/5/53**NC**	161,353 miles Axle examined for flaws only
22/6/53-8/8/53**HI**	166,143 miles Repainted BR Green, front casing removed, 252 steel stays riveted over, 6 fusible plugs renewed, 33 new tubes, 8 new superheaters
5/3/54-20/3/54**LC**	205,486 miles, Test 2137, safety valve casings, Test 2242, coupling rods replaced
10/2/55-19/3/55**GO**	246,303 miles, 'Test 2242' twenty-two modifications, modified driving crank pin, boiler pressure reduced, safety valves resited
6/12/55-14/1/56**LC-HC**	44,963 miles, two modifications, fitted with new type of crank pin, plain coupling rods
11/6/56-30/6/56**LC**	65,626 miles
8/10/56-3/11/56**LI**	87,484 miles, four modifications,TIA recorder not fitted and connections blanked off
16/1/57-19/1/57**LC**	102,309 miles, T2207 and left-hand side bogie spring renewed
8/1/58-1/2/58**LI**	157,010 miles,one modification T2207, drainpipe fitted to Tender TIA Doser tank
7/11/58-29/11/58**LC**	210,582 miles
11/6/59-29/8/59**GO**	246,513 miles, eleven modifications, three tests BR type AWS fitted, anti glare shield, rebuilt having run 859,784 miles, tender tank rebuilt to 5,250 gallons to DRG.E50504, 2nd BR tender emblem, PV spindle pockets

22/11/60-17/1/61**LC**	At Exmouth Junction shed
22/8/61-30/9/61**LI-HI**	139,772 miles, speedometer fitted and two tests
26/3/62-14/4/62**NC-LC**	179,579 miles
4/4/63-25/5/63**LI-GO**	228,110 miles 'Tests 2296, 2305', spark arrester fitted
13/1/64-25/1/64**LC**	34,813 miles, Tests 2296, 2305, 2326
17/8/64-16/9/64**LC**	
19/5/65-2/7/65**I**	
5/1/67**NC**	

Experiments listed on BR9215 card: 2133 2207 2241 2242 2296 2305 2307 2326 2362

Withdrawn July 1967 having run 1,131,793 miles, 272,009 as a rebuild, stored at Nine Elms shed to about October.

21C3 ROYAL MAIL (nothing to do with the Post Office!) on the rarely-photographed Exmouth Junction turntable about 1947; malachite, the rib for the 'limpet board' sides part of the lining as it were. Original cab, larger smoke deflectors. Photograph John Robertson, www.transporttreasury.co.uk

35003 ROYAL MAIL in blue at Andover on 21 June 1950. In blue livery with black 'skirt'; batten for 'Devon Belle' plate and 'limpet board rib' no longer part of the lining. Photograph W. Hermiston, www.transporttreasury.co.uk

Waterloo station on 2 August 1960. 35003 ROYAL MAIL (small 'pockets' inside the smoke deflectors prominent from this vantage point) waits to leave with the 5pm train for the West of England while Schools 30908 WESTMINSTER is on a local for Basingstoke. At the time 35003 was still an Exmouth Junction engine and 30908 had been at Basingstoke for just over a year. 35003 after a number of transfers ended up at Nine Elms shed and survived right until the end of Southern steam. Photograph D.C. Ovenden, Paul Chancellor Collection.

Out on the road with ROYAL MAIL. 35003 just a few months apart in 1964; firstly, on 27 April it was ostensibly a WR loco, working out of Exmouth Junction shed of course, coming through Wimbledon on the 7.30am Exeter Central-Waterloo, a duty it had worked throughout. Secondly, it has the down Bournemouth Belle passing Raynes Park a short while after departure at 12.30pm from Waterloo, on 24 September. It had just moved from Nine Elms to Bournemouth shed. Photographs John Scrace.

Looking down at heel at Eastleigh on 24 March 1963. The following year 35003 was working well on the Atlantic Coast Express until Thursday 11 June 1964 when a hot inside big end made its presence felt with uncomfortable force at Clapham Junction. On staggering into Waterloo the motion was found to be distorted and ROYAL MAIL had to literally cool its heels for some hours before being towed away to Nine Elms. Photograph Stephen Gradidge.

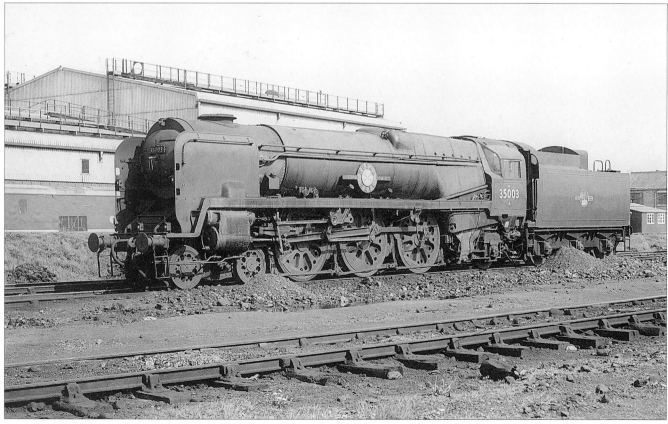

In Eastleigh shed yard with rebodied tender on 5 May 1965, a couple of weeks before it entered the nearby Works for an intermediate service. Speedometer cable by the rear driving wheel and under the cab can be seen the turbo-generator that powered the headlamps. Photograph Peter Groom.

21C4 CUNARD WHITE STAR

Entered traffic 29 October 1941 to works order No.1068 in Malachite Green livery.
Named at Charing Cross station on 1/1/42 by Sir P.E. Bates, Chairman of Cunard White Star.
On loan to Nine Elms shed in place of 21C14, on 16 October 1946, 21C4 took a Pullman special from Waterloo-Southampton Docks for the first passenger sailing of 'Queen Elizabeth'. A trial run with ten Pullmans twelve days before had seen the first visit of the class to Southampton Docks.
Renumbered 35004 19/4/48.

Tenders
3114 28/10/41
3113 24/1/44
3121 31/10/65

Boilers
1093 28/10/41
1110 27/4/46
1095 29/10/55
1121 5/7/58
1113 20/4/63

Allocations
Salisbury 10/41
Exmouth Jct. Autumn 1942
Salisbury p/e 13/11/48.
Exmouth Jct. p/e 4/2/50
Salisbury p/e 1/4/57
Bournemouth p/e 14/9/64

Works: 1

27/12/41-31/12/41**D**	1,415	
7/3/42-23/5/42**D**		
22/7/42-31/7/42**C**		
20/8/42-29/8/42**B**	Tender only	
1/10/42-3/10/42**D**		
15/12/42-29/12/42**C**	24,496	
10/6/43-2/7/43**B**	48,588 Wartime Black livery	
5/8/43-10/8/43**C**		
7/12/43-24/1/44	73,236 miles, balancing pipes added to equalise pressure between ends of steam chests, tender fitted with additional wash plates, flared deflectors	
28/7/44-2/8/44**C**	93,226 Separate top cowl	
19/4/45-28/7/45**A**	124,306 New left-hand side cylinder and equalising pipes	
21/2/46-27/4/46**B**	27,044 Repainted Malachite Green, lamp brackets added to smokebox door	
15/5/46-25/5/46**C**	27,044	
7/10/46-12/10/46**D**	45,998 Standard deflectors	
10/2/47-1/3/47**C**	59,446	
1/3/48-17/4/48**A**	106,115 Renumbered, Malachite Green, yellow lines, 'Sunshine' style numerals, BR lettering	
24/4/48**D**	No mileage recorded	
30/5/49-24/6/59**LI**	59,371	
30/8/50-27/10/50**A**	115,464 Modified cab, speedometer fitted, repainted BR Blue	
5/2/51-9/2/51**LC**	11,759	
20/9/51-24/10/51**LC**	54,112	
25/3/52-26/4/52**LI**	81,813 396 steel stays riveted over, fusible plugs, 20 secondhand superheaters expanded and rebeaded	

(cont overleaf)

The Book of the Merchant Navy Pacifics

Works: 2
(Mileages = since last General Overhaul)

22/1/53-14/2/53**HI**	121,524 miles Repainted BR Green, 1,120 steel stays riveted over, fusible plugs, 41 new tubes, 'Howell' 22 new superheaters, sliding covers for whistle and manifold valves, front casing removed
31/3/53-15/4/53**LC**	126,136 miles
12/5/53-14/5/53**NC**	128,155 miles Axle examined for flaws only
27/7/53-7/8/53**NC**	146,510 miles
17/11/53-28/11/53**LC**	161,753 miles
2/6/54-26/6/54**LI**	181,258 miles, ten modifications and boiler pressure reduced, 475 steel stays riveted over, 6 fusible plugs, 30 new tubes 'Howell' 4 new superheaters
28/9/55-29/10/55**GO**	248,081 miles, twelve modifications, two tests, resited safety valves, additional washout plugs to barrel DRG.E.47882, 84 monel metal renewed, 553 steel renewed and 72 crown stays renewed, 6 fusible plugs renewed, 2 crown patches, foundation ring, 4 patches fitted, set new tubes and superheaters
7/3/56-24/3/56**LC**	27,315 miles
7/3/57-30/3/57**LI-HI**	89,845 miles, two modifications, one test, 345 steel stays riveted over, 6 fusible plugs, 16 new tubes 'Howell'
27/8/57-31/8/57**NC**	116,457 miles
21/2/58-26/2/58**NC**	142,890 miles
16/5/58-5/7/58**GO**	156,914 miles, nine modifications, rebuilt having run 750,886 miles, spring links and hanger pins, anti glare shield, 2nd BR tender emblem, 30 monel metal, 87 steel and 16 flexible stays renewed, 6 fusible plugs renewed, 124 new tubes 'Stewart and Lloyds', 40 new superheaters
20/10/59-27/10/59**NC**	92,761 miles, BR type AWS fitted
30/12/59-23/1/60**LI**	104,647 miles, three tests, speedometer fitted, 360 steel stays riveted over, 6 fusible plugs, 1 syphon neck patch fitted and welded, 16 new tubes 'Tube products'
11/5/60-19/5/60**NC**	121,868 miles, 'T2319, 2321, 2322'
18/4/61-13/5/61**LI-HI**	185,943 miles, one modification and three tests, 200 steel stays riveted over, 6 fusible plugs renewed, 2 syphon patches, bottom and back, 30 new tubes 'Stewart and Lloyds', 8 second hand superheaters welded
23/8/62-15/9/62**NC-LC**	254,407 miles, PV spindle pockets
13/3/63-20/4/63**GO**	272,537 miles, spark arrester gear fitted
7/9/64-13/10/64**LC**	
26/8/65-1/10/65**LC**	

Plain coupling rods before 3/1956
Experiments listed on BR9215 card: 2081 2133 2264 2268 2274 2277 2296 2305 2319 2322 2326

Withdrawn October 1965 having run 1,129,417 miles, 378,531 as a rebuild, stored at Eastleigh Works from 9/65-1/66. Scrapped at Eastleigh shed (presumably it was unfit to move by rail) in February 1966.

35004 had just been through the works, repaired and weighed, between 26 August and 14 October 1965 and had its mileage extended for a further 10,000 miles. It then had the mischance to slip severely near Hook while in charge of the 7.24am Bournemouth Central-Waterloo on 28 October and fail with broken and buckled coupling rods. Damage was relatively minor but such was the policy regarding steam stock that repairs were not authorised. It was this that spurred the creation of the Merchant Navy Locomotive Preservation Society (MNLPS) and eventually led to the purchase of 35028 from BR.

Exmouth Junction's 35004 CUNARD WHITE STAR in its 'final original form' as it were, in BR dark green. Note the notorious third rail which in the confines of the running platforms were well protected by wooden battens. Steam locos were not allowed to use the sanders when departing from Waterloo station as this might interfere with the track circuits. So we witnessed many a spectacular departure when a Pacific would slip, to accompanying deafening pyrotechnics.

CUNARD WHITE STAR at Nine Elms in 1946. Note the unusual footsteps cut into the plating at the front and the roundel (21C1 and 21C2 were the only two that carried the inverted horseshoe) with the legend EASTLEIGH 1941 cast in the lower part. It was never a Nine Elms engine and the closest shed it had to London was Salisbury; 21C4 has run out of Waterloo light (note the tail lamp) and run forward from Loco Junction down that sloping curve to arrive at the coaling roads. It will run forward and turn before working back to Waterloo. The ground is littered in the typical Nine Elms debris but the loco from up country is clean with number and Southern in the shaded lettering of the period. This front view shows up well the hood and first smoke deflectors designed to get rid of the drifting exhaust. At least access to the smokebox is a little easier with the short ladders either side of the front buffer beam and those inset footsteps either side of the front running number. Photograph www.transporttreasury.co.uk

21C4/35004, at Exmouth Junction off (firstly) the Devon Belle on 14 September 1947 and the Atlantic Coast Express on 7 July a year later. This was the engine shot at by a German raiding aircraft near Whimple in November 1942. Photographs R.C. Riley, www.transporttreasury.co.uk and J.H. Aston.

Works: 2
(Mileages = since last General Overhaul)

30/5/52-5/7/52**LI**	117,801 miles Sliding covers for whistle and manifold valves, front casing removed
17/2/53-28/2/53**LC**	140,008 miles
13/5/53-29/5/53**LC**	144,758 miles Axles checked for flaws at Ashford Works
10/11/53-28/11/53**LC**	163,824 miles
1/1/54-13/2/54**GO**	165,589 miles, valve chain adjustment, resited safety valves and modified steam reverser, repainted BR Green
29/4/54-29/5/54**LC**	5,721 miles, new inside cylinder, boiler pressure reduced
7/12/54-18/12/54**LC-HC**	38,335 miles, 'T2265', plain coupling rods
14/2/55	Gauge wires fitted to coupling rod oil syphons at Eastleigh shed
5/7/55-13/8/55**LI**	55,020 miles, three modifications and three tests, TIA recorder removed also pipes valve blanked off
21/10/55-29/10/55	**Return** for previous **LI** 63,871 miles, three tests
24/2/56-10/3/56**LC**	86,770 miles, one modification, three tests
27/7/56-8/9/56**LI-HI**	106,857 miles, right-hand cylinder replaced after cracks noted
28/6/57-2/8/57**LC**	151,008 miles
1/11/57-30/11/57**LI**	164,250 miles
13/3/58-2/4/58**LC**	183,644 miles
18/6/58-29/7/58**LC-HC**	196,167 miles
2/4/59-30/5/59**GO**	227,317 miles, ten modifications, four tests, rebuilt having run 632,322 miles, tender tank rebodied to DRG.E.50504, anti glare shields, regulator shroud and cast iron valve seating, 2nd BR tender emblem, PV spindle extensions, 76 monel metal, 170 steel renewed and 20 crown stays renewed, 6 fusible plugs, 124 new tubes 'Stewart and Lloyds', 40 new superheaters
14/11/60-3/12/60**LI**	98,641 miles, AWS and speedometer fitted, 500 steel stays riveted over, 6 fusible plugs, 21 new tubes 'Stewart and Lloyds'
9/4/62-12/5/62**LI**	190,736 miles 650 steel stays riveted over, 6 fusible plugs, 15 new tubes 'Stewart and Lloyds', 5 new superheaters
26/2/63-16/3/63**LC**	240,012 miles
28/11/63-1/2/64**LI-HI**	282,038 miles, spark arrester fitted, 558 steel stays riveted over, 56 new tubes 'Tube Products', 10 second hand superheater tubes welded
	Experiments listed on BR9215 card: 2196 2207 2242 2265 2274 2296 2305 2307 2341

Withdrawn 10/10/65 with tender no.3348 after running 976,806 miles, 344,484 as a rebuild, stored at Feltham 10/65-1/66 and Weymouth 1-3/66 sold to Woodham Brothers, Barry where it stayed 4/66-3/73, spent a number of years at Steamtown Carnforth before eventual restoration (with tender no.3119, ex-35009) on the Great Central Railway at Loughborough, now on the Mid-Hants Railway.

35005 CANADIAN PACIFIC in green, at Waterloo in the mid-1950s, by which time the coupling rods were plain section. The line of square marks climbing up the casing are the relics of the recording equipment attachments, put on during the Rugby trials. Curl retaining cap for connecting rod crankpin replaced by plain cap secured with four studs. The latter would be employed for the return crank of the future Walschaerts valve gear. Photograph T.R. Smith, www.transporttreasury.co.uk

Newly resplendent at Eastleigh in May 1959 with rebodied tender and small 'pockets'. These were confined to the inside of the smoke deflectors; the far one can just be discerned.

35005 CANADIAN PACIFIC in green, at Exmouth Junction with a Battle of Britain light Pacific behind, on 20 August 1957; coupling rods by now plain section. The old boarding forming the casing is showing its age a bit, with many of the rivets standing out a bit too prominently. Photograph K.C.H. Fairey.

After rebuilding in 1959 35005 moved to Bournemouth shed and bade farewell to workings in the West; this is Dorchester South on 12 June 1964 and CANADIAN PACIFIC is working up from Weymouth on the 1.30pm train to Waterloo. The train had come in from the main line on the left, to then reverse into the terminus part of the station. it will now continue with its five coach train, part of duty 384, to Bournemouth. Three months later it transferred to its final shed, Weymouth. Photograph John Scrace.

Late in the day and by now a Weymouth engine, but nevertheless resplendent for its WRS (Warwickshire Railway Society) special CANADIAN PACIFIC (there is a good view of the large right-hand outside 'pocket') sits ready in the shed yard on 23 May 1965. New diesel shunters over to the right... Photograph Alec Swain, www.transporttreasury.co.uk

21C6 PENINSULAR & ORIENTAL S.N.Co.

Entered traffic 14 January 1942 to order No.1068 in Malachite Green livery.
Named at Ashford Works on 4/6/42 by Sir W. Currie, Chairman of the line.
When working an evening Exeter-Salisbury goods near Honiton on 17 December 1942 the chain parted in the oil bath on 21C6; the resulting fires had to be dealt with by the local fire brigade.
Renumbered 11/12/48 as 35006.

Tenders
3116 31/12/41 all its working life

Boilers
1095 31/12/41
1093 21/9/46
1111 4/12/48
1100 4/9/53
1119 9/7/55

Allocation
At Salisbury all its working life.

Works: 1

23/4/42-27/5/42**C**	Wartime Black livery
25/9/42**D**	
19/11/42	Not repaired
5/1/43-30/1/43**C**	35,992 Attention to chain drive gear, small cracks electrically welded
10/6/43-19/6/43**C**	64,009 miles At Nine Elms shed
17/2/44-27/4/44**A**	100,104 miles, hood fitted over smokebox, flared deflectors, fitted with corrugated steel piping to replace 7inch smokebox steam pipes, 118 monel metal stays renewed, small cracks welded, 6 drop plugs, new pattern of oil bath fitted
1/7/44-12/7/44**C**	10,415 Modified hydraulic locking cylinder, 59 steel stays renewed, split and leaking small tubes expanded and welded at Salisbury shed
14/8/44-19/8/44**C**	13,299
29/12/44-10/1/45**C**	33,227 20 monel metal renewed and 437 steel stay recaulked, leaks, stays and flaws repaired at Salisbury shed
12/2/45-20/4/45**B**	41,768 6 drop plugs, set of new tubes and set of new superheaters
14/5/45-18/5/45**C**	41,768
1/12/45-9/2/46**B**	72,960 miles, new left hand cylinder and equalising pipes, 3 experimental fusible plugs fitted
12/8/46-21/9/46**A**	96,408 repainted Malachite Green, new steel firebox
30/6/47-19/7/46**B**	46,024 Standard deflectors
2/2/48-9/2/48**D**	73,440
21/10/48-4/12/48**A**	108,274 renumbered, Malachite Green, yellow lines, BR Gill Sans numerals and lettering
16/12/49-18/1/50**LC**	62,970
31/1/50	62,970 Weighing
14/2/51-17/3/51**HI**	127,092 Modified cab fitted, repainted BR Blue

Works: 2
(Mileages = since last General Overhaul)

12/8/52-12/9/52**HI**	212,263 miles
12/5/53-14/5/53**NC**	245,369 miles Examined for flaws in axles only
31/7/53-4/9/53**GO**	256,429 miles Boiler pressure reduced, repainted BR Green, new steel firebox, front casing removed
14/12/53-19/12/53**LC**	18,522 miles
2/6/54-4/6/54**NC**	45,471 miles, two modifications, 'T2195 and 2242'
26/8/54	62,242 miles, weighing one day
13/1/55-12/2/55**LI**	80,121 miles, ten modifications, 'T2195 and 2242'
2/6/55-9/7/55**LC-HC**	97,345 miles, three modifications, 'T2195 and 2242', safety valves resited, 168 steel and 16 roof stays renewed, 6 fusible plugs, 124 new tubes 'Stewart and Lloyds' and 40 new superheaters, safety valves resited
19/4/56-5/5/56**LC-HC**	134,790 miles, plain coupling rods
2/10/56-3/11/56**LI-HI**	158,440 miles, eight modifications, 'T2195 2207, 2242', TIA recorder not fitted and connections blanked off, 2 monel metal renewed and 345 steel stays riveted over, 2 syphon elbow patches fitted and welded, 6 fusible plugs, 16 new tubes 'Howell'
4/10/57-18/10/57**NC**	213,374 miles, modifications include, steam chest pressure gauge pipe repositioned, cab handrails, left and right piston valve guide bushes, piston valve spindles and tail ends, platform clearance for reversing screw grease nipple
1/7/58-16/8/58**LI**	253,172 miles, one modification, two tests, Briquette container changed, 3 monel metal renewed and 450 steel stays riveted over, 6 fusible plugs, 2 large elbow patches fitted and welded to syphon,, 30 new tubes 'Stewart and Lloyd' and 24 new superheaters.
10/3/59-3/4/59**NC-LC**	282,954 miles, 7 monel metal renewed, 650 steel riveted over and 36 roof stays repaired
5/8/59-10/10/59**GO**	301,506 miles, ten modifications, five tests, BR type AWS fitted, rebuilt having run 962,757 miles, anti glare shield, tender rebodied, 30 monel metal, 160 steel and 20 roof stays renewed, 6 fusible plugs, 2 pipe portions fitted and welded, 124 new tubes 'Stewart and Lloyds', 40 second hand welded superheaters, 2nd BR tender emblem, PV spindle pockets

14/12/60-21/1/61**LI**   84,308 miles, 'T2304 MN and WC inside big end cotters (new test)', speedometer fitted,, 350 steel stays riveted over, 6 fusible plugs, 17 new tubes 'Stewart and Lloyds'

11/4/62-5/5/62**NC-LC**   178,728 miles

14/2/63-23/3/63**LI**   216,496 miles, 565 steel stays riveted over, right and left hand neck patches fitted, 6 fusible plugs, right and left bottom of pipe fitted to syphons,19 new tubes 'Stewart and Lloyds' 8 new superheaters

Experiments listed on BR9215 card: 2190 2195 2207 2242 2282 2296 2305 2304 2305 2307 2318 2326

Withdrawn in August 1964 after running 1,134,319 miles, 271,562 as a rebuild, stored at Eastleigh shed 9/64-2/65 and moved to Woodham Brothers, Barry in 3/65. Left there in 3/83 for a new life on the Glos. & Warwickshire Railway, Toddington where it has been undergoing a comprehensive overhaul. It needed a new tender.

Wrong line working on Honiton bank, August 1955; this would have gone down very badly in the summer season. 35006 PENINSULAR & ORIENTAL S.N.Co. has a short train; probably the 8.12am Salisbury to Ilfracombe stopper – a Salisbury working to Exeter. The lamp has been overlooked after backing on to the coaches in Salisbury station. 35006 was of course based at Salisbury all its working life. Horizontal rib strengthening the casing. As with almost anything where the Merchant Navys were concerned, the nameplate plaques had their own inconsistencies. Generally they were specifically left or right, fluttering in the wind towards the rear of the locomotive. Exceptions were 35006 and 35029 which had identical plates each side, so that the flag on one side (actually the right-hand) fluttered to the front. 35012 had right and left plates until 1951, when they were redesigned, the new ones being identical both sides. Photograph W. Hermiston, www.transporttreasury.co.uk

35006 wet and woebegone at Eastleigh in August 1958 despite having been in for a light intermediate repair (obviously no painting involved) only days before. It would be another year before its next general and rebuilding and it would sadly run only five years in rebuilt condition. Livery worn and the air smoothed 'limpet' casing just tired. The aircraft visible is from Eastleigh airport one assumes. Photograph T. Wright.

35006 a few months later on 16 November 1958 on what is probably the 1.0am Waterloo-West of England train, passing Andover Junction. This was in effect the final days of haulage by a Merchant Navy in original condition. PENINSULAR & ORIENTAL S.N.Co. was a particularly consistent Merchant Navy and was employed on top link work almost to the day it went for rebuilding. Some remedial work has been done to the front portion of the smoke deflector. Photograph Les Elsey.

A rebuilt 35006 at Clapham cutting on one of those time honoured workings for the class, with that unmistakable West of England headcode, on 25 July 1964. PENINSULAR & ORIENTAL S.N. Co. has only a short service time left. It was withdrawn in August; there followed grim years at Woodhams yard but it may yet turn a wheel at Toddington in Gloucestershire where restoration has been ongoing. Photograph Peter Groom.

35006 PENINSULAR & ORIENTAL S.N.Co. at Exmouth Junction shed on 27 July 1961. Good view of the six washout plugs at the top of the firebox, gap for mudhole door at base of cab, handrail running the length of the boiler and the hand holds cut in the smoke deflectors. Photograph Stephen Gradidge.

Both pictures. **From our Irwell Press magazine,** *British Railways Illustrated,* **Volume 13 No.3, December 2003, an item entitled** *Canberra Conundrum:* **The pair of photographs of 35006 PENINSULAR & ORIENTAL S.N. Co. at Waterloo have their origins in the design of a locomotive headboard to mark the maiden voyage of S.S. CANBERRA from Southampton. There was always a strong link between railway, be it London & South Western, Southern or BR Southern Region, and the shipping companies which the railway liked to foster, hence the provision of one, or more, headboards to mark the occasion. Normally ocean liner trains were worked between London Waterloo and Southampton Docks by Lord Nelson or West Country class locomotives rather than the Merchant Navy Pacifics, an arrangement which obviated any embarrassment of having, say, The Cunarder hauled by 35012 UNITED STATES LINES. In any case there was no need for the power of the larger Pacifics on the comparatively easy timings of these trains. However, in this case engine 35006 has been brought up from Salisbury shed to haul the special trains. By the look of it Nine Elms shed has made a good job of cleaning the locomotive, providing pristine duty discs (SPL 4) into the bargain. One assumes this was the principal special train from Waterloo to Southampton New Docks, via Millbrook. The second picture has 35006 in travel-stained condition on arrival at Waterloo rather than departing. It is close to the buffer**

stops and one of the water columns supplying arriving engines. In the background is a pannier tank interloper. 35006 has its rear lamp in position and is ready to go to Nine Elms shed. The first conundrum is why two photographs of the headboard should be needed. There appears to be no difference in design although in the second picture it seems to have a lighter coloured ground and is also free of the travel stains marking the rest of the engine. Next, both photographs are annotated by the Publicity Department on the reverse: *P&O Orient Lines. S.S. "CANBERRA". SPECIAL TRAIN FOR GUESTS, Photograph shows engine headboard.* Both are dated 23 May 1961 and each carries the reference D9130; why was the same number adopted for both pictures? Did 35006 do a round trip on 23 May or, as the state of 35006 in the second picture suggests, were the trips on different days? It would have to have been a rough old day indeed to pick up that much grime in one trip to Southampton and back. From reports in the press it is known that on 16 May 300-400 guests were on board CANBERRA for a trip down Southampton Water and on 21 May seaborne trials were taking place in western waters. The maiden voyage started in June so neither of these photographs relate to that but might have a connection with the earlier sailing in May. The date on the pictures might be that of entering into a register, rather than the date of photographing, as has happened on other occasions. A trap for the unwary!

21C7 ABERDEEN COMMONWEALTH

Entered traffic June 1942 to order No.1068 in Malachite Green
livery. Separate smoke deflectors c.1943.
Named on 30/7/42 at Victoria station by Lord Essendon, Chairman
of the Company.
Renumbered 35007 25/12/48.

Tenders
3117 3/6/42
3114 1/5/44
3127 23/9/66

Boilers
1096 3/6/42
1108 19/7/47
1105 24/3/50
1118 18/6/55
1106 31/5/58

Allocations
Salisbury 6/1942
Weymouth p/e 18/1/65
Nine Elms p/e 17/4/67

Works: 1

3/6/42	Within a short space of time repainted Wartime Black
27/7/42-29/7/42**D**	
17/9/42-15/10/42**C**	250 steel stays riveted over, firebox welded at left syphon pipe on throat plate, 2 large tubes expanded
12/1/43-26/1/43**C**	23,892
23/4/43**D**	
19/6/43-29/7/43**B**	59,311 new right hand cylinder
1/5/44**D**	
2/6/44-17/8/44**A**	100,647 hood fitted over smokebox, flared deflectors, 98 monel metal renewed and 79 steel stay riveted over, 6 drop fuse plugs, 5 new tubes
248/44-25/8/44**C**	100,647
9/10/44-10/10/44**D**	
11/12/44-22/12/44**C**	8,4852 monel metal stays renewed, 34 new tubes and 11 large tubes renewed at Salisbury shed
26/3/45-8/4/45**C**	29,028 43 monel metal stays renewed, 18 small cracks welded on sides and backplate, 6 drop plugs, 6 new tubes at Salisbury shed
21/6/45-25/8/1945**B**	138,575 new left hand cylinder and equalising pipes, 312 steel stays caulked, patch right side of firebox, all superheater tubes expanded
1/3/46-1/4/46**C**	58,352 at Salisbury shed
19/8/46-7/9/46**C**	79,376 extension of mileage 5,000
16/1/47-25/1/47**D**	93,490 60 steel stays replaced, new firebox with old repaired syphon
4/6/47-19/7/47**A**	106,304 Inside cylinder replaced, repainted Malachite Green, standard deflectors
12/11/48-18/12/48**B**	73,761Inside cylinder replaced again after fracture, 11 monel metal renewed and 350 steel stays riveted over, 6 drop plugs, renumbered, Malachite green, yellow lines, SR style numerals
11/1/49-5/2/49**C**	73,775
9/2/50-24/3/50**A**	129,867 Modified cab, repainted BR Blue, new steel firebox and syphons repaired
15/6/51-3/8/51**LI**	87,253 560 steel stays riveted over, fusible plugs renewed, 30 new tubes 'Howell'

Works: 2
(Mileages = since last General Overhaul)

13/11/52-13/12/52**LI**	173,854 miles Repainted BR Green, front casing removed, 625 steel stays riveted over, patch on syphon and fusible plugs renewed, 47 new tubes, 'Howell' and 19 new superheaters, sliding covers on whistle and manifold valves, front casing removed
12/5/53-20/5/53**LC**	199,072 miles Driving axle examined for flaws
24/11/53-24/12/53**HI**	231,769 miles 2 monel metal renewed and 820 steel stays riveted over, 24 cracks welded between stay
holes, lead plugs,	55 new tubes 'Stewart and Lloyds' and 16 secondhand superheaters welded
9/5/55-18/6/55**GO**	298,694 miles, four modifications,'T2268 and 2274', resited safety valves, boiler pressure reduced, modified crank pin
16/8/56-8/9/56**LI**	79,402 miles, six modifications, two tests, tender rebodied, plain coupling rods
15/4/58-31/5/58**GO**	183,787 miles, eight modifications, four tests, rebuilt after running 799,299 miles, modified Briquette container fitted, grease lubrication to pony truck, anti glare shield, 2nd BR tender emblem
9/9/59-26/9/59**LI**	92,117 miles, outside cylinder barrel lubrication, BR type AWS fitted
4/7/60-7/7/60**NC-LC**	143,038 miles
7/3/61-8/4/61**LI-HI**	182,382 miles, 'T2305', speedometer fitted
7/9/62-13/10/62**LI**	272,724 miles, PV spindle pockets
22/4/64-6/8/64**LI-HI**	
5/7/65-9/7/65**LC**	
11/8/66-23/9/66**LC**	

Experiments listed on BR9215 card: 2081 2242 2258 2264 2274 2277 2289 2296 2305 2345

Withdrawn July 1967, due to broken cylinder, having run 1,318,765
miles, 519,466 as a rebuild; stored at Nine Elms until about March
1968 and sold for scrap.

21C7 ABERDEEN COMMONWEALTH on 24 June 1948 leaving Sidmouth Junction on the down Devon Belle; malachite green lined livery, from a repaint in July 1947. Photo Millbrook House Ltd.

35007 ABERDEEN COMMONWEALTH, forging its way up Honiton bank with the all-Pullman Devon Belle; early cab, BR smokebox number but SOUTHERN on tender and 35007 on cab in SR lettering. Photograph W. Hermiston, www.transporttreasury.co.uk

35007 ABERDEEN COMMONWEALTH off the down Devon Belle at Exmouth Junction on 8 July 1949. Photograph H.C. Casserley, courtesy R.M. Casserley.

Although the Devon Belle was advertised as running 'non stop' there were no water troughs on the Southern so a run from Waterloo to Exeter meant a loco change or water stop at least once, which effectively meant Salisbury. To maintain the illusion of non-stop working the Devon Belle locos were changed west of Salisbury at the little country station of Wilton South. This is the 1952 season and 35007, in blue with some of the lining painted over after repairs, is backing into the siding to await the arrival of the down train in the adjacent platform. The engine off that train will pull forward and be running back light on the up line (far left) just as the train gets underway behind ABERDEEN COMMONWEALTH. Photograph www.transporttreasury.co.uk

35007 ABERDEEN COMMONWEALTH passing Exmouth Junction shed on 8 July 1949 with the down train, having taken over at Wilton. This Merchant Navy was always a great favourite for the Pullman down to Exeter. Photograph H.C. Casserley, courtesy R.M. Casserley.

35007 ABERDEEN COMMONWEALTH on Honiton bank, 3 August 1955, in BR green and new cab. It was as 21C7 that the engine had some strange experimental smoke lifting measures applied in 1943. This involved a much wider gap under the 'widow's peak' and two rather flimsy, bolted-on deflector plates. Like the similar tinkerings with Gresley Pacifics, Royal Scots and so on, it was to no avail. Photograph W. Hermiston, www.transporttreasury.co.uk

Sent among the heathens; 35007 at York shed on Sunday 11 October 1964, after working a Birmingham Railway Society special. Photograph www.transporttreasury.co.uk

In truly disgraceful external condition, 35007 ABERDEEN COMMONWEALTH looks grateful for the imminent ending of its journey, coming through Clapham Junction with an up train on 28 June 1965. Despite its grim looks, it worked through to July 1967. Photograph Stephen Gradidge.

21C8 ORIENT LINE

Entered traffic 16 June 1942 to order No.1068 in Wartime Black livery.
Named on 2/11/42 at Waterloo station by Mr. I.C. Geddes, Chairman of the Company.
Renumbered 35008 20/7/49.

Tenders
3118 15/7/49
3343 3/2/62
3118 7/10/64

Boilers
1097 16/6/42
1092 28/8/47
1106 10/10/53
1102 25/5/57
1112 3/2/62

Allocations
Salisbury 6/42
Bournemouth p/e 8/2/54
Exmouth Jct. p/e 20/8/54
Bournemouth p/e 10/3/60
Weymouth p/e 17/10/66
Nine Elms p/e 17/4/67

Works: 1
4/8/42D
26/10/42-31/10/42**D**
23/11/42-12/12/42**C** 24,625
23/3/43-3/6/43**B** 58,698 hood fitted over smokebox, additional plates to deflect the exhaust clear of the cab
24/8/43-22/10/43**C** 71,804
1/5/44-7/5/44**C** 96,516
25/7/44-6/8/44**C** 107,564 50 steel stays replaced by monel metal at Salisbury shed
15/9/44-4/11/44**A** 113,569 new left hand cylinder and equalising pipes, 32 steel stays renewed, short cracks welded in fire area on side throats and back plates, 6 fusible plugs, 15 new small tubes
24/4/45-3/5/45**C** 11,733 39 steel stays renewed, all tubes and superheaters renewed at Salisbury shed
17/9/45-13/10/45**C** 27,733
9/1/45-18/11/45**C** 37,847 at Salisbury shed
27/6/46**C** 61,416 at Salisbury shed
11/12/46-18/1/47**C** 90,966 54 steel stays renewed, extension of mileage 20,000
1/7/47-28/8/47**A** 107,364 After collision with electric stock at Waterloo 10 June 1947, it was repaired with wedge shaped cab and still with a two window cab and boiler No.1092, repainted Malachite Green, new steel firebox, standard deflectors
10/5/49-15/7/49**A** 93,085 Fitted with three window cab, repainted BR Blue, Gill Sans numerals, Large BR crest, renumbered
20/12/49-13/1/50**LC** 27,355 New left-hand side cylinder
18/1/50 'This small repair was not recorded by Erecting Shop'
1/1/51-3/2/51**LI** 93,372

Works: 2
(Mileages = since last General Overhaul)
22/4/52-17/5/52**LI** 173,389 miles Repainted BR Green, sliding covers for whistle and manifold valves
12/5/53-20/5/53**LC** 231,039 miles Driving axle examined for flaws
4/9/53-10/10/53**GO** 251,429 miles Safety valves resited, front casing removed,
3/2/54-5/2/54**NC** 22,084 miles, 'T2081', regulator valve seating
19/8/54-4/9/54**NC-LC** 46,000 miles, 'Modification 176, T2081', boiler pressure reduced
22/11/54-27/11/54**LC** 49,542 miles
14/2/55**NC** Gauge wires fitted to coupling rod oil syphons at Eastleigh shed
14/4/55-7/5/55**LI** 70,677 miles, six modifications, 'T2081 and 2242'
1/5/56-19/5/56**LC** 115,054 miles, plain coupling rods
15/10/56-10/11/56**LI** 140,392 miles, five modifications, three tests, TIA recorder removed and connections blanked off
12/4/57-25/5/57**GO** 164,967 miles, ten modifications, six tests, rebuilt having run 730,712 miles, Doser tank on tender had drain pipe and clips fitted, briquette container fitted, 2nd BR tender emblem
25/11/58-20/12/58**LI** 119,725 miles
23/3/60-23/4/60**LI** 209,216 miles, AWS and speedometer fitted, PV spindle pockets
7/2/61-22/3/61**LC** At Bricklayers Arms shed
24/11/61-3/2/62**LI-GO** 314,700 miles, tender no.3343 had self weighing equipment removed and tender rebodied
W/E 3/2/62 'Test 2305', driving coupling rod bushes
13/12/63-1/2/64**LI-HI** 94,542 miles, spark arrester fitted
13/8/65-1/10/65**LI**
Experiment numbers listed on BR9215 card: 2064 2081 2190 2207 2242 2264 2277 2281 2282 2292 2296 2305 2310 2322 2341.

Withdrawn in July 1967 having run 1,286,418 miles 555,706 as a rebuild, stored at Nine Elms shed 7/67-3/68 before sold for scrap.

Although still showing signs of Southern ownership it is July 1948 and 21C8 at Exmouth Junction is now a BR loco. Repainting in malachite green had taken place the previous year and when fully lined out this livery certainly suited the class. ORIENT LINE has now got the smokebox hood and the standard version of the smoke deflectors. Modified cab but two windows only.

ORIENT LINE at Eastleigh on 19 June 1947, after its contretemps with the electric train at Waterloo two or three weeks earlier. The front of the smoke deflectors and casing is off revealing a mangled collection of lubrication pipes between the frames, along with the Stones generator, in its original site. Looks like the remaining deflector section is a recent 'unfinished' addition, in undercoat.

35008 in drab BR green at Eastleigh about 1955, the coal looking a bit precarious; cab windows now three sliding sections.

35008 ORIENT LINE, up from Exeter for the day, on the ash road at Nine Elms. This picture is undated but the engine was rebuilt in May 1957; no pockets yet. It was the fitting side of things that derived the most benefit from the rebuilding of the Merchant Navys but though there was talk of valves and pistons going back to Eastleigh by the cartload before rebuilding it was never quite as bad as that. After rebuilding it is true that the sheds could deal with much more of the work, but this has to be balanced against the increased preparation time on the part of the driver – work, after all which Bulleid had sought to greatly reduce. This aspect is one of several brought out in the testimonial to Bulleid on his retirement, compiled by Driver Pistell. A generous extract appears in the volume *Bulleid of the Southern* and should be compulsory reading for critics of Bulleid's Pacifics before they put pen to paper. Photograph W. Hermiston, www.transporttreasury.co.uk

Amid the 'ash sea' at Nine Elms on 5 May 1963. The tender is no.3343 (6000 gallons, modified from coal weigher in 1952 and rebodied in 1962) which was attached to 35008 in February 1962 during a light intermediate that became a general. Photograph Peter Groom.

35008 at Nine Elms on 25 May 1963 when the class was still intact and apart from works visits you could have found any one of them on shed that Saturday. ORIENT LINE at the time was a Bournemouth loco and was only based (in name at least) at Nine Elms in the last months of Southern steam. Photograph Stephen Gradidge.

Out on the road with the 1.30pm Waterloo-Weymouth at Micheldever, 9 September 1966; tender 3118 rebodied with 5,250 gallon tank. Photograph John Scrace.

Life at the last; 35008 (this page and opposite) in powerful mood at Nine Elms, 16 October 1965. ORIENT LINE survived right until the end of steam and although despatched to South Wales for scrap it was not purchased by Woodhams, so sank into the melting pot in October 1968. Like many photographers of the period, Stephen Gradidge could not resist a few close-ups, for steam was getting scarcer by the week, and we would miss all that dirt, oil and grease. Photographs Stephen Gradidge.

Clear view of the method of attaching the return crank. Many Merchant Navys, before rebuilding, had the crankpin modified with the four studs with the future rebuilding in mind. Photographs Stephen Gradidge.

21C9 SHAW SAVILL

Entered traffic 25 June, 1942 to order No.1068 in Wartime Black
livery.
Named at Victoria station on 30/7/42 by Lord Essendon, Shaw
Savill Chairman.
Renumbered 35009 31/8/49.

Tenders
3119 25/6/42 all its working life

Boilers
1098 25/6/42
1097 29/11/47
1102 27/2/53
1117 16/3/57
1108 16/9/61

Allocations
Salisbury 6/1942
Exmouth Jct. p/e 1/4/57
WR 1/1/63

Works: 1

27/7/42-29/7/42**D**	
12/11/42-13/11/42**D**	26,802 miles
2/6/43-9/6/43**C**	53,603 miles, smokebox hood, flared deflectors
4/8/43-16/8/43**C**	57,400
18/4/44-17/6/44**A**	103,501
1/2/45-12/2/45**C**	26,090 at Salisbury shed
5/7/45-22/9/45**B**	49,673, new left hand cylinder and equalising pipes, extension of mileage 10,000
15/10/45-25/10/45**C**	49,673
21/11/45-7/12/45**C**	52,393 at Salisbury shed
6/5/46-28/5/46**C**	72,884
11/11/46-7/12/46**B**	95,192 repainted Malachite Green, standard smoke deflectors, extension of mileage 25,000
14/10/47-29/11/1947**A**	131,291 New steel firebox with repaired syphons
18/3/49	66,121 weighing
28/6/49-26/8/49**A**	84,270 new inside cylinder, repainted BR blue, Gill Sans numerals, large BR crest, boiler off for fitters, 320 steel stays repaired, 6 fusible plugs renewed, renumbered
1/11/50-8/12/50**LI**	77,315 580 steel stays repaired, fusible plugs renewed, 55 new tubes, 14 new superheaters
4/4/51-8/12/50**NC**	96,364 weighing only
3/8/51-24/8/51**NC**	120,771 weighing only
2/11/51-21/11/51**HC**	133,727
24/1/52-16/2/52**LC**	139,133 New right-hand cylinder

Works: 2
(Mileages = since last General Overhaul)

20/1/53-27/2/53**GO**	183,064 miles Cab modified, repainted BR Green, sliding covers for whistle and manifold valves, front casing removed
13/5/53-22/5/53**LC**	10,370 miles Driving axle examined for flaws
20/10/53	Weighing only
30/12/53	42,890 miles Weighing only
5/5/54-12/6/54**LC**	62,031 miles, broken cylinder, modification No.81. boiler pressure reduced
17/6/54-9/7/54	62,031 miles, '**Return**' for previous **LC**
19/8/54-11/9/54**LI**	67,712 miles, eleven modifications
23/12/55-28/1/56**LI**	133,610 miles, five modifications, 'T2268, 2274', TIA recorder removed and connections blanked off, plain coupling rods
12/2/57-16/3/57**GO**	182,356 miles, six modifications, seven tests, rebuilt having run 684,482 miles, Briquette container fitted, 2nd BR tender emblem
15/8/58-13/9/58**LI**	114,363 miles
22/1/60-13/2/60**LI**	201,478 miles, 'T2304 inside big end cotters, speedometer fitted, T2310 eccentric strap bolts and locking plates, T2322 inside cylinder lubrication'
18/10/60-22/10/60**NC**	245,301 miles, AWS fitted
25/7/61-16/9/61**GO**	296,461 miles, 178 monel metal, 984 steel renewed and 45 roof stays renewed, 2 front end patches, 2 back end patches and 2 3/4 sides all fitted and welded, 2 back end to crown patches fitted and welded, 6 fusible plugs, 124 new tubes 'Stewart and Lloyds' and 40 new superheaters
20/11/61-6/1/62**NC-LC**	9,562 miles
7/11/62-15/12/62**LI-HI**	76,329 miles, 108 steel stays riveted over, 6 fusible plugs, 15 new tubes 'Stewart and Lloyds', PV spindle pockets
14/3/63-21/3/63**NC-LC**	

Experiments listed on BR9215 card: 2081 2264 2268 2274 2277 2281 2282 2296 2304 2305 2310 2322 2326

**Withdrawn in September 1964 having run 1,127,542 miles, 442,970
as a rebuild with the same tender, stored at Exmouth Junction
shed 10/64-2/65. Sold to Woodham Brothers, Barry where it stayed
3/65-2/89. After a number of years at Brighton it is now owned by
Ian Riley but awaits restoration.**

35009 SHAW SAVILL (it had been renumbered in August 1949) at Exmouth Junction shed on 22 June 1950; Southern Railway style of headboard that fitted neatly just above the front buffer beam. BR lined blue, looking a bit worn here. Photograph J.Robertson, www.transporttreasury.co.uk

The more prosaic style of board on 35009, now in BR lined green, on home shed Salisbury on 31 July 1954. With a tender full of coal the loco must be awaiting departure to Wilton to take up the down working. A late decision in 1955 not to run the Devon Belle meant that 1954 was the last year it operated. Photo A.R. Carpenter, www.transporttreasury.co.uk

The rebuilt SHAW SAVILL at Exmouth Junction shed in August 1957; it had recently gone there after many years at Salisbury, where it had spent the great part of its 'air-smoothed' days. It was rebuilt in March 1957, the tender (3119 which it had throughout its life) modified at the same time. Parts from the original locos included the wheels, the outside cylinders and the smokebox door. The new inside Walschaerts valve gear and cylinder meant extra work for the driver of course, for he now had more oiling round to do and this would normally require an inspection pit unless he had an agile and willing fireman. In its original form 35009 ran for fifteen years but only seven as a rebuild. Photograph J. Robertson, www.transporttreasury.co.uk

What might 35009 be doing at Folkestone? It was always based in the West though somehow it has been pinched by the Eastern Section. In the absence of anything in the Record the only suggestion is that it had been sent round to Bricklayers Arms shop for attention and is now running in – the repair was never entered in the engine history card. The period is not recorded but it is before the early part of 1960 when the speedometer was fitted. Right under the cab side can be seen the ¾hp turbo generator that supplied the electricity for the headlights and the cab lights. A box was handily placed above to hold the fuses. Photo A.H. Lucas, www.transporttreasury.co.uk

35009 SHAW SAVILL at Axminster with an up Waterloo train about 1960, doubtless connecting with a Lyme Regis train, in the bay behind. Photograph B.K.B. Green, Initial Photographics.

21C10 BLUE STAR

Entered traffic 31 July 1942 to order No.1068 in Wartime Black livery.
Named 18/12/42 at Waterloo station by Lord Vestry, Chairman of the Company.
December 1942 saw it at Eastleigh Works in the unlikely role of mobile test bed, in the hope of curing the problems of drifting smoke. The outcome was an experimental hood fitted early in 1943 and, in the March, separate smoke deflectors.
Renumbered 35010 13/12/48.

Tenders
3120 31/7/42
3122 12/64

Boilers
1099 31/7/42
1090 3/1/48
1101 11/11/49
1124 12/5/51
1112 5/1/57
1105 25/11/61

Allocations
Salisbury 7/1942
Nine Elms p/e 4/2/50
Bournemouth p/e 29/1/56
Exmouth Jct. p/e 10/3/60
Western Region stock 1/1/63
Bournemouth p/e 14/9/64

Works: 1
28/8/42**D**	
12/12/42-16/12/42**D**	24,224
23/3/43-8/4/43**C**	Separate top cowl and flared smoke deflectors
23/10/43-22/12/43**B**	74,891
8/8/44-21/8/44**C**	104,390 at Salisbury shed
2211/44-24/2/45**A**	120,033 modified hydraulic locking cylinder
9/4/45-17/4/45**C**	644
12/11/45-22/12/45**B**	34,948
28/3/46-6/4/46**C**	46,298 at Salisbury shed
19/8/46-31/8/46**C**	63,683
11/2/47-15/3/47**B**	85,600 standard smoke deflectors, new right hand cylinder and equalising pipes
23/5/47-7/6/47**D**	91,081 repainted Malachite Green
16/10/47-3/1/48**A**	105,051new steel firebox, renumbered, Malachite Green, yellow lines, SR style numerals
24/11/48-18/12/48**D**	53,572
5/10/49-11/11/49**A**	92,988 cab modified, repainted BR Blue,
6/4/51-12/5/51**GO**	74,826
12/6/51-28/6/51**Return**	1,317
31/3/52-12/4/52**LC**	49,960

35010 BLUE STAR in dark green at Exmouth Junction in August 1955, coaled up and tail lamp on ready to back down to Exeter Central for the up ACE. Modified cap for big end. Photograph W. Hermiston, www.transporttreasury.co.uk

Works: 2
(Mileages = since last General Overhaul)

16/10/52-15/11/52**LI**	76,182 miles Sliding covers, repainted BR Green, front casing removed, sliding covers for whistle and manifold valves
26/1/53-14/2/53**LC**	84,789 miles
9/4/53-15/4/53 **Return**	89,372 miles
13/5/43-16/5/53**NC**	99,434 miles Driving axle examined for flaws at Ashford Works
20/4/54-15/5/54**LI**	139,655 miles, fourteen modifications, three tests, boiler pressure reduced
5/5/55-3/6/55**LI-HI**	198,085 miles, five modifications, four tests, modified crank axle to DRG.W.11247
21/11/56-5/1/57**GO**	270,276 miles, rebuilt having run 663,174 miles, extensive replacement of the main frames in front of the cylinders, resited safety valves
8/5/58-31/5/58**LI**	95,448 miles
7/7/59-15/8/59**LI**	181,810 miles, BR type AWS fitted
5/10/61-25/11/61**GO**	337,822 miles, speedometer fitted, plain coupling rods, 2nd BR tender emblem, 90 monel metal renewed, 928 steel renewed and 41 roof stays renewed, 6 fusible plugs, 2 pipe portions, 2 back end patches and 2 diaphragms fitted and welded to syphons, 124 new tubes 'Stewart and Lloyds' 40 new superheaters
W/E 2/12/61	Briquette tube feeder fitted
21/3/62-7/4/62**NC-LC**	17,371 miles, PV spindle pockets
14/8/62-11/10/62**LC**	At Exmouth Junction shed
12/3/63**LC**	At Stewarts Lane shed
3/7/63-7/9/63**LI**	96,341 miles, spark arrester fitted, 397 steel stays riveted over, 6 fusible plugs, 8 new tubes 'Stewart and Lloyds'
11/10/65-12/11/65**LC**	
17/3/66-18/3/66**NC**	

Experiments listed on BR9215 card: 2190 2204 2207 2265 2268 2274 2301 2305

Withdrawn September, 1966, the main reason being a damaged right-hand cylinder. Mileage run 1,241,299, with 578,775 as a rebuild, stored at Eastleigh shed 9/66-3/67. Sold to Woodham Brothers, Barry where it stayed 4/67-1/85. First moved to North Woolwich it is now resident at Chappel & Wakes Colne, Essex, undergoing restoration.

35010 BLUE STAR at Eastleigh with a prototype BR Atlantic Coast Express headboard based, obviously, on the enamel station signs that were being introduced across BR as standard. Interestingly, for comparative photographic purposes, the board was mounted on a light Pacific, a King Arthur, a Lord Nelson and – well you never know – an S15!

Top left. 35010, with Exmouth Junction plate, looking rather forlorn in 'BR grey' livery in the howling wastes of the Nine Elms shed yard, 17 February 1962. This was a Saturday and according to the front buffer (times are hard!) 35010 is due out on working 525. Photograph A.Swain, www.transporttreasury.co.uk

Above. At Basingstoke on 21 July 1962, the grey getting greyer and the grime grimier, with 35010 in charge of the 3pm Waterloo to the West of England. Photograph A.Swain, www.transporttreasury.co.uk

Left. To end on a brighter note, with BLUE STAR leaves Axminster in a cloud of steam under that distinctive bridge with an up passenger. It's only a slightly brighter note though – BLUE STAR has a least had a rag dragged over it in the last few weeks and although there is no date for the photograph 35010 carries the WR 83D code for its home shed, Exmouth Junction; so it is after September 1963 and before September 1964 when the loco transferred to Bournemouth. During that time it was officially 'WR stock' but this meant nothing other than in the paper sense. Photograph David Anderson.

21C11 GENERAL STEAM NAVIGATION

Entered traffic 30 December 1944 to order No.1189 in Wartime Black livery.
Named on 20/2/45 at Waterloo station by Mr. R. Kelso, Chairman of the Company. Never received blue livery.
Renumbered 35011 6/11/48.

Tenders
3121 31/12/44
3129 10/65

Boilers
1100 31/12/44
1111 11/1/47
1112 6/11/48
1104 29/9/50
1090 29/3/56
1097 4/7/59

Allocations
Nine Elms 12/1944
Bournemouth p/e 8/2/54
Nine Elms p/e 13/5/54
Exmouth Jct. p/e 12/6/57
Bournemouth p/e 10/3/60

Works: 1

9/2/45-10/2/45**D**		
24/3/45-12/5/45**C**	8,673	
29/9/45‑12/10/45**C**	27,733	
18/11/46-11/1/47**A**	84,768 repainted Malachite Green, standard deflectors	
3/1/48-27/1/48**C**	58,178	
29/9/48-6/11/48**A**	84,650 renumbered, Malachite Green, yellow lines, BR Gill Sans numerals and lettering	
7/9/49-7/10/49**HI**	48,222	
1/8/50-29/9/50**HC**	83,460 552 monel metal stays renewed, new steel firebox, new top 1/2 syphons, 124 new tubes 'Howell', 40 new superheaters, Boiler record card.: Internal examination extended to 9/56.Ref. M.1163. 7/1/55, modified cab, new steel firebox	
12/10/51-17/11/51**LI**	132,986 400 steel stays repaired, lead plugs, 30 new tubes 'Howell', repainted BR Green	

Works: 2
(Mileages = since last General Overhaul)

17/4/53-16/5/5H3**LI**	203,241 miles 456 steel stays repaired, slight pit holes on tubeplate welded, lead plugs renewed and holes welded, 15 new tubes 'Howell' 2 new superheaters, sliding covers for whistle and manifold valves, front casing removed
5/1/54-23/1/54**LC**	231,085 miles, Modification No.89, 'T2133' 3inch Ross safety valves, T2204; LMR steam heating relief valve
14/5/54-5/6/54**LC**	239,460 miles, two modifications, boiler pressure reduced
2/7/54-9/7/54**LC**	242,138 miles, was a 'return' i.e. for readjustment to the work
25/1/55-19/2/55**HI**	267,520 miles, eleven modifications, three tests, 280 steel stays repaired, lead plugs, 16 new tubes 'Stewart and Lloyds', 6 new superheaters, balanced crank axle to DRG.W.11247
16/2/56-29/3/56**GO**	320,422 miles, twelve modifications, two tests, plain coupling rods, TIA recorder removed and connections blanked off
19/9/56-5/10/56**NC-LC**	31,394 miles
19/6/57-3/8/57**LI**	68,076 miles, four modifications, two tests. Tender modified.
9/10/58-25/10/58**LC**	154,086 miles
5/12/58-13/12/58**LC**	159,051 miles
7/5/59-4/7/59**GO**	180,942 miles, eleven modifications, four tests, rebuilt having run 670,782 miles, 2nd BR tender emblem, PV spindle pockets, ashpan watering pipes, anti glare shield, regulator shroud and CI valve seat, 42 monel metal and 350 steel stays renewed, 6 fusible plugs, 2 diaphragm neck patches, 124 new tubes 'Stewart and Lloyds' 40 second hand superheaters, PV spindle pockets
20/4/61-20/5/61**LI-HI**	120,574 miles, AWS and speedometer fitted, 400 steel stays riveted over, mudhole seating fitted, 22 new tubes 'Stewart and Lloyds'
17/10/62-1/12/62**LI**	218,584 miles, 720 steel stays riveted over, 6 fusible plugs, syphons right and left bottom patches fitted, 25 new tubes 'Stewart and Lloyds', 6 new superheaters
13/6/63-29/6/63**NC-LC**	248,839 miles, spark arrester fitted, 655 steel stays riveted over, 6 fusible plugs, 21 second hand welded superheaters
20/2/64-21/3/64**LC**	
2/2/65-19/3/65**LC**	150 steel stays riveted over, 6 fusible plugs, 88 new tubes 'Stewart and Lloyds', 15 new and 16 second hand welded superheaters. Boiler record card: Internal examination extended to 6/66 M1163 7/4/65

Experiments listed on BR9215 card: 2133 2204 2207 2242 2274 2282 2296 2305 2307 2326

Withdrawn February, 1966 having run 1,069,128 miles 398,346 as a rebuild, stored at Eastleigh Works 2/66, sold to Woodham Brothers, Barry and stayed there 3/67-3/89, moved to Brighton and now stored at Sellinge in Kent. This loco, peculiarly, went for scrap with no middle crank axle.

21C11 GENERAL STEAM NAVIGATION at Nine Elms on 8 September 1945, accompanied by 0-8-0T 949 HECATE. Photograph H.C. Casserley, courtesy R.M. Casserley.

Still in its original wartime black, 21C11 at Eastleigh on 22 September 1945. Shadow from the next lamp along on the casing. Photograph H.C. Casserley, courtesy R.M. Casserley.

21C11 GENERAL STEAM NAVIGATION at Earlsmoor on 12 June 1948. It was at Nine Elms for the first ten years from building, the first of the second batch delivered at the very end of 1944, in black. By now it is in malachite green. The modified cab did not appear until 1950. 21C11 is on a Bournemouth line train; it spent its time at Bournemouth and Nine Elms sheds save for a short period at Exmouth Junction. Bulbous casing below front fairing now absent. The 21C11 did not give way to 35011 till November 1948. Photograph www.transporttreasury.co.uk

35011 in the Nine Elms shed yard; it carries a Bournemouth 71B plate which helps but little in determining the period, for it went there in 1960 and continued to work from Bournemouth until withdrawal in 1966. As a rebuild it lasted only 6½ years, covering some 400,000 miles in that time.

35011 GENERAL STEAM NAVIGATION at Salisbury with everyone anxious for the off. It ran like this for a relatively short time, from late 1948 to the autumn of 1951. Photograph George Heiron, courtesy Mrs Shirley Heiron, www.transporttreasury.co.uk

35011 GENERAL STEAM NAVIGATION backing down onto its train at Waterloo station – in the final years of Southern steam; very grubby loco, painted-on 70F Bournemouth code and Warship (not better than a Merchant Navy in power or reliability) over in the sidings by the old turntable. The Warships on the Exeter diagrams retired there before the next down working rather than take a trip to Nine Elms, not needing to turn of course. Photograph www.transporttreasury.co.uk

35011 GENERAL STEAM NAVIGATION in perfect condition at Salisbury shed, 6 September 1959. It has worked up from Exeter and is on the coaling roads, tail lamp still up from the short light working back from the station. Photograph B.K.B. Green, Initial Photographics.

35011 at Nine Elms on 1 June 1962, a nice summer Friday; rebuilt in 1959 it was now in its second period at Bournemouth shed. Photograph www.transporttreasury.co.uk

GENERAL STEAM NAVIGATION on a Monday with the down Bournemouth Belle approaching Clapham Junction, 25 October 1965. Photograph Stephen Gradidge.

21C12 UNITED STATES LINES

Entered traffic 13 January 1945 to order No.1189 in Wartime Black livery.
Named at Waterloo station on 10/4/45 by Admiral Schuirman of the United States Navy.
Renumbered 35012 17/3/49.

The nameplate was changed in 1951, the original emblem changing from a flag to a capstan and flag.

Tenders
3122 16/1/45
3120 12/12/64
3343 change 7/1952 not shown on Engine record Card

Boilers
1101 16/1/45
1106 8/3/47
1104 11/3/49
1096 24/2/50
1101 5/7/52
1124 28/2/57
1120 21/4/62

Allocations
Nine Elms 1/1945
Bournemouth p/e 8/2/54
Nine Elms p/e 13/5/54
Weymouth p/e 14/9/64
Nine Elms p/e 17/4/67

Withdrawn April 1967 due to leaking boiler barrel joint, after running 1,134,836 miles, 570,015 as a rebuild, stored at Nine Elms shed 4-6/67 and at Weymouth shed 7/67-3/68. Sold to J. Cashmores, Newport and scrapped 4-9/68.
On 24 April 1964 A4 60008 DWIGHT D.EISENHOWER, destined for the American Railroad Museum at Green Bay, was towed to Southampton Docks by 35012, which in gleaming condition had also hauled all the dignitaries down from Waterloo. The museum's president made it known that upon withdrawal, they would very much welcome the addition of 35012, but the request fell on deaf ears and the loco was scrapped.

Works: 1
7/2/45-14/2/45**D**	
3/4/45-7/4/45**D**	1,373 Broken chain, repainted Malachite Green
1946	Early this year, no date given, loco. ran light engine to Feltham shed via Putney for light repairs, suffering from a hot radial bearing
31/1/47-8/3/47**A**	102,314 standard smoke deflectors
26/5/48-23/6/48**C**	52,876 at Nine Elms shed, leading sand pipes blanked off
25/1/49-11/3/49**A**	78,696 81 steel stays renewed, 130 cracks welded, 2 syphon plates, seams caulked, 6 drop plugs, 124 new tubes 'Howell', 40 new superheaters, modified cab, renumbered, Malachite Green, yellow lines, BR Gill Sans numerals
26/4/49-4/5/49	93 33 steel stays renewed, 10 splits in firebox cut out and welded, 6 fusible plugs at Nine Elms shed
8/1/50-24/2/50**HC**	32,419 500 steel stays repaired
12/1/51-10/2/51**LI**	84,837 fitted with self-cleaning smokebox, repainted BR Blue, 400 steel stays repaired, 6 fusible plugs renewed, 31 new tubes
22/8/51-31/8/51**LI**	111,979 'Replica of company's House flag corrected'
27/12/51-5/1/52**LC**	124,761

Works: 2
(Mileages = since last General Overhaul)
6/5/52-5/7/52**GO**	144,506 miles Boiler pressure reduced, repainted BR Green, tender modified, sliding covers for whistle and manifold valves, front casing removed, new steel firebox, modifications to steam chest liners and morse chains
11/4/53	Seen under repair at Exmouth Junction shed
13/5/53-17/5/53**NC**	58,009 miles
4/6/53-12/6/53**LC**	57,353 miles Driving axle replaced
20/11/53-19/12/53**HI**	79,325 miles
23/12/54-22/1/55**LI**	138,262 miles, two modifications, eight tests
20/1/56-18/2/56**LI**	191,657 miles, seven modifications, ten tests, plain coupling rods
25/1/57-28/2/57**GO**	239,340 miles, six modifications, nine tests, rebuilt having run 564,821 miles
4/12/57-21/12/57**HC-LC**	54,976 miles
2/12/58-24/12/58**LI**	116,773 miles
27/10/59-7/11/59**NC**	179,695 miles, BR type AWS fitted
19/12/59-18/1/60**LC**	Done at Exmouth Junction shed
11/8/60-3/9/60**LI-HI**	228,381 miles, speedometer fitted, PV spindle pockets
7/3/62-21/4/62**GO**	315,907 miles, 2nd BR tender emblem, foundation ring modified, 124 new tubes 'Stewart and Lloyds' and 40 second hand welded superheaters
11/10/62-27/10/62**LC**	26,238 miles
17/5/63-1/6/63**LC**	57,349 miles
26/2/64-18/4/64**LI**	2 monel metal and 671 steel renewed, also 33 roof stays repaired, 6 fusible plugs, 2 neck patches and 2 bottom 1/2 portions fitted and welded to syphons, 17 new tubes 'Tube Products' and fractures in heads of 5 superheaters cut out and welded
29/7/64-19/8/64**LC**	
11/2/66-10/3/66**NC-LC**	

Boiler record card: Internal extended from 4/67 to 10/67. M1163 5/4/67.

A postcard of 21C12 UNITED STATES LINES at Worting Junction, on a West of England train. That inverted horseshoe was no more than a short-lived detail on 21C1 and 21C2. Also apart from a very short time on 21C1, the '21C' number was *always* above the bufferbeam. Short version of the smoke deflectors.

35012 UNITED STATES LINES (note the plural – other renditions are incorrect!) at Waterloo on 4 April 1956. The first Pacifics to appear at Waterloo were of course the Merchant Navys but as the first ten were allocated to Exmouth Junction or Salisbury sheds not a lot was seen of them in London especially as engine changing took place at Salisbury. It was not until the second batch (of which 21C12 UNITED STATES LINES was the second) came to Nine Elms that they really became familiar in the capital. Photograph J.H. Aston.

35012 UNITED STATES LINES at Nine Elms shed with the ACE headboard, 21 May 1957; it had emerged from Eastleigh in rebuilt condition just a few months before. No speedometer yet of course. Photograph J. Robertson, www.transporttreasury.co.uk

Not long after rebuilding, 35012 passes Millbrook with the down Bournemouth Belle. Photograph Brian Wadey.

On 18 June 1957 the new rebuild is on a down working at Bournemouth Central, duty no.29. This is an unusual view, taken from the running shed and thus the reverse of the very many we see from the down platform, looking across to 71B. Note the situation of the signalbox and the elevated walkway which allowed the signalmen a good view of what was happening down below. Do any photos exist taken from that vantage point? Photograph T.R. Smith, www.transporttreasury.co.uk

The down ACE approaching Vauxhall behind 35012 UNITED STATES LINES. Photograph Peter Groom.

In Eastleigh shed yard, 1 June 1963. Photograph Peter Groom.

A steamy UNITED STATES LINES at Nine Elms; it carries the shed code 70G so this is the period after September 1964 when Weymouth had a number of the class allocated until right at the end of Southern steam when a number were officially moved back to Nine Elms shed. Photograph www.transporttreasury.co.uk

Weymouth shed, an old GWR establishment, on 25 May 1966. 35012 UNITED STATES LINES on left, followed by 35026 LAMPORT & HOLT LINE and Standard 4-6-0 73002. Photograph John Scrace.

21C13 BLUE FUNNEL

Entered traffic 5 February 1945 to order No.1189 in Wartime Black livery.

Named at Waterloo station on 17/4/45 by Mr. L. Holt as BLUE FUNNEL LINE but these plates were soon removed; new plates read simply BLUE FUNNEL followed in Latin in smaller letters CERTUM PETE FINEM.

On 22 February 1945 worked the 8.30am down train from Waterloo station. On 19/1/47 took part in fifteen coach 500 ton test trains working between Norwood Junction and Brighton.

Renumbered 35013 10/8/48.

Tenders
3123 3/2/45
3124 16/8/50

Boilers
1104 3/2/45
1093 5/2/49
1112 13/12/52
1105 19/5/56
1119 20/5/61

Allocations
Nine Elms 2/1945
Exmouth Jct. p/e 19/3/54
Western Region stock 1/1/63
Bournemouth p/e 14/9/64
Weymouth p/e 17/10/66
Nine Elms p/e 17/4/67

Withdrawn in July, 1967 having run 1,114,658 miles, 596,743 as a rebuild, stored at Nine Elms shed 7-9/67 and then sold for scrap.

By January 1967 many of the SR engineering works and speed restrictions had been lifted, and crews took the opportunity to 'have a last fling' with steam. On 28 April 35013 left Waterloo fourteen minutes late with twelve coaches and a van, and reached Winchester *one minute early*. The speed recorder was firmly jammed at 104mph. More was to come and on 26 June 1967 35013 attained 106mph!

Works: 1

11/4/45-14/4/45**D**	2,928
22/10/4236-18/11/46**A**	85,747 4 steel renewed and 600 steel stays riveted over, lead plugs, 50 new tubes 'Jarrow'; 32 new superheaters, repainted Malachite Green, standard smoke deflectors
8/5/47-24/5/47**D**	22,417 works visit due to boiler lagging fire
5/7/48-7/8/48**C**	67,101renumbered
24/12/48-5/2/49**A**	80,133 repainted Malachite Green, yellow lines, BR Gill Sans numerals
8/6/50-16/8/50**HI**	66,435 repainted BR Blue
29/6/51-17/8/51**HI**	115,555

Works: 2
(Mileages = since last General Overhaul)

24/10/52-13/12/52**GO**	181,789 miles Modified cab, repainted BR Green, sliding covers for whistle and manifold valves, front casing removed. Tender modified.
13/5/53-6/6/53**LC**	31,154 miles Axle checked for flaws at Ashford Works
16/2/54-27/3/54**LI**	69,919 miles, had to await cylinders, new inside one fitted
15/10/54-21/10/54**LC-NC**	107,737 miles, Boiler pressure reduced
28/1/55-26/2/55**LI-HI**	120,576 miles, two modifications, eight tests
12/1/56-4/2/56**LC-HC**	160,120 miles, eight tests, one modification
6/4/56-19/5/56**GO**	170,246 miles, rebuilt having run 517,915 miles, bogie spring gear to DRG.W.12587, safety valves resited, 90 monel metal renewed, 57 steel renewed, 16 flexible longitudinal renewed and 15 roof stays renewed, copper tube, ½ throat welded, copper firehole, 1/2 back welded, copper wrapping 2 x ½ sides welded, 6 fusible plugs and mudhole seating riveted, 124 new tubes 'Howell' and 40 new superheater tubes, 2 syphon patches 12", 2 pipe end patches and 2 1/2 diaphragm patches all welded
20/7/56-26/7/56**NC-LC**	10,012 miles
3/10/56	Driving shaft and axle box examinations at Bricklayers Arms shed
5/11/56-9/11/56**NC**	28,173 miles, five tests
7/1/57-11/1/57**LC**	40,444 miles
18/6/57-29/6/57**LC**	67,043 miles
6/3/58-29/3/58**LI**	116,883 miles, 4 monel metal renewed and 360 steel stays riveted over, 6 fusible plugs and bottom back portion of syphons renewed and welded, 16 new tubes 'Stewart and Lloyds'
3/3/59-9/4/59**LC**	At Exmouth Junction shed
20/10/59-14/11/59**LI**	237,881 miles, BR type AWS fitted, 2 monel steel renewed and 360 steel stays riveted over, 6 fusible plugs, 45 new tubes 'Tube Products' and 31 secondhand welded superheaters
17/3/61-20/5/61**GO**	325,057 miles, speedometer fitted, 2nd BR tender emblem, 231 monel metal, 1,143 steel and 45 roof stays renewed, 6 fusible plugs, 2 syphon patches fitted and welded, mudhole plugs fitted, 124 new tubes'Tube Products' and 40 new superheaters
8/3/62-17/3/62**NC**	48,687 miles
22/10/62-8/11/62**LC**	92,258 miles, PV spindle pockets
30/1/64-21/3/64**LC-LI**	'W/E 8/2/64, now holding, possible scrap', spark arrester fitted and three tests, 1 monel metal, 16 roof renewed and 766 steel stays riveted over, 6 fusible plugs, 2 small crown patches fitted and welded to back end, 2 neck patches and 2 complete back portions fitted and welded to syphons, 5 fractured heads of superheaters cut out and welded
29/12/65-25/2/66**LC**	Boiler record card: Internal extended from 5/66 to 12/66. M1163 dated 5/5/66 Internal extended from 6/67 to 10/67. M1163 dated 17/5/67
	Experiments listed on the back of the BR 9215 card: 2081 2133 2191 2204 2228 2231 2232 2242 2246 2249 2264 2268 2277 2281 2282 2296 2305 2310 2322

35013 in blue (though you'd never know it) taking the down Atlantic Coast Express over Hurstbourne viaduct (east of Andover) on 24 November 1950. Single line working was in force over the viaduct as up and down lines were separately excavated and re-laid after the structure underneath was repaired.

21C13 in its original black; early cab and cover over the trailing truck, short smoke deflectors. It first bore the name BLUE FUNNEL LINE in April 1945 but because this was, strictly, incorrect, soon after was replaced by new plaques with a Latin phrase, to read BLUE FUNNEL CERTUM PETE FINEM, omitting LINE at the same time. A simple BLUE FUNNEL was its customary sobriquet, not many of us being capable of pronouncing the latter part.

Taking coal at Nine Elms, 8 September 1945. Photograph H.C. Casserley, courtesy R.M. Casserley.

BLUE FUNNEL at Waterloo in September 1952, its last few weeks in BR blue.

In Southern malachite green with the down Bournemouth Belle at Clapham Junction. Photograph Ted's Dad.

A dirty but noisy BLUE FUNNEL at Yeovil Junction on 5 May 1957. Photograph A.E. Bennett, www.transporttreasury.co.uk.

BLUE FUNNEL backing out of Waterloo – at an unknown date unfortunately. AWS was fitted in the autumn of 1959 but though 35013 has the protector shield for the screw coupling below the buffer there is no battery box between the frames – it can only be concluded that it has been part-fitted and the batteries will follow in due course. Photograph B.H. Fletcher, www.transporttreasury.co.uk

Two more of the down Bournemouth Belle at Clapham Junction; BLUE FUNNEL in charge on 31 March 1965 and 25 October 1965 respectively. Photographs Stephen Gradidge.

21C14 NEDERLAND LINE

Entered traffic 13 February 1945 to order No.1189 in Wartime Black
Livery. Never received blue livery.
Named at Waterloo station on 27/11/45 by Mr.A.F. Bronsing,
Managing Director of the line.
*Week ending 28/9/46 used on coal tests between Exeter and
Salisbury, sixteen coaches and twelve the following week. On
1/10/46 it covered the 88 miles Exeter-Salisbury in 86 minutes on
The 10.25am Exeter Central to Waterloo. Return working was the
2.43pm Salisbury-Exeter. Replaced by 21C4 (on loan) at Nine Elms
Shed.*
Renumbered 35014 3/5/49

Tenders
3124 13/2/45
3123 23/6/50
3343 8/11/52
3126 7/7/56
3345 6/3/65
3115 12/4/66 [according to Engine record Card]

Boilers
1106 13/2/45
1100 1/2/47
1106 6/5/49
1107 25/8/51
1103 7/11/53
1123 7/7/56
1116 17/3/62

Allocations
Nine Elms 2/1945
Exmouth Jct. p/e 13/5/54
Bournemouth p/e 10/8/54
Stewarts Lane p/e 4/6/55
Nine Elms p/e 5/6/56
Weymouth p/e 14/9/64

Works: 1

7/4/4520/4/45**C**	2,386 new inside cylinder
16/11/45-24/11/45**C**	37,970 repainted Malachite Green
4/7/46-19/7/46**C**	3,768
30/11/46-1/2/47**A**	89,493 standard smoke deflectors
16/12/47-3/1/48**C**	43,560 cab and firebox sheeting damaged, repaired at Nine Elms shed
1/4/4822/4/48**C**	56,074
1/3/49-6/5/49**A**	95,444 modified cab fitted, renumbered, Malachite Green, yellow lines, BR Gill Sans numerals
2/5/5023/6/50**HI**	53,519 carrying plate: 'Test no.2161. Bronze Bushes, Anti-Attrition Co'
3/7/51-25/8/51**A**	107,409 repainted BR Green, new steel firebox
27/9/51-28/9/51	781

Works: 2
(Mileages = since last General Overhaul)

22/5/52-23/5/52**NC**	45,035 miles
14/10/52-8/11/52**LI**	68,008 miles Front casing removed
24/2/53-27/2/53**LC**	82,756 miles
12/5/53-26/5/53**LC**	102,332 miles Axle checked for flaws at Ashford Works
1/10/53-7/11/53**GO**	116,005 miles 142 steel renewed and 6 roof stays renewed, 2 diaphragm patches and 2 syphon patches, lead plugs, 124 new tubes 'Howell' and 40 new superheaters, sliding covers for whistle and manifold valves
17/6/54-3/7/54**LC**	30,828 miles, Modifications 81 and 176, T2204', boiler pressure reduced, safety valves resited
11/3/55-9/4/55**LI**	71,156 miles, 156 steel stays caulked, lead plugs, 15 second hand tubes, four modifications, standard valve renewal
2/3/56-30/3/56**LC**	At Bricklayers Arms shed
18/5/56-7/7/56**GO**	108,460 miles, rebuilt having run 516,811 miles, boiler modified and safety valves resited, 78 monel metal, 562 steel and 15 roof renewed also 16 flexible stays, 6 fusible plugs, mudhole seating fitted, 2 x 1/2 diaphragm patches, 2 elbow patches 9" and 2 pipe end patches fitted and welded to syphons, foundation ring, 4 corner patches fitted and welded, 124 new tubes 'Howell' and 40 new superheaters.
6/6/57-15/6/57**LC**	68,976 miles, six tests
2/6/58-28/6/58**LI**	136,675 miles, 230 steel stays riveted over, 6 fusible plugs, 2 small elbow patches fitted and welded to syphons, 17 new tubes 'Stewart and Lloyds'
22/9/59-17/10/59**LI**	236,082 miles, BR type AWS fitted, Briquette container fitted, modern lubrication to rubbing blocks, outside cylinder barrel lubrication, 1 monel metal renewed and 450 steel stays riveted over, 6 fusible plugs, 2 back patches and 2 bottom patches fitted and welded to syphons, 30 new tubes 'Stewart and Lloyds' and 12 secondhand welded superheaters

(cont. overleaf)

11/11/60-3/12/60**LC-HI**	308,354 miles, AWS overhauled and speedometer fitted, 560 steel stays riveted over, 6 fusible plugs, 30 new tubes 'Stewart and Lloyds' and 28 secondhand welded superheaters
	Boiler record card: Internal examination extended from 7/61 to 11/61: M.1163 18/11/60
1/6/61-1/7/61**LC**	335,897 miles. New right-hand cylinder
	Boiler record card: Internal examination extended from 11/61 to 2/62. M1163 25/9/61
	Boiler record card: Internal examination extended from 2/62 to 7/62. M1163 10/1/62
31/1/62-17/3/62**GO**	375,945 miles, 2nd BR tender emblem, 301 monel metal, 1,151 steel and 84 roof stays renewed, firehole, 2 new foundation corners, patch fitted back end of crown plate, patch fitted at crown to syphons, left and right hand sides, 6 fusible plugs, 124 new tubes 'Stewart and Lloyds' 40 new superheaters, PV spindle pockets
4/9/63-26/10/63**LI-HI**	88,686 miles, 714 steel stays riveted over, 2 complete back patches and 2 neck patches fitted and welded to syphons, 6 superheaters with split heads to be welded
14/3/65	Railway Magazine [6/65] reported loco under repair at Redhill shed, April 23rd l/e through Purley
2/7/65	'No work carried out'
	Boiler record card: Internal exam extended from 3/67 to 9/67. M.1163
	20/2/67
17/3/66-12/4/66**LC**	
25/5/56-8/6/66**N**	

Experiments listed on back of BR9215 card: 2081 2162 2204 2264 2277 2281 2282 2296 2304 2305 2313

Withdrawn in March, 1967 having run 1,062,394 miles, 545,583 as a rebuild, stored at Weymouth shed, 6-8/67.

35014 NEDERLAND LINE leaves Blackboy Tunnel in August 1954. It is approaching Exmouth Junction with a West of England to Waterloo express and the beginnings of the Exmouth Junction complex are up there on the right. The engine has the coal weighing tender with which it ran from October 1952 until July 1956. The footpath above the van once served the long-closed Mount Pleasant Halt. Photograph John Robertson, www.transporttreasury.co.uk

21C14 NEDERLAND LINE at Waterloo with the Devon Belle about 1948; it was not renumbered until well into the following year. No malachite green Merchant Navy ever did get the BR crest. Notice once again the boarded in third rail, which meant sanding when starting away from here was prohibited.

After working the down Belle on 16 September 1950 NEDERLAND LINE has come on to Bournemouth shed for attention; something's amiss for the crew are peering over the Belle headboard at the mechanical lubricators (as they were sited then). This was one of the class that did not receive BR blue, so it is a BR loco running in malachite green; the change to dark green took place in August 1951.

A year later and 35014 is ex-works at Eastleigh on 30 August 1951, resplendent in the BR dark green livery complete with the black 'skirt' along the lower side of loco and tender. NEDERLAND LINE will soon be returning to its home shed of Nine Elms and once again be a regular to Bournemouth and the West of England. Photograph B.K.B. Green, Initial Photographics.

At home shed Nine Elms a few years later, on 21 August 1954; some hard work has burnt the smokebox door. Comparison with the picture above shows how the appearance suffered without the front fairing. Tender now cut down too. Modellers love a spare set of wheels in a wagon on a shed layout but too rarely do we see this in practice. Lo, there on the right are driving wheels bound for/arrived from Eastleigh.

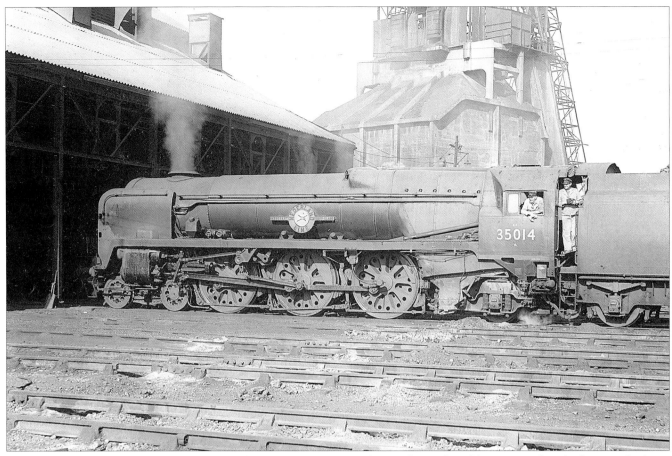

Nine Elms; after January 1957 at least 24 of them were, at separate times, allocated to this great London shed. 35014 had two periods working there. This day, 10 September 1966, it is plainly ready for its next duty, with the crew attempting a nonchalant pose. The same month had seen 35014 get tender no.3115, re-bodied in May 1959 when its then 'owning' loco, 35005, had been rebuilt. Photograph Peter Groom.

With the down Bournemouth Belle in Clapham cutting on 1 August 1964. Photograph Peter Groom.

On the Belle again, at Waterloo on 14 December 1957; no pockets yet of course, nor AWS. Photograph B.K.B. Green, Initial Photographics.

Down relief to the Atlantic Coast Express (with section for Bude) approaching Vauxhall on 30 August 1961; AWS protector plate but no battery box... Photograph Peter Groom.

NEDERLAND LINE with that distinctive solid gait, bringing the down Atlantic Coast Express into Salisbury station on 13 October 1962. Photograph A.E. Bennett, www.transporttreasury.co.uk

Tucked away with other survivors at Nine Elms on 16 October 1965; NEDERLAND LINE was finally withdrawn, from Weymouth shed, in March 1967. Rebodied tender no.3115. Photograph Stephen Gradidge.

21C15 ROTTERDAM LLOYD

Entered traffic 5 March 1945 to order No.1189 in Wartime Black livery.
Named at Waterloo station on 27/11/45 by Mr W. Ruys, Managing Director of the Company.
Worked the inaugural Devon Belle on 20/6/47 to and from Wilton.
Renumbered 35015 8/6/49.

Tenders
3126 6/3/45
3343 6/7/56
3123 14/6/58

Boilers
1105 6/3/45
1107 22/2/47
1121 3/6/49
1099 24/4/54
1113 14/6/58
1091 16/6/62

Allocations
Nine Elms 3/1945
Stewarts Lane p/e 5/6/56
Nine Elms p/e 14/6/59
'Stored unserviceable 6/1/64'

Works: 1

21/4/45-1/5/45**D**	990	
10/9/45-15/9/45**C**	21,482	
15/11/45-24/11/45**D**	31,712 repainted Malachite Green	
9/1/47-22/2/47**A**	94,620 standard smoke deflectors	
6/8/47-23/8/47**C**	18,160 at Nine Elms shed	
30/9/47-25/10/47**B**	25,685 new right hand cylinder	
21/11/47-28/11/47**D**	26,351	
13/4/49-3/6/49**A**	91,899 modified cab, new inside cylinder, renumbered, Malachite Green, yellow lines, BR Gill Sans numerals	
24/1/50-24/2/50**LC**	40,826 second new right hand cylinder, 350 steel stays repaired, 49 smoke tubes and 6 superheater tubes re-welded	
4/5/50-12/5/50**LC**	48,791	
4/1/51-10/2/51**HI**	74,892 repainted BR Blue, 860 steel stays repaired, 6 new fusible plugs, 42 smoke tubes and 15 superheater tubes re-welded	
18/3/52-24/4/52**LI**	135,049 700 steel and 52 roof stays repaired, fusible plugs renewed, 38 tubes renewed, 22 superheater tubes and 3 brackets welded, sliding covers for whistle and manifold valves	

Works: 2
(Mileages = since last General Overhaul)

7/5/53-6/6/53**HI**	193,278 miles Repainted BR Green, 432 steel stays repaired, 6 fusible plugs renewed, 30 small tubes and 6 superheater tubes renewed, front casing removed
9/11/53-28/11/53**LC**	215,728 miles
23/3/54-24/4/54**GO**	229,860 miles, fifteen modifications, boiler pressure reduced, resited safety valves, modified crank pin
1/6/54-12/6/54**NC**	2,754 miles, three tests, oil pump examined and replaced
8/12/55-23/12/55**LC**	At Bricklayers Arms shed
29/5/56-30/6/56**LI-HI**	81,033 miles, two tests, eight modifications, TIA recorder not fitted and connections blanked off, Briquette tube feeder, plain coupling rods
19/6/57-6/7/57**LC**	115,587 miles, 'T2265 and 2268', left-hand cylinder from 35016
1/5/58-14/6/58**GO**	133,392 miles, ten modifications, three tests, new left-hand cylinder, rebuilt having run 549,706 miles, 2nd BR tender emblem
27/10/59-7/11/59**NC**	49,027 miles, BR type AWS fitted
2/1/60-29/1/60**LC**	At Nine Elms shed
25/5/60-18/6/60**LI-HI**	81,987 miles, speedometer fitted, modified cylinder lubrication, whistle gear
5/10/61-16/12/61**LC**	At Bricklayers Arms shed
14/5/62-16/6/62**HC**	188,485 miles, PV spindle pockets
28/12/62-9/1/63**LC**	211,890 miles 'To be stored unserviceable 6/1/64'

Experiments listed on back of BR9215 card: 2081 2133 2264 2265 2268 2277 2282 2304 2305

Withdrawn February 1964 having run 813,950 miles, 264,250 as a rebuild, stored at Nine Elms shed 1-7/64 and then sold for scrap.

35015 ROTTERDAM LLOYD, just ex-works and newly renumbered in June 1949, at Eastleigh. Another engine which spent its first ten years at Nine Elms; covered slidebars, Devon Belle batten; no legend on tender. It later ran with the coal weighing tender. Sufficient superlatives, it must be said, hardly exist to do justice to the exquisite condition of many of the originals in these years. This was the last time a Merchant Navy was repainted in malachite green – a quite beautiful sight. (As a matter of interest, all of the 21C11-21C20 batch went new to Nine Elms and stayed there for years.) Photograph W. Hermiston, www.transporttreasury.co.uk

A very dilapidated 35015 ROTTERDAM LLOYD at Eastleigh works almost certainly in April 1958 when called in for rebuilding. Attached is the coal weighing tender no.3343 with which it had run since July 1956. All side rods removed as well as the left-hand piston. Cylinder drains bent all ways, doubtless by the boots of a fitter standing on them when dismantling the cylinder. Photograph J. Davenport, Initial Photographics.

ROTTERDAM LLOYD went to the Eastern Section from 1956 to 1959, the only time it spent away from Nine Elms, though it was only based a five minute walk away at Stewarts Lane. Rebuilt while down the road with the 'Battersea lot', here it is made ready at Stewarts Lane for 'the Arrer' on 21 March 1959. Photograph R.C. Riley, www.transporttreasury.co.uk

35015 at home shed Stewarts Lane alongside a Dover King Arthur, about 1958-59, before 35015 moved back to Nine Elms in June 1959. ROTTERDAM LLOYD was rebuilt in the summer of 1958 and returned to Stewarts Lane. It had first gone there in June 1956 and was one of the few to work on the Kent routes; it was especially well known for its haulage of the Golden Arrow.

ROTTERDAM LLOYD at Folkestone Junction between boat trains, 28 February 1959. This description of another Merchant Navy, from the original 'Book Of', comes to mind: *from whatever angle there is a look of limitless power, of an engine ready to spring away at an instant with that boiler of vast power. That wide firebox so responsible for the prodigious steam raising powers took/takes a ton of coal just to cover the grate in order to light up!* Mark Arscott, much involved early on in the preservation and running of CLAN LINE adds: *This does not make them very popular on preserved lines – a truly caged lion!* This was steam production on another level altogether really and, detail considerations aside, in the rebuilt Merchant Navys we might well have the apogee of Pacific power in this country. Tested in 1956, after one of the first rebuildings, the boffins could find hardly a trace of carbon monoxide in the smokebox of BIBBY LINE – indicating almost complete combustion. And yet, and yet. They were formidable things, certainly, but after conversion coal, in service, wasn't saved on the scale expected, if at all. Even in ideal test conditions it was only around 10%. Photograph D.W. Winkworth.

Repatriated to Nine Elms, 35015 took up its as-nature-intended duties on the Bournemouth and Exeter lines. At Bournemouth shed on 21 February 1960 it is turned and coaled ready for the return to London. Note the carrying bolts on the smoke deflectors for the actual *fleche d'or*. Photograph Alec Swain, www.transporttreasury.co.uk

ROTTERDAM LLOYD on shed at Exmouth Junction, 18 April 1960. Photograph Stephen Gradidge.

A day at Waterloo, 4 March 1961. 35015 ROTTERDAM LLOYD, looking well cared for, backs on to the stock of the Bournemouth Belle and while the duty number and Bournemouth line discs are put up fellow Nine Elms Pacific 34020 SEATON has appeared on the adjacent train, another Bournemouth line working. Photographs Paul Chancellor Collection.

21C16 ELDERS FYFFES

Entered traffic 14 March 1945 to order No.1189 in Wartime Black livery.
15th March 1945 capacities of tender tested at Eastleigh Works. [Bradley page 18].
Named on 5/7/45 at Waterloo station by Mr H. Stockley, managing director of the Company.
On 23 March 1945 it worked the 9.54am Waterloo to Basingstoke –
'...this seems to be the regular test run for these locomotives.'
Renumbered 35016 23/10/48

Tenders
3125 14/3/45 carried all its working life

Boilers
1107 14/3/45
1112 25/1/47
1094 16/10/48
1111 27/8/54
1110 17/4/57
1124 18/8/62

Allocations
Nine Elms 3/1945
Weymouth p/e 14/9/64

Works: 1

22/5/45-9/6/45**C**	2,117 attention to middle cylinder and oil bath
29/6/45**D**	5,630
22/11/46-25/1/47**A**	86,121 all cylinders re-bored, repainted Malachite Green, yellow lines, standard smoke deflectors
1/9/48-16/10/48**A**	75,447 new steel firebox, renumbered, Malachite Green, yellow lines BR Gill Sans numerals and lettering
29/8/48**C**	75,447 at Nine Elms shed
9/11/48-11/11/48**D**	75,447
24/5/49-17/6/49**LC**	30,917 modified cab, Southern style numerals applied
14/4/50-19/5/50**LI**	65,318 repainted BR Blue, new cab with 'V' front windows
16/6/50-23/6/50**NC**	66,447
6/9/51-12/10/51**HI**	133,047

Works: 2
(Mileages = since last General Overhaul)

16/2/53-14/3/53**LI**	198,485 miles Repainted BR Green
30/6/53-10/7/53**NC**	216,130 miles
18/1/54-30/1/54**LC**	245,586 miles, 'Modification No.89'
6/7/54-27/8/54**GO**	274,356 miles, twelve modifications, boiler pressure reduced and safety valves resited
23/11/55-31/12/55**LI**	61,695 miles, awaited new axle boxes – on 16/11/55 fractures occurred on all four coupling rods and cracks appeared in axleboxes near Gillingham, Dorset. The result was a redesign of the coupling rods and steel axleboxes on the rebuilds, new type crank pins
28/8/56-15/9/56**NC-LC**	102,074 miles, valve and piston exam, plain coupling rods
13/3/57-17/4/57**GO**	117,667 miles, eight modifications, five tests, rebuilt having run 467,091 miles, including new left-hand cylinder, 2nd BR tender emblem
25/9/58-18/10/59**LI**	101,610 miles, fitted with a set of coupled springs similar to Britannia class
15/10/59-7/11/59**LI**	170,265 miles, BR type AWS fitted
31/1/61-25/3/61**LI-HI**	251,080 miles, speedometer fitted
21/6/62-18/8/62**GO**	323,115 miles
26/9/62-29/9/62**NC**	
30/5/63-31/7/63**LC**	At Bricklayers Arms shed
2/3/64-4/4/64**LC**	
25/11/64-18/12/64**NC-LC**	

Withdrawn 8 August 1965 having run 900,637 miles, 433,456 as a rebuild, stored at Weymouth shed 8-11/65 and then sent for scrap.

21C16 ELDERS FYFFES at Waterloo in 1947; malachite green applied at the start of the year. This was one of the class that worked with the same tender throughout its life, no.3125.

A striking, beautiful blue 35016 ELDERS FYFFES at Eastleigh in 1950, alongside the vast water tank building (still with wartime whitewash); sanding abandoned on front wheel though top sliding hatch still looks usable. Photograph W. Hermiston, www.transporttreasury.co.uk

35016 was rebuilt in the spring of 1957 having run 467,091 miles in its original form. Here it is on the 10.30 train out of Waterloo at Vauxhall, 30 August 1961. Photograph Peter Groom.

ELDERS FYFFES in that classic location, the bombed site of the 'Old Shed' at Nine Elms, 22 August 1958. The work of rebuilding was directed by R.G. Jarvis at Brighton, working under H.H. Swift, who had succeeded Bulleid. The original outside cylinders were retained and only the inside cylinder replaced, though where outside cylinders were in poor condition they were replaced by new ones cast off the old pattern. Photograph W. Hermiston, www.transporttreasury.co.uk

35016 in Nine Elms shed yard on 17 July 1964, looking a bit scruffy but still with the same tender, modified at the same time as the rebuilding. Two months later ELDERS FYFFES moved to Weymouth shed from where it was withdrawn in August 1965. Photograph Peter Groom.

35016 ELDERS FYFFES leaving Waterloo with the 4.22pm for Bournemouth, Friday 4 June 1965. 'Old Bananas' had just two months to go before withdrawal – not that the occupants of the flats (from where this photograph was taken) had much reason to mourn the decline of Southern steam. Photograph Peter Groom.

21C17 BELGIAN MARINE

Entered traffic 17 April 1945 to order No.1189 in wartime Black livery.
Named at Victoria station 22/10/45 by Monsieur G. Rongvaux, then Belgian Minister of Communications.
Renumbered 35017 24/4/48.

Tenders
3127 17/4/45
LMS 10123 17/4/48
3127 12/6/48

Boilers
1108 17/4/45
1101 27/6/46
1122 8/7/49
1114 31/7/54
1107 30/3/57
1109 21/9/63

Allocations
Nine Elms 4/1945
Weymouth p/e 14/9/64

Works: 1

12/10/45-20/10/45**D**	23,545 repainted Malachite Green, yellow lines, SR style numerals
12/11/46-3/12/46**C**	87,789 20 steel stays renewed, 4 cracks on firebox plates welded, 50 tubes renewed at Nine Elms shed
23/2/47-17/3/47**C**	96,128 15 steel renewed and 60 steel stays riveted over, 6 new fusible plugs, 26 tubes renewed and 20 superheaters renewed at Nine Elms shed. Standard smoke deflectors.
16/5/47-27/6/47**A**	100,809 66 monel metal renewed and 650 steel stays riveted over, tubeplate and cracks in firebox welded, plug holes welded, fusible plugs renewed, 124 new tubes and 40 new superheaters
10/3/48-17/4/48**C**	34,409 prepared for the Locomotive Exchanges, fitted with Flaman speed recorder, modified cab, LMS tender 10123 fitted w/e 24/4/48, worked Kings Cross-Leeds and Euston-Carlisle, renumbered, Malachite Green, yellow lines, SR style numerals
10/6/48-12/6/48**D**	36,396
12/5/49-8/7/49**A**	81,327 repainted BR Blue
8/8/49-12/8/49	None recorded
19/1/50-27/1/50**D**	24,312
23/6/50-13/7/50**LC**	52,688 new left-hand cylinder
26/10/50-2/12/50**HI**	64,350
9/8/518/9/51**HI**	

Works: 2
(Mileages = since last General Overhaul)

5/3/53-28/3/53**LI**	203,720 miles Repainted BR Green
13/5/53-6/6/53**LC**	209,752 miles Axles checked for flaws at Ashford Works
15/6/54-31/7/54**GO**	278,616 miles, thirteen modifications, boiler pressure reduced, safety valves resited, 168 steel and 15 crown roof stays renewed, 6 fusible plugs, 124 new tubes 'Howell' and 40 new superheaters
14/11/55-10/12/55**LI-HI**	72,587 miles, seven modifications, three tests, plain coupling rods, new type crank pins, 306 renewed and 4 roof stays repaired, 2 syphon elbow patches, lead plugs, 15 new tubes 'Stewart and Lloyds'
26/2/57-30/3/57**GO**	135,397 miles, seven modifications, six tests, rebuilt having run 594,522 miles, 2nd BR tender emblem, anti glare shield
20/5/58-21/6/58**LC-HI**	80,758 miles, two modifications, three tests
28/9/59-24/10/59**LI**	163,007 miles, outside cylinder barrel lubrication, BR type AWS fitted
22/2/61-1/4/61**LI**	243,723 miles, speedometer fitted
13/4/62-5/5/62**LC**	297,132 miles
5/7/63-21/9/63**GO**	333,177 miles, spark arrester fitted
30/3/65-14/5/65**LI**	

Experiments listed on back of BR9215 card: 2081 2190 2212 2264 2268 2274 2277 2281 2282 2296 2305 2312

Withdrawn in July 1966 having run 1,017,754 miles, 423,232 as a rebuild, stored at Weymouth shed 7-8/66 and then sent for scrap.

35017 BELGIAN MARINE approaching Finsbury Park with the 7.50am from Leeds, during the Locomotive Exchanges, 26 May 1948. Photograph J.C. Flemons, www.transporttreasury.co.uk

35017 in green at an Eastleigh Open Day in early August 1954; behind is Battle of Britain 34055 **FIGHTER PILOT**. In the right background can just be glimpsed the tender of 70004 **WILLIAM SHAKEPEARE**.

35017 BELGIAN MARINE, rebuilt in the early part of 1957, outside the 'New Shed' at Nine Elms, 6 September 1958. That is the ashpan operating handle being handed down from the footplate. The general idea was to keep what was regarded as good, which was a very large part of the design, and jettison only what was 'bad'. Rebuilding thus kept the great glory at the heart of the original design, the tremendous steam producing capacity of its boiler. Whatever the advantages of the rebuilds so far as maintenance and repair were concerned, everything had a price and the benefits of the transition should not be wildly overstated; daily preparation time increased of course and the need to fit 'stink bomb' detectors (they released an intense aniseed smell when overheated) to the inside big ends speaks for itself. Out on the road, too, the advantages were less clear cut than has often been claimed; the new screw reverser could physically test the older and stouter driver and certainly the new locos were less free running and smooth riding than the originals, while not all firemen approved of the power-operated firehole doors being removed. Photograph R.C. Riley, www.transporttreasury.co.uk

A famous Belgian at last – 35017 BELGIAN MARINE at Nine Elms on 31 May 1960. Photograph Peter Groom.

Just to prove they could still turn out locomotives to astonishing standards well into the 1960s, here are some detail photographs of 35017 BELGIAN MARINE in September 1963, after a General at Eastleigh. 35017 chalked on tender to make sure it went back on the right Merchant Navy! Photograph Paul Hocquard, www.transporttreasury.co.uk

Flag fluttering correctly. Photograph Paul Hocquard, www.transporttreasury.co.uk

Rear coupling rod on the right-hand side of 35017. The coupling rod has 35017 stamped into it and what looks like a date of 1-12-55. The large nut holding the coupling rod onto the driving wheel is stamped 35002. Photograph Paul Hocquard, www.transporttreasury.co.uk

Note large size spindle 'pockets' ahead of the right-hand cylinder. That whistle connection looked dangerously flimsy yet seemed to work alright! Photograph Paul Hocquard, www.transporttreasury.co.uk

The Walschaerts valve gear as clean as it will ever be; even the ashpan has a gloss paint finish. Photograph Paul Hocquard, www.transporttreasury.co.uk

The lining out of the BR green livery shows up well here. The original fluted coupling rods have been replaced by ones of rectangular section. Photograph Paul Hocquard, www.transporttreasury.co.uk

Quite a way from the glorious condition we've just seen, 35017 BELGIAN MARINE at home in more usual state at Nine Elms where it spent over nineteen years, on 25 May 1963. Photograph Stephen Gradidge.

21C18 BRITISH INDIA LINE

Entered traffic 7 May 1945 to order No.1189 in wartime Black livery.
Named at Waterloo station 13/12/45 by Mr. A.J. Lang, Managing
Director of the British India Steam Navigation Co. Ltd.
When new the driving wheels were fabricated and in 4/47 were
replaced by standard cast type; worked the first post-war
Bournemouth Belle on 7/10/46.
Renumbered 35018 in 29/5/48.

Tenders
3129 7/5/45
3343 11/7/52
3346 14/10/52
3118 13/1/62
3343 10/64*
after loco withdrawn

Boilers
1109 7/5/45
1105 26/4/47
1100 23/9/49
1109 7/7/51
1116 14/2/56
1117 13/1/62

Allocations
Nine Elms 5/1945
Bournemouth p/e 24/11/60
Nine Elms p/e 17/1/61

Works: 1

10/8/45-25/8/45**D**	9,391 repainted Malachite Green, yellow lines, numerals and lettering 'Sunshine' style
4/12/45-8/12/45**D**	27,159
12/646-21/6/46**C**	61,231 rearward extension of smoke deflectors
17/10/46-31/10/46**C**	82,970 at Nine Elms shed
6/11/46-24/11/46**C**	83,759 at Nine Elms shed
19/3/47-26/4/47**A**	96,346 fabricated driving wheels replaced by standard cast type, 106 monel metal renewed and 1108 steel stays riveted over, lead plugs renewed, Foundation ring caulked, 124 new tubes and 40 new superheaters
4/5/48-22/5/48**D**	43,789 Flaman speed recorder fitted, cab modified for the Locomotive Exchanges which 35018 worked Waterloo-Exeter, 19 monel metal renewed and 650 steel stays riveted over, crack welded on sides and syphons, fusible plugs renewed, 88 smoke tubes re-welded and 9 superheater tubes re-welded, renumbered, Malachite Green, yellow lines, 'Sunshine' style for lettering and numerals
30/8/48-22/9/48**C**	58,799 7 steel renewed stays, 18 splits in firebox plates cut out and welded, 124 new tubes and 5 new superheaters at Nine Elms shed
16/5/49-23/9/49**A**	91,744 repainted BR Blue
11/7/50-18/8/50**LC**	51,647 new right-hand cylinder
29/5/51-7/7/51**GO**	90,937 repainted BR Green, new steel firebox
12/11/51-22/11/51**LC**	23,121

(cont. overleaf)

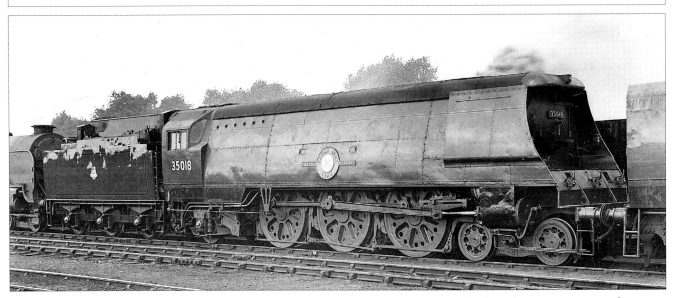

BRITISH INDIA LINE at Eastleigh on 12 July 1952 having just finished a brief non-classified repair, a consequence of a return back to works to sort out some minor complication following a light casual. It was attached to no.3343, the coal weighing tender looking markedly cleaner then the loco. Later in the year this was exchanged for tender no.3346 which had started out with 35024 in April 1949. Loco in BR green, still with speedometer. Photograph Les Elsey.

21C18 BRITISH INDIA LINE at Southampton Central about 1945. The unique fabricated driving wheels – discarded in 1947 – with which it was built can be clearly seen. Original short smoke deflectors, the rear of which were in line with the rear of the cylinders.

Works: 2
(Mileages = since last General Overhaul)

10/6/52-4/7/52**LC**	61,735 miles Front casing removed
29/9/52-14/10/52**NC**	72,748 miles
8/4/53-2/5/53**LI**	97,264 miles
4/6/53-12/6/53**LC**	100,319 miles Driving axle replaced
2/12/53-16/12/53**LC**	131,276 miles
28/6/54-7/8/54**LI-HI**	163,214 miles, fourteen modifications, boiler pressure reduced
6/11/55-14/2/56**GO**	First of class to be rebuilt, having run 504,900 miles, 16 monel metal, 164 steel and 13 roof stays renewed, lead plugs, mudhole door seating fitted, 124 new tubes 'Stewart and Lloyds', 40 new superheaters, Boiler modified to HO.7998, safety valves resited
16/4/56-17/4/56**NC**	5,478 miles, return due to lubrication trouble
25/9/56-4/10/56	Valve and piston exam at Brighton Works
8/3/57-13/3/57**LC**	65,288 miles, five tests
14/5/58-14/6/58**LI**	141,359 miles, five tests, 1 monel metal renewed, 400 steel riveted over and 24 crown stays repaired, 6 fusible plugs. 2 large elbow patches fitted and welded to syphons, 16 new tubes 'Stewart and Lloyds'. Boiler record card: Internal examination extended from 2/61 to 8/61. Ref. M1163. 6/1/60
24/4/59-8/5/59**NC**	208,857 miles, 2nd BR tender emblem, PV spindle pockets [smaller type, retained until withdrawn]
14/1/60-6/2/60**LI**	230,295 miles, speedometer fitted, four tests, 2 monel metal renewed and 600 steel stays riveted over, 6 fusible plugs, 2 back patches, 2 bottom patches and 2 diaphragm necks fitted and welded to syphons,40 new tubes 'Tube products' and 11 secondhand welded superheaters. Boiler record card: Internal examination extended from 8/61 to 10/61. M1163. 5/9/61
2/12/60-10/12/60**NC**	299,519 miles, AWS fitted, three tests
7/11/61-13/1/62**GO**	329,263 miles
10/4/62-19/4/62**NC**	3,894 miles, four tests
17/5/63-12/7/63**LC**	At Bricklayers Arms shed
23/8/63-7/9/63**LC**	82,681 miles, four tests

Withdrawn in August, 1964 having run 956,544 miles, 451,644 as a rebuild, stored at Nine Elms shed 8/64-2/65. Sold to Woodham Brothers, Barry and stored there, with tender no.3343 3/65-3/80. Sold to the Mid-Hants Railway with tender no.3350 and now undergoing long term restoration in Dorset. (Tank from tender no.3350 later sold to the 35025 Brocklebank Line Association.)

21C18 at Salisbury on 21 September 1946 showing the unique short extensions to the smoke deflectors that were added in June 1946. The rear of these were in line with a vertical join in the casing (compare with previous picture).

Getting underway with the down Bournemouth Belle in the middle 1950s – before the tower blocks prominent in later pictures arose – see elsewhere in the book.

Engines could hardly appear in a cleaner condition than this; it is almost unreal (it had been specially prepared for BR official photographs) and is beautifully captured by the photographer in the clear winter light. 35018 BRITISH INDIA LINE stands blinking in the sunlight in the works yard, 7 February 1956. Note how the feed pipes to the clack valves take that sudden change of direction and the curiously high front sand filler, different from the other rebuilds. The first to be rebuilt, BRITISH INDIA LINE was slightly different from the production run and always easy to spot for these reasons. This was true from the other side too, where the bend in the ejector pipe came above the left-hand nameplate. On all the others the bend occurred just to the rear of the smokebox. Note – deflector handrails have not yet been fitted. Photograph Les Elsey.

Belle headboard slightly awry, BRITISH INDIA LINE heads the famous old train past Wimbledon, bound for the seaside.

A quiet Sunday at Nine Elms, 5 May 1963; still that unique and rather odd front sand filler stands out. A week or so after this it left for a light casual at Bricklayers Arms only to be in Eastleigh Works within a few weeks for another light casual. That would be its last visit, for withdrawal came a year later. Rebodied tender attached December 1961. As the first rebuild it should have been preserved and indeed it eventually was, after fifteen years in the open at Barry. Photograph Peter Groom.

Amid what looks like the debris of a ruined brick arch as well as ash, clinker and plenty of rejected 'cobbles' BRITISH INDIA LINE nevertheless looks in fine fettle in Eastleigh shed yard. It had been released after a light casual only a week before; paint on the (clean) wheels and clean motion indicate work below the running plate rather than above, where the surfaces remain a bit grubby. Coal is piled high on the tender as 35018 awaits return to its home shed Nine Elms. Photograph Stephen Gradidge.

Nine Elms on 24 June 1964 and BRITISH INDIA LINE is more or less in black livery, so filthy is it. Photograph Stephen Gradidge.

21C19 FRENCH LINE C.G.T.

Entered traffic 7 June 1945 to order No.1189 in wartime Black livery.
Named at Southampton Docks 22/9/45 by Monsieur de Malglaive, director of the line.
Took part in the 1948 Locomotive Exchanges fitted with a modified cab, a Flaman speed recorder and LMS tender 10219. It worked Kings Cross-Leeds for two days before suffering firebox defects and after attention worked Paddington-Plymouth
Renumbered 35019 11/5/48 (Was s21C19 in Eastleigh Works in March, but emerged fully renumbered.)

Tenders
3128 7/6/45
LMS 10219 13/4/48
3128 29/5/48

Boilers
1103 7/6/45
1102 13/1/50
1108 22/6/51
1100 14/10/55
1092 15/5/59

Allocations
Nine Elms 6/1945
Weymouth p/e 4/9/64

Works: 1

7/6/45-20/8/45	Boiler no.1103 new in 11/1944, repainted Malachite Green, yellow lines, SR style numerals
1/9/45-20/9/45**D**	11,871
1/4/46-4/4/46**D**	44,019 6 drop plugs renewed, 40 smoke tubes and 2 superheater tubes rewelded
10/9/46-4/10/46**C**	76,926 63 small tubes renewed at Nine Elms shed
26/10/46-14/11/46**C**	77,861 at Nine Elms shed
23/6/47-1/8/47**A**	106,463 78 monel metal renewed and 950 stays caulked, tubeplate and firebox cracks welded, fusible plug holes welded and plugs renewed, cylinders rebored due to excessive wear
8/9/47-13/9/47**D**	'None yet recorded'
10/3/48-13/4/48**C**	23,356 6 monel metal, 1 steel renewed and 600 steel stays riveted over, firebox cracks welded, 6 lead plugs, beads rewelded, speedometer fitted, cab modified (as 35019) to suit LMS tender No.10219 w/e 17/4/48
28/5/48-29/5/48**D**	24,636 works visit after loco exchanges and original tender fitted
25/3/49-13/5/49**LC**	66,119 600 steel stays riveted over, firebox cracks welded, 6 lead plugs.
17/11/49-13/1/50**A**	87,932 repainted BR Blue, new steel firebox
8/5/51-23/6/51**GO**	75,177 new steel firebox, single nozzle blastpipe and chimney fitted. BR Green
2/8/51-3/8/51**NC**	574 'Arrived for further adjustment' sandboxes and piping for leading coupled wheels removed, liner inserted in chimney,
15/8/51-17/8/51**NC**	1,187
25/9/51-27/9/51**NC**	3,327
18/1/52-19/1/52**NC**	10,837Chimney alteration included a flared skirt to the petticoat 'with its single exhaust, when working hard, it gave a very creditable imitation of a Paddlebox in full cry'

Works: 2
(Mileages = since last General Overhaul)

13/5/53-6/6/53**HI**	79,241 miles, 552 steel renewed and 559 steel stays riveted over, lead plugs, 15 new tubes Howell'.
3/12/53-24/12/53**LC**1	06,696 miles
18/2/54-27/2/54**LC**	114,787 miles, steam heating relief valve repositioned, single blast pipe and small diameter chimney
9/8/54-4/9/54**LI-HI**	139,752 miles, Boiler pressure reduced, fifteen modifications, 318 steel stays riveted over, lead plugs, 19 new tubes, 'Stewart and Lloyds',10 new superheaters, multiple blastpipe refitted
13/4/55-30/4/55**LC-HC**	175,633 miles, modern crank axle sprocket, wheel and deflector plate fitted to diagram W11228
26/7/55-14/10/55**LC-GO**	182,950 miles, converted to General Overhaul after boiler failure, seven modifications, resited safety valves
1/3/56-17/3/56**LC**	31,525 miles, chimney and blastpipe converted to standard plain coupling rods
7/9/56-6/10/56**LI**	61,438 miles, three modifications, two tests
11/9/57-5/10/57**LI**	109,465 miles, two modifications, three tests, mechanical lubrication arrangement modified
24/10/58-8/11/58**LC**	158,087 miles
17/3/59-15/5/59**GO**	164,868 miles, ten modifications, two tests, rebuilt having run 617,368 miles plus three new cylinders, 2nd BR tender emblem, PV spindle extensions, anti glare shield
9/10/59-16/10/59**NC**	30,824 miles, BR type AWS fitted
11/3/60-26/3/60**LI-NC**	52,407 miles, inside big end heat detector modified
12/1/61-11/2/61**LI-HI**	106,608 miles, speedometer fitted
15/3/62-24/3/62**NC**	175,506 miles, three tests
11/2/63-16/3/63**LI**	220,458 miles, three tests
27/5/64-26/6/64**NC-LC**	

Experiments listed on back of BR9215 card: 2204 2207 2219 2274 2285 2296 2302 2307

Withdrawn 5 September 1965 having run 947,344 miles, 329,976 as a rebuild, stored at Weymouth shed 9-12/65 and at Salisbury shed 1/66. Scrapped in January, 1966.

21C19 FRENCH LINE CGT newly outshopped at Eastleigh in shimmering malachite, in September 1945. Photograph H.C. Casserley, courtesy R.M. Casserley.

Subdued livery now, with BR number in SR style, at Nine Elms, 17 June 1948. Photograph H.C. Casserley, courtesy R.M. Casserley.

35019 FRENCH LINE C.G.T. with LMS tender during the Locomotive Exchanges, near Acton with the 1.30pm from Paddington to Plymouth, 21 April 1948. Appreciative lineside audience to the left. Photograph J.C. Flemons, www.transporttreasury.co.uk

35019 FRENCH LINE C.G.T. now on the Great Northern, leaving Hadley South tunnel with the 7.50am from Leeds, 18 May 1948. The double line would later be enlarged to four lines and a new tunnel built. Photograph J.C. Flemons, www.transporttreasury.co.uk

An almost unreal and blue 35019 FRENCH LINE C.G.T., burnished and honed at Dover shed to a quite astonishing degree; a condition only appropriate of course, to French notions of *la gloire*: apparently the French president was on board for this all-Pullman trip to London Victoria on 7 March 1950, the little-known (to us) Vincent Jules Auriol.

A rather more sombre 35019 FRENCH LINE C.G.T. (the initials stood for 'Compagnie Generale Transatlantique') in BR green at Waterloo on 21 December 1951; it retains the front fairing. On works in March 1948 it was noted with the number s21C19 but it never ran thus.

Above. Bournemouth shed on 8 July 1953 with 35019 with cylinder fairing removed; 34095 BRENTOR also in original form. Photograph J.C. Hillmer.

Left. This is far from a perfect picture but it is unusual to catch one of the locos furiously slipping – and what a sight and sound it was. It wouldn't have done the fire any good; the fireman doesn't seem too pleased either. Salisbury, November 1955. Photograph J.T. Rendell, www.transporttreasury.co.uk

35019 FRENCH LINE C.G.T. at Nine Elms, as usual among the stumps left over from the old coaling stage, on 16 October 1960; it had been rebuilt in May the previous year. The first part of the name, oddly, was in a joined-up 'ooh la la' jaunty script; this was unexpected but, it turns out, the Southern was merely reproducing the shipping company's own style. Its second series 5,100 gallon tender was rebuilt at the same time as the loco, emerging with the later BR emblem from the first. Extended valve spindles but no pockets – just clearance holes in sloping front. Photograph J. Davenport, Initial Photographics.

FRENCH LINE's jolly style of lettering, 22 September 1945. Photograph H.C. Casserley, courtesy R.M. Casserley.

FFRENCH LINE C.G.T. 35019 in blue pauses at Templecombe in March 1950. The fireman has climbed onto the tender and is taking the opportunity to rake the coal forward for the onward journey to Exeter Central. A.E. West, courtesy M.S. King.

21C20 BIBBY LINE

Entered traffic 30 June 1945 to order No.1189 in wartime Black livery.
Named at Waterloo station 18/10/45 by Mr H. Bibby, Chairman of the Company.
Prepared for the Locomotive Exchanges by having a modified cab, a Flaman speed recorder extra long smoke deflectors which were retained until rebuilding and LMS tender (No.10373) but did not take part.
Renumbered 35020 11/5/48.

Tenders
3130 30/6/45
LMS 10373 8/5/48
3130 3/6/48
3347 21/6/52
3345 25/5/56
3344 14/7/56

Boilers
1102 30/6/45
1109 5/7/47
1103 26/5/50
1096 2/7/53
1108 28/4/56
1100 29/4/61

Allocations
Nine Elms 7/1945
Weymouth p/e 14/9/64

Works: 1

Date		Notes
13/7/45-21/7/45**C**		
9/8/45-20/8/45**D**	418	repainted Malachite Green, yellow lines SR style numerals
9/10/45-16/10/45**D**	5,867	
25/5/47-5/7/47**A**	94,134	standard smoke deflectors
21/4/48-8/5/48**C**	34,061	extra long smoke deflectors, cab modified, renumbered, Malachite Green, yellow lines, SR style numerals
31/5/48-3/6/48**D**	36,240	visit after Locomotive Exchanges, fitted with original tender
3/2/49-3/3/49**C**	70,892	
5/7/49-19/8/49**LI**	82,214	
14/3/50-26/5/50**A**	104,880	552 monel metal stays renewed, new steel firebox, top and bottom plates on syphons, 30 new tubes 'Howell', new steel firebox, TIA water treatment equipment fitted and new inside cylinder, Flaman speed recorder removed, repainted BR Blue
16/5/51-9/6/51**LI**	54,253	340 steel stays caulked, 6 lead plugs

BIBBY LINE was the spare for the Locomotive Exchanges and, not needed in the event, stayed at home. It was fitted out for work in the event of failure among the other three and thus ran like this on the Southern (this is Southampton Central) equipped with speed recorder and Stanier tender – the giant deflectors are out of view.

Works: 2
(Mileages = since last General Overhaul)

19/5/52-21/6/52**LI** sliding covers	105,059 miles 350 steel stays caulked, lead plugs, 16 second hand tubes welded, 8 new superheaters, whistle and manifold cover, repainted BR Green, front casing removed
1/5/53-2/7/53**GO**	155,573 miles Safety valves resited, admitted to works after driving axle fractured on 24/4/53 at speed near Crewkerne, smoke deflector plates '..extended rearward by about two feet', 101 monel metal, 592 steel and 12 roof stays renewed, 2 diaphragm patches fitted and welded, two new cylinder drain valves [three previously]
18/5/54-21/5/54**NC**	66,076 miles, 'Modification No.176', boiler pressure reduced. 'truncated lower half of a large BR emblem is clearly visible through the well rubbed paintwork on one side of the tender'
5/11/54-27/11/54**LI-HI**	83,025 miles, seven modifications and tests, 407 steel stays riveted over, 6 new plugs, 15 new tubes 'Stewart and Lloyds'
25/7/55-20/8/55**LC-HC**	118,734 miles, two modifications, six tests, new inside cylinder
15/3/56-28/4/56**GO**	153,451 miles, rebuilt having run 507,958 miles, tender 3345 attached 2/6/56; anti glare shield, spring links, mechanical lubrication arrangement modified, 8 monel metal, 176 steel renewed and 17 roof stays renewed, 2 syphon patches, safety valves repositioned, mud hole seating fitted, barrel patch, Boiler modified to HO.7998, 124 new tubes 'Howell' and 40 new superheaters
28/9/56	At Bricklayers Arms shed, driving shaft and axle box examinations
20/5/57-1/6/57**LC**	60,018 miles
4/7/56	Boiler Record Card shows 1 Crown roof stay renewed
11/2/58-8/3/58**LI**	113,007 miles, modified whistle valve springs, hind boiler support brackets modified, 2 monel metal renewed and 506 steel stays riveted over, 6 fusible plugs, 124 new tubes 'Stewart and Lloyds'
4/5/59-15/5/59**LC**	191,469 miles
26/6/59-1/8/59**LI**	195,017 miles, BR type AWS fitted, 600 steel stays riveted over, 6 fusible plugs, 2 bottom pipes fitted and welded to syphons, 18 new tubes 'Stewart and Lloyds' 6 new superheaters
2/3/61-29/4/61**GO**	289,003 miles, speedometer fitted, 2nd BR tender emblem
18/2/63-23/3/63**LI-HI**	91,750 miles. PV spindle pockets
11/2/65**LI**	

Experiments listed on back of BR9215 card: 2081 2133 2223 2231 2232 2242 2243 2249 2264 2274 2277 2281 2282 2296 2300 2305 2310 2316 2322 2326

Withdrawn February 1965 having run 981,479 miles, 473,521 as a rebuild, stored and cut up at Eastleigh Works 3/65. Only one of the class to be scrapped at its place of birth. (Record Card says 'Scrap at Eastleigh 20/2/65')

35020 BIBBY LINE, in blue and equipped for the Devon Belle. At Nine Elms for almost all its life, it is standing in Salisbury shed yard ready to run back to Wilton and collect the up working of the observation car Pullman train. The Flaman speed recorder, the bracket for which survives, was fitted when the engine was made 'spare' for the 1948 Locomotive Exchanges. Date (note slidebar cover) is about 1950. Photograph W. Hermiston, www.transporttreasury.co.uk

BIBBY LINE at Nine Elms with the temporary high sided tender fitted for dynamometer car tests between Waterloo and Exeter in May-June 1956. This tender was employed (rather than a modified one) because it could better retain the cables between engine and car.

35020 BIBBY LINE passing Millbrook on 5 May 1957. When BIBBY LINE was rebuilt in 1956 it was chosen for testing on the road, to compare a rebuilt engine with the original that had been so exhaustively examined back in 1953, 35022 HOLLAND-AMERICA LINE. The results were happy in the extreme, with almost perfect combustion and an increase in cylinder efficiency of something like a fifth, though the comparison had hardly been fair. 35022 had been driven, thrashed even, to the limit, as evidenced by the bent coupling rods. 35020 on the other hand was driven in text book style with no heroics and was in first class condition. The wonder was that the efficiency improvement wasn't greater than 20 per cent. An Exmouth Junction Top Link fireman, asked about coal used on rebuilds, told Eric Youldon: 'We haven't noticed any difference'. Test result need to be approached with some reserve. Photograph Les Elsey.

35020 BIBBY LINE with 6,000 gallon tender, in Clapham cutting in the early 1960s 1961. It has shorter necks to its sand fillers – the initial long necks in the rebuilds also made for sand spillage, and some, at least, were changed. Photograph J.G. Walmsley, www.transporttreasury.co.uk.

Some odd painting on the smokebox door hinge bolts on BIBBY LINE, approaching Vauxhall with the down 10.30 from Waterloo, 7 August 1963. AWS, battery box and speedometer. Photograph Peter Groom.

35021 NEW ZEALAND LINE

Entered traffic 11 September 1948 to order No.3393 in unlined Malachite Green.
Named at Waterloo station on 24/11/48 by Mr. H.S. Whitehouse, Chairman of the Company.
Boiler 1098 had been carried by 21C9 from 6/42-11/47 and the firebox was renewed. This third series of the class had wedge shaped cabs, three side windows and fabricated rear truck. Ashford built the frames and cylinders, Brighton the boilers and tenders (all with TIA water treatment) while Eastleigh constructed the remainder of the parts and undertook assembly of all the 'third batch'.
In the 1960s the left-hand leading coupling rod fractured at Winchester, fortunately without serious consequences.

Tenders
3333 11/9/48
3342 13/11/48
3126 23/10/65

Boilers
1098 11/9/48
1091 8/10/54
1098 13/6/59

Allocations
Exmouth Jct. 9/48
Nine Elms p/e 12/5/51
Bournemouth p/e 12/6/57

Works: 1

23/9/48-30/9/48**D**	Not recorded
16/11/48-18/11/48**D**	325 Malachite Green, yellow lining, BR Gill Sans lettering
21/5/49	Wooden battens on smoke deflectors to carry 'Devon Belle' side boards
2/12/49-9/12/49**D**	59,033
19/1/50-15/3/50**LC**	65,437
11/10/50-22/11/50**LI**	109,324 repainted BR Blue
1/2/52-29/2/52**LI**	184,099 tender no.3343 upper side sheets removed thus easier to swing hose of a water column over when watering. lining out was also revised, sliding covers whistle and manifold valves, repainted BR Green. Retained front casing until 7/53. From 3/52 until then, 35021 was the only example of front casing on a Bulleid Pacific with a cut down tender.

Works: 2
(Mileages = since last General Overhaul)

5/5/52-10/5/52**Return**	189,998 miles
9/1/53-21/1/53**LC**	241,128 miles
8/7/53-22/8/53**HI**	262,019 miles Front casing removed
4/2/54-19/2/54**LC**	293,512 miles, Modification 'No.169', modified crank pin and plate, 'T2231' tender raves and tool pockets.
22/5/54-11/6/54**LC**	306,066 miles, Modification 'No.81, T2231' boiler pressure reduced
26/8/54-8/10/54**GO**	314,960 miles, thirteen modifications, 'T2231', boiler pressure reduced [change of boiler] safety valves resited
23/9/55-8/10/55**LC**	62,020 miles, two modifications, 'T2231', plain coupling rods
13/1/56-17/2/56**LI**	80,104 miles, seven modifications, two tests, TIA recorder removed and connections blanked off, plain coupling rods
17/1/57-9/2/57**LI**	135,516 miles, two modifications, three tests
30/8/57-14/9/57**LC**	177,700 miles
25/3/58-25/4/58**LI-HI**	203,188 miles, three modifications, 'T2285'
23/4/59-13/6/59**GO**	260,033 miles, ten modifications, three tests, rebuilt having travelled 575,993 miles, 2nd BR tender emblem, PV spindle pockets, anti glare shield, ashpan watering pipes, manganese liners and modified lubrication
24/3/61-22/4/61**LI**	113,468 miles, AWS gear and speedometer fitted
2/11/62-8/12/62**LI**	209,472 miles
14/2/64-21/3/64**LC**	

Experiments listed on back of BR9215 card: 2231 2274 2277 2285 2296 2305 2307 2326 2335

Withdrawn 8 August 1965 having run 859,661 miles, 283,668 as a rebuild, stored at Eastleigh Works 9/65 and later scrapped with tender no.3126 in October 1965.

35021 NEW ZEALAND LINE new in September 1948, in part varnished but unlined malachite green; delays in building the tenders at Brighton meant several Merchant Navys started life with light Pacific tenders. Full Bulleid livery arrived with its 6,000 gallon tender two months later. Point of interest: while photographs of 35021 in 'as built' condition are rather plentiful, a similar photograph of 35022 has *never* surfaced in over sixty years!

The last ten Merchant Navys came into service under BR and so did not carry Bulleid's weird and wonderful numbering system. 35021 NEW ZEALAND LINE at Southampton on 15 August 1951 now has its proper 6,000 gallon tender no.3342.

NEW ZEALAND LINE at Nine Elms, 17 August 1956, with its correct third series 6,000 gallon tender, now cut down. BR green with rectangular panels on the cab (low placed number) and modified tender. On a cut down tender the emblem had to be the small version. Front sand filler resolutely blocked off and hardly any trace left. Photograph J. Robertson, www.transporttreasury.co.uk

35021 NEW ZEALAND LINE with the down Bournemouth Belle at Vauxhall, 3 May 1960. Photograph John Scrace.

It is not often you would find a Merchant Navy taking on water at Brockenhurst for although facilities existed here for the locos working the Lymington Boat trains the turntable was only 50ft in diameter and could not turn any Bulleid Pacifics. 35021 by now is a Bournemouth loco, having transferred there in June 1957, two years before it was rebuilt. Photograph Dr Ian C. Allen, www.transporttreasury.co.uk.

35021 NEW ZEALAND LINE with the 12.15pm for Waterloo at Southampton Central, 27 July 1963. AWS fitted by now, though the Southern was something of a laggard when it came to this system – all that third rail around could make for some extraordinary 'magnetic field interference' problems. Some Merchant Navys had still not been equipped even by 1962, and some never got it, whatever the cards say. Photograph Alec Swain, www.transporttreasury.co.uk

NEW ZEALAND LINE hurrying along at Esher, 29 August 1964. Photograph Stephen Gradidge.

35022 HOLLAND AMERICA LINE

Entered traffic 9 October 1948 to order No.3393 in unlined Malachite Green.
Named at Southampton Docks on 24/1/49 by Mr W.H. de Monchy, Managing Director of the shipping line.

Tenders
3335 9/10/48
3345 8/1/49
3347 16/6/56

Boilers
1099 9/10/48
1107 21/11/53
1109 16/6/56
1123 28/7/62

Allocations
Exmouth Jct. 10/1948
Bournemouth p/e 22/6/54
Exmouth Jct. p/e 10/3/60
Western Region stock 1/1/63
Nine Elms p/e 2/3/64
Weymouth p/e 14/9/64

Proof – no hyphen between Holland and America.
Photograph Hamish Stevenson.

Works: 1

31/12/48-8/1/49**D**	4,493	
21/5/49	Wooden battens on smoke deflectors to carry 'Devon Belle' side boards	
11/1949	Malachite Green, yellow lining	
15/5/50-5/7/50**HI**	92,805 repainted BR Blue	
10/4/51	Trains Illustrated reported loco ran light engine to Newton Abbot for weighing	
10/12/51-8/2/52**LI**	188,928 repainted BR Green	
4/3/52	Ran light engine from Willesden shed to Rugby Testing Station	

Works: 2
(Mileages = since last General Overhaul)

18/5/53-28/5/53**LC**	194,165 miles Single nozzle blastpipe – Rugby Trials, front casing removed
22/7/53-8/8/53**LC**	204,792 miles
22/10/53-21/11/53**HC**	212,325 miles
9/12/54-10/12/54**NC**	240,281 miles Ultrasonic testing, 1 day
19/1/55-12/2/55**LI**	254,612 miles, Six modifications, four tests, Boiler pressure reduced
27/4/56-16/6/56**GO**	329,083 miles, rebuilt having run 329,083 miles, resited safety valves, Briquette tube feeder
11/5/57-24/5/57**LC**	78,899 miles
5/12/57-11/1/58**LI**	123,134 miles, Valve spindle extended, experimental pockets.
17/2/58-22/2/58**NC-LC**	124,184 miles
10/3/59-11/4/59**LI**	210,233 miles
3/6/59-6/6/59**NC**	213,047 miles, five tests, 'T2296', bogie and coupled springs, 2nd BR tender emblem, PV spindle pockets, steel bogie and pony truck spring gear.
5/10/59-10/10/59**NC**	242,137 miles, BR type AWS fitted
22/9/60-15/10/60**LI-HI**	294,501 miles, speedometer fitted
2/12/60-10/12/60**NC**	314,000 miles
23/5/62-28/7/62**GO**	397,016 miles
13/4/64-30/5/64**LI**	350 steel stays riveted over, 6 fusible plugs, Flaws in syphons at junction to crown plate cut out and welded
30/12/65-11/1/66**NC**	
6/4/66-7/4/66**NC**	

Experiments listed on back of BR9215 card: 2081 2196 2204 2207 2212 2242 2264 2277 2281 2282 2289 2296 2300 2304 2305 2315 2341

Withdrawn May 1966 having run 903,542 miles, 574,459 as a rebuild, stored at Weymouth shed 6-11/66 and then at Woodham Brothers, Barry 11/66-3/86. A number of years were spent in store on the Swanage Railway. Now planned as spares for 35027 which is in private ownership. Currently at Southall shed.

Lined malachite 35022 HOLLAND AMERICA LINE on home ground climbing Honiton bank, between May 1949 when the wooden battens were fixed on the smoke deflectors to carry the Devon Belle 'wings' and May 1950 when it entered Eastleigh, to emerge two months later in blue. Unlettered tender. This was the engine which spent so much time on Rugby Test Plant and took 'the largest number of bogie coaches ever operated' over the Skipton-Carlisle route. Photograph W. Hermiston, www.transporttreasury.co.uk

35022 HOLLAND AMERICA LINE (there never was a hyphen, despite it often being written thus, not least in the first edition of this book!) at Basingstoke with the 1.30pm Waterloo-Bournemouth on a rather dismal 2 April 1955; just over a year to go before rebuilding. 30860 LORD HAWKE stands in the bay. For its sins HOLLAND-AMERICA LINE covered 329,083 miles in its original form but over ten years as a rebuild managed 574,459. Photograph Philip J. Kelley.

35022 HOLLAND AMERICA LINE was rebuilt in May 1956; here it is at the Eastleigh coaling stage with a Lord Nelson 4-6-0 a few weeks later, on 21 June 1956. This was another one that ran more miles as a rebuild than in original form. When rebuilt it received tender no.3347, itself modernised in June 1953 and taken from 35020. Photograph K.C.H. Fairey.

35022 at Nine Elms shed amid those familiar concrete stumps, 6 October 1957. They could double, it is clear, as handy if crude benches – observe the driver and his oil bottle. First BR emblem, with paint worn away by a combination of water and coal dust draining off the tender. Further oil bottles on running plate by smoke deflectors; tail lamp up ready for the run to Waterloo. Photograph A.E. Bennett, www.transporttreasury.co.uk

The ground shudders underneath as 35022 HOLLAND AMERICA LINE races by at Clapham Junction with the down 'Belle' on 20 November 1959. Once again we see the curious 'part-fitted' AWS – protector plate recently fitted but no battery box as yet. Photograph John Scrace.

The rebuilt 35022 HOLLAND AMERICA LINE at Nine Elms shed on 24 May 1960, still only part-fitted with AWS – still no battery box between the frames. It had moved from Bournemouth to Exmouth Junction a few weeks before and the new owners had not got around to fitting 72A plates. Proving that no detail development is immune to its own peculiar deviation, the 'pockets' for the valve spindle extensions are, on 35022, cylindrical not rectangular. Photograph Peter Groom.

Basingstoke station on 14 October 1962 with two locos on West of England duties. Exmouth Junction 'Merchant' 35022 HOLLAND AMERICA LINE is thundering through on the fast line past 73088 JOYOUS GARD then of Nine Elms. Photograph A.E. Bennett' www.transporttreasury.co.uk.

35023 HOLLAND-AFRIKA LINE

**Entered traffic 6 November 1948 to order No.3393 in Malachite Green livery. Never carried blue livery.
Named at Southampton Docks on 24/1/49 by Mr M.A. Pelt, Managing Director of the Line.**

Tenders
3341 6/11/48

Boilers
1113 6/11/48
1092 15/10/54
1115 9/2/57
1102 17/11/62

Allocations
Exmouth Jct. 11/1948
Bournemouth p/e 10/3/60
Weymouth p/e 17/10/66
Nine Elms p/e 17/4/67

Correctly fluttering flag and this time a hyphen.

Works: 1
6/11/48	Tender 6,000 gallon capacity on trial
17/1/49-22/1/49**D**	1,506
21/5/49	Wooden battens on smoke deflectors to carry 'Devon Belle' sideboards
10/3/50-17/3/50**D**	74,737
2/10/50-3/11/50**LI**	92,706
25/2/52-22/3/52**LI**	179,699 sliding covers, whistle and manifold valves, repainted BR Green

Works: 2
(Mileages = since last General Overhaul)
11/4/53-2/5/53**LI**	246,335 miles Front casing removed
13/5/53-22/5/53**LC**	246,335 miles Driving axle examined for flaws and replaced
21/9/53-26/9/53**NC**	264,826 miles
10/5/54-29/5/54**NC**	294,781 miles, three modifications, boiler pressure reduced
7/9/54-15/10/54**GO**	306,964 miles, fifteen modifications, resited safety valves, modified crank pin
28/11/55-31/12/55**LI**	66,879 miles, three modifications, 'T2274, 2282', plain coupling rods
19/11/56-1/12/56**LC**	122,091 miles
7/1/57-9/2/57**GO**	126,952 miles, seven modifications, five tests, rebuilt having run 433,833 miles, 106 monel metal and 583 steel renewed with 15 roof stays renewed, firehole patch welded, 6 fusible plugs, 2 pipe end patches, 2 back end patches and 2 1/2 diaphragm patches all welded to syphons, 124 new tubes 'Howell' 40 new superheaters, boiler modified, mudhole seating fitted, safety valves resited
10/9/57-14/9/57**LC**	177,700 miles, three tests
22/4/58-10/5/58**LC**	92,374 miles, six tests
3/2/59-28/2/59**LI**	151,045 miles. 'T2283 and 2293', 3 monel metal renewed and 350 steel stays riveted over, 6 fusible plugs, 2 patches fitted and welded to syphons, 30 new tubes 'Stewart and Lloyds' 23 secondhand welded superheaters
8/4/60-23/4/60**NC**	220,361 miles
4/7/60-7/7/60**NC**	230,623 miles
6/9/60-1/10/60**LI-HI**	241,430 miles, AWS and speedometer fitted, 490 steel stays riveted over, 6 fusible plugs, 59 new tubes 'Stewart and Lloyds' 9 secondhand welded superheaters. Boiler record card: Internal examination extended from 2/62-6/62. M1163. 23/1/62, then from 6/62 to 12/62. M1163
29/5/62	'Coupled axle box guide face oil pipes with section of nylon tubing to eliminate fractures due to vibration.'
6/9/61-14/10/61**LC**	295,908 miles, spark arrester gear fitted
5/12/61-16/12/61**NC**	299,380 miles, 'T2341' new floorboards to diagram 52266
20/9/62-17/11/62**GO**	339,225 miles, 2nd BR tender emblem, PV spindle pockets, new steel firebox
21/5/64-27/6/64**LI**	'tests cancelled'
30/3/66-12/5/66**HC**	

Experiments listed on back of BR9215 card: 2081 2137 2264 2274 2277 2281 2282 2293 2296 2305 2341 2347

Withdrawn July 1967 having run 941,326 miles, 507,493 as a rebuild, stored at Nine Elms shed 7/67-3/68 and then sold for scrap.

Malachite green 35023 HOLLAND-AFRIKA LINE (this one *did* have a hyphen) climbs Honiton bank in early BR days. Gill sans 35023 and BRITISH RAILWAYS on tender; it did not lose the malachite until 1952, making it the last to run in it. Photograph W. Hermiston, www.transporttreasury.co.uk

Rebuilt 35023 HOLLAND-AFRIKA LINE (TIA box just visible on tender back) at Exmouth Junction on 15 August 1957. Photograph W. Hermiston, www.transporttreasury.co.uk

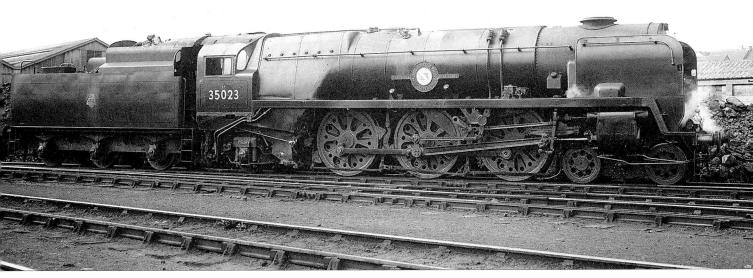

A year later at Nine Elms, on 22 August 1958, HOLLAND-AFRIKA LINE with empty bunker has worked up from Exeter with the ACE. With headboard still in place 35023 will work back on the down ACE the next day – in fact all main Merchant Navy diagrams to/from Exeter involved a return to the home shed the same day. The Merchant Navy off the up ACE returned on the 9.10pm goods from Nine Elms to Exmouth Junction, for instance. The light Pacific behind is 34010 SIDMOUTH; a Nine Elms loco, it would be rebuilt within a few months. Photograph W. Hermiston, www.transporttreasury.co.uk

35023 at Exmouth Junction on 24 June 1958. That smokebox, retaining the original prominent oval door and forming such a strong feature of the rebuilt engines was central to the look. It was properly circular for a start, resting on a saddle which was formed partly of a new fabricated saddle stretcher and partly of the new steel inside cylinder casting below. This gave much greater strength to the framing at the front end. Photograph J. Davenport, Initial Photographics.

35023 at Nine Elms on 13 October 1964. Photograph Stephen Gradidge.

Deep into diesel days on the West of England line, a filthy 35023 HOLLAND-AFRIKA LINE leaves Waterloo with the 14.45 relief to Exeter, 4 June 1965. Photograph Peter Groom.

At the last. Plateless at Waterloo on 10 June 1967. This Merchant Navy was withdrawn as one of the last a few weeks later. Photograph Stephen Gradidge.

35024 EAST ASIATIC COMPANY

Entered traffic 13 November 1948 to order No.3393 in unlined Malachite Green.
Named at Waterloo station 5/5/49 by HRH Prince Axel of Denmark, Chairman of the Company.

Tenders
3333 13/11/48
3346 12/2/49
3123 30/10/52
3343 14/5/58
3346 21/12/61

Boilers
1114 13/11/48
1097 15/5/54
1099 25/4/59

Allocations
Exmouth Jct 11/1948
Bournemouth p/e 1/5/59
Nine Elms p/e 1/2/62
Weymouth p/e 14/9/64

Works: 1
31/1/49-12/2/49**D**   3,039 dark blue livery, horizontal crimson bands, hand painted tender emblem
2/3/49-29/3/49**D**   7,724cab side numerals straw colour, tender emblem moved in line with running number,
                    two black bands with white lining. BR blue was inspected by the Railway Executive at Brighton Works
29/4/49-6/5/49**D**   8,798 Wheels painted black, narrow black splash skirt added
21/5/49   Wooden battens on smoke deflectors to carry 'Devon Belle' side boards
11/7/50-18/8/50**LC** 88,621
13/9/50-6/10/50**LC** 88,621
17/5/51-15/6/51**LI** 130,579 repainted BR Green, 270 steel stays renewed, 6 lead plugs,
                    30 new tubes 'Howell' 3 superheater tubes

Works: 2
(Mileages = since last General Overhaul)
30/9/52-30/10/52**HI** 219,232 miles 220 steel stays riveted over, 6 lead plugs, 124 new tubes 'Howell' 40 new superheaters.
Boiler record card: 'Internal examinations extended to 11/54. C40/2293'
12/5/53-22/5/53**LC** 247,347 miles Axle examined for flaws and replaced
5/4/54-15/5/54**GO**   289,428 miles, sixteen modifications, boiler pressure reduced, 562 steel, 26 flexible and 31 roof stays
                    renewed, 2 diaphragm syphon patches fitted, foundation ring renewed and 4 patches fitted in corners, set of
                    new tubes and superheaters
4/7/55-30/7/55**LC-HC** 54,264 miles, four tests
10/2/56-1/3/56**LC**   82,917 miles, one modification, four tests, plain coupling rods
6/9/56-29/9/56**LI**   118,639 miles, seven modifications, five tests, TIA recorder not fitted and connections blanked off, 340 steel
                    stays riveted over, 6 fusible plugs, 16 new tubes 'Howell'
19/11/57-14/12/57**LI** 195,951 miles, one modification, three tests, drain pipe and clip to TIA Doser tank, 340 steel stays riveted
                    over, 6 fusible plugs, 2 diaphragm neck patches, 34 new tubes 'Stewart and Lloyds' 11 new superheaters
5/5/58-14/5/58**LC**   223,158 miles, three tests
26/2/59-25/4/59**GO** 262,625 miles, nine modifications, 'T2265', safety valves resited, rebuilt having run 552,053 miles, 2nd BR
                    tender emblem, PV spindle extensions, ashpan watering pipes, regulator shroud and cast iron valve seat,
steel   axleboxes and manganese liners, modified lubrication
13/10/59-20/10/59**NC** 35,594 miles, BR type AWS fitted
1/11/60-26/11/60**LI** 110,151 miles, speedometer fitted
20/12/61-21/12/61**LC** 181,864 miles, two tests
7/6/63-27/7/63**LI**   249,685 miles, spark arrester gear fitted, two tests
Experiments listed on back of BR9215 card: 2204 2207 2242 2265 2268 2296 2315 2316 2326

Withdrawn January 1965 having run 839,415 miles, 287,362 as a rebuild. Scrapped May 1965.

With the coal weighing tender, at Nine Elms on 6 September 1958. The air smoothed casing is definitely looking a bit ropey by now. It had enjoyed mixed fortunes in the livery stakes; it had been the first of the class to get BR blue, in February 1949 with horizontal red bands, only for these to be promptly replaced by 'two lines in black with a fine white lining'. It was the first to get the dark green and with that BR seem to have concluded it had spent enough on paint for EAST ASIATIC COMPANY for a while. It got the coal weighing tender, no.3343, in May 1958, keeping it on rebuilding only to lose it in December 1961 during a light casual. The cylinder drain cocks have been opened in particularly impressive fashion. Photograph R.C. Riley, www.transporttreasury.co.uk

35024 EAST ASIATIC COMPANY, in BR dark green, calling at Basingstoke on 28 August 1954.

35024 EAST ASIATIC COMPANY, off the down Atlantic Coast Express, taking coal at Exmouth Junction on 21 May 1957. Photograph J. Robertson, www.transporttreasury.co.uk

35024 EAST ASIATIC COMPANY at Exmouth Junction on 1 May 1951. The strange shapes are not two malformed fitters but one man only; he is on the left, reaching up under the casing while a length of lagging is draped over the connecting rod. Photograph J. Davenport, Initial Photographics.

Immaculate 35024 EAST ASIATIC COMPANY emerged from works in the new rebuilt guise in 1959, still with the 6,000 gallon coal weighing tender. Photograph Les Elsey.

35024 EAST ASIATIC COMPANY at Nine Elms, 4 October 1964; note the odd 'edge' effect along the top of the boiler, a consequence of the cleaners not being able to reach that far. Tender is now cut down 6,000 gallon no.3346. Photograph Colin Stacey, Initial Photographics.

35025 BROCKLEBANK LINE

Entered traffic 27 November 1948 to order No.3393 in Malachite Green.
Named at Waterloo station 20/9/49 by Colonel D.H. Bates, Chairman of the Company.

Tenders
3343 27/11/48
3350 7/6/52

Boilers
1115 27/11/48
1110 3/11/50
1104 12/12/56

Allocations
Bournemouth 11/1948
Stewarts Lane p/e 25/3/50
Exmouth Jct. p/e 19/3/52
Nine Elms p/e 22/6/54
Bournemouth p/e 5/6/56
Exmouth Jct. p/e 10/3/60
Western Region stock 1/1/63

Works: 1

13/9/49-16/9/49**D**	44,382 repainted BR Blue	
15/9/50-3/11/50**A**	110,880	
4/3/52-29/3/52**LI**	49,745 sliding covers for whistle and manifold valves	

Works: 2
(Mileages = since last General Overhaul)

12/5/52-6/7/52**LC**	57,590 miles Repainted BR Green
14/5/53-25/5/53**LC**	111,361 miles Driving axle examined for flaws and replaced
21/9/53-17/10/53**HI**	130,769 miles Boiler pressure reduced
3/5/54-8/5/54**LC**	158,792 miles
4/1/55-5/2/55**LC-LI**	183,159 miles. On 10 December, 1954 35025 had fractured the inside connecting rod, damaging the oil bath (as well as the track). The leaking oil set fire to the boiler lagging. Three modifications, 'T2242'; coupling rods, new pattern
6/4/55-22/4/55**NC-LC**	193,780 miles, 'T2081, 2242'
30/12/55-21/1/56**LC**	228,278 miles. 'T2081, 2242'. Plain coupling rods
30/10/56-12/12/56**GO**	258,749 miles, rebuilt having run 419,374 miles, 16 monel metal and 164 steel and 15 roof stays renewed, 2 syphons back end and 2 diaphragm neck patches fitted [welded], 6 fusible plugs, protection patch front barrel, 124 new tubes 'Howell' 40 new superheaters, safety valves repositioned, mudhole seating fitted [Boiler modification]
9/7/57-13/7/57**NC**	49,288 miles, modifications to diagrams E30560 and E401, four tests. There followed a visit to Swindon Works Stationary Test Plant for investigation into a 'knock' that had developed after running 35,000 miles, modifications to file M.1173 [Drgs.E30560 and E.401]
30/9/57-12/10/57**LC**	59,235 miles, steam chest pressure gauge pipe repositioned, cab handrails, left and right piston valve guide bushed, piston valve spindle at tail end. platform [the running board, that is] clearance for reversing screw grease nipple
12/11/57-23/11/57**LC-NC**	63,155 miles, five tests
17/12/58-10/1/59**LI**	127,340 miles, two tests, 350 steel stays repaired, 6 fusible plugs, 2 new bottom pipe portions fitted and welded to syphons, 16 new tubes 'Stewart and Lloyds'
22/10/59-31/10/59**NC**	174,201 miles, BR type AWS fitted
30/5/60-25/6/60**LI**	210,054 miles, ' T2305 driving coupling rod bushes, T2292 vacuum ejector cones, T2307 mechanical lubrication drive, T2282 boiler water gauge and drain cocks, speedometer fitted, 600 steel stays repaired, fusible plugs, 15 new tubes 'Howell' 10 second hand welded superheaters, Briquette tube feeder, bogie and pony truck spring gear
3/10/60-8/10/60**NC-LC**	223,538 miles, three tests, 21 steel renewed and 150 steel stays repaired, bulged plate on LH side of firebox cut out and new patch fitted and welded in place
18/1/61-23/2/61**LC**	At Exmouth Junction shed
15/11/61-16/11/61**LC-NC**	298,057 miles, three tests. Boiler Record Card: Internal examination extended from 12/61 to 6/62. M.1163 1/12/61
17/1/62-10/3/62**GO**	310,948 miles, 170 steel and 16 roof stays renewed, 6 fusible plugs, Foundation ring and rivets on LH and RH back renewed, 124 new tubes 'Stewart and Lloyds' 40 new superheaters, 2nd BR tender emblem
26/7/63-14/9/63**LI**	93,635 miles, 250 steel renewed and 232 steel stays repaired, 6 fusible plugs 2 neck patches fitted to syphons, 19 new tubes 'Stewart and Lloyds' Experiments on listed on back of BR9215 card: 2081 2150 2242 2264 2277 2281 2281 2296 2305

Withdrawn in September 1964 after 884,081 miles, 420,041 as a rebuild, stored at Exmouth Junction shed 2/65 and moved to Woodham Brothers, Barry in 3/65. Based at Sellinge, Kent undergoing long term restoration.

35025 BROCKLEBANK LINE in 1948 in lined malachite green waiting to depart Bournemouth with an up train. Nameplate covered for its naming ceremony in September 1949, when it would be ex-works in blue.

35025 BROCKLEBANK LINE drifting down Honiton bank in August 1955. It carries the new BR green (applied during a casual 12/5/52-6/7/52 which mistakenly was shown as 12/2/52 in the original 'Book of...') and looks to be in beautiful condition. Though the new engines were by no means immune to slipping, the originals continued to demonstrate their extraordinary contradictions throughout the 1950s, to the wonder of observers. In the same year for instance, 1955, only a few days after this photograph and in wet conditions, 35022 slipped for *eleven miles* lurching between 26mph and 40mph; once it got a grip the engine suddenly tore away to nearly 90mph. The driver could not understand why anyone should be interested in such routine events and, genuinely puzzled, assured the *Railway Observer* correspondent that there was 'nothing wrong'. 'Curious engines!' wrote the correspondent... Photograph J. Robertson, www.transporttreasury.co.uk

Above. For two years – March 1950 to March 1952 – 35025 BROCKLEBANK LINE worked out of Stewarts Lane but was on the Western section for the rest of its time. On 21 May 1957 it is at Nine Elms where the usual shortage of staff to clear the ash and clinker seems to have been worse than ever, the piles reaching heroic proportions. The cylinder drains are bent all ways! Photograph J. Robertson, www.transporttreasury.co.uk

Left. In an unusual turn of events in July-August 1957, not long after rebuilding, BROCKLEBANK LINE was packed off to the Swindon testing plant for investigation of 'a knock'. Presumably all was well, eventually. Here it is still 'wired up' somewhere in the works on 18 August 1957. Photograph R. Wilson, www.transporttreasury.co.uk

'On the milk'; 35025 with down tanks at Basingstoke, 2 August 1962. There was always an Exmouth Junction loco on this working, though a light Pacific in original form was more often in command. Photograph Paul Chancellor collection.

35025 BROCKLEBANK LINE at Esher, 29 August 1964. Photograph Stephen Gradidge.

From February 1950 when through working became more common between Exeter and London it was crews, rather than locos, that changed over at Salisbury. Six minutes were allowed to take on water and often both crews set to in order to get some coal forward in the allotted time. This is the penultimate summer Saturday before withdrawal of Waterloo-West of England steam expresses, 29 August 1964 and both crews are hard at it on 35025 BROCKLEBANK LINE at Salisbury before it continues on its way west with the 3.0pm Waterloo-Plymouth/North Devon train. The work would be accomplished in the six minutes allowed; a classic sight. Photograph S.P. Derek.

35026 LAMPORT & HOLT LINE

Entered traffic 4 December 1948 to order No.3393 in unlined Malachite Green.
Named jointly with 35028 at Southampton Docks 15/1/51 by Mr S.H. Mercer, the London Manager of the Company.

Tenders
3260 4/12/48
3350 1/7/49
3130 14/6/52
3349 20/3/65
3111 4/65

Boilers
1116 4/12/48
1117 29/1/55
1103 24/8/57
1111 20/10/62

Allocations
Bournemouth 12/1948
Stewarts Lane p/e 25/3/50
Exmouth Jct. p/e 25/1/57
Bournemouth p/e 12/6/57
Exmouth Jct. p/e 1/5/59
Western Region stock 1/1/63
Nine Elms p/e 2/3/64
Weymouth p/e 14/9/64

Works: 1

18/12/48-24/12/48**D**	Not recorded	
30/6/49-1/7/49**D**	18,182 repainted BR Blue, became standard livery for the class	
6/2/50-10/2/50**LC**	59,910	
1/1/51-13/1/51**NC**	91,401 200 steel stays riveted over, 6 lead plugs, 30 new tubes 'Howell'	
24/1/51-24/2/51**LI**	92,869	

Works: 2
(Mileages = since last General Overhaul)

13/5/52-14/6/52**LI** Green, front	143,416 miles Self cleaning smokebox fitted, sliding covers for whistle and manifold valves, repainted BR casing removed, 264 steel stays riveted over, 6 fusible plugs, 20 new tubes 'Howell' 3 new superheaters
9/1/53-31/1/53**LC**	179,315 miles
8/6/53-13/6/53**LC**	191,709 miles Driving axle replaced
21/9/53-16/10/53**LC**	202,514 miles
28/12/53-29/1/54**LI**	207,669 miles, modifications; 'T2133, casings at safety valve, T2195 self-cleaning smokebox gear, T2242 coupling rods MN class', 368 steel stays riveted over, 6 fusible plugs, 83 new tubes 'Stewart and Lloyds' 16 second hand welded superheaters.
	Boiler record card: Internal examinations extended to 5/55. Ref. M.1163. 29/11/54
27/4/54-30/4/54**NC**	219,303 miles, 'T 2133, 2194, 2242'
20/12/54-29/1/55**GO**	245,662 miles, seven modifications, two tests, modified balanced crank axle, boiler pressure reduced, safety valves resited, plain coupling rods
11/5/56-2/6/56**LC**	51,054 miles
13/12/56-26/1/57**GO**	65,401 miles, nine modifications, five tests, safety valves resited, rebuilt having run 311,063 miles, 184 steel and 15 roof stays renewed, 1 syphon patch complete, 2 back patches and 1 1/2 diaphragm patch welded, 6 fusible plugs, 124 new tubes 'Howell' 40 new superheaters
	Boiler modified: Safety valves repositioned and mudhole seating fitted and riveted to hind barrel
9/8/57-24/8/57**LC**	43,995 miles, four tests
20/10/58-8/11/58**LI**	128,908 miles, 306 steel stays riveted over, 6 fusible plugs, 16 new tubes 'Stewart and Lloyds'.
27/10/59-21/11/59**LI**	205,051 miles, BR type AWS fitted, 400 steel stays riveted over, 6 fusible plugs, pipe portion fitted and welded to LH syphon, 16 new tubes 'Tube Products', 6 second hand welded superheaters
18/10/60-29/10/60**LC**	274,182 miles 'T2302', Speedometer fitted
14/3/61-15/4/61**LI-HI**	99,853 miles, 390 steel stays riveted over, 6 fusible plugs, 30 new tubes 'Tube Products' 5 new superheaters
6/12/61-2/3/62**LC**	At Exmouth Junction shed
	Boiler record card: Internal examination extended from 1/62-9/62. M1163. 22/2/61
29/8/62-20/10/62**GO**	387,171 miles, 2nd BR tender emblem, PV spindle pockets, 124 new tubes 'Stewart and Lloyds' 40 new superheaters
13/3/64-17/4/64**NC**.	
28/9/65-5/11/65**LI**	
7/9/66-8/9/66**NC**	

Withdrawn in March 1967, due to loose driving wheel tyre, having run 858,784 miles, 547,721 as a rebuild.

35026 LAMPORT & HOLT LINE at Abbotscliff on 6 August 1956, during its spell on the Eastern Section 1950-1957. Photograph J. Robertson, www.transporttreasury.co.uk

35026 LAMPORT & HOLT LINE in original form working an express near Ashford, Kent on 29 August 1956. It had been at Stewarts Lane since March 1950. A majestic signal gantry in the background indicates a train soon in the other direction. Our train seems to be a Victoria to Folkestone or Dover express made up of Maunsell coaches. Photo A.W. Battson, www.transporttreasury.co.uk

35026 LAMPORT & HOLT LINE south of Worting Junction, 3 August 1957. The Royal Wessex was a Waterloo-Bournemouth and Weymouth (with M7s on to Swanage!) train, one of several special sets to mark the Festival of Britain of 1951. 35026 had actually gone to Bournemouth (along with 35021) for the accelerated two hour expresses of 1957. After its long spell on the Eastern Section it had first gone to Exmouth Junction in January 1957 and after two years as one of Bournemouth's finest went back to Exmouth Junction. After takeover by the WR it moved to Nine Elms in 1964 and then on to Weymouth. Photograph Les Elsey.

LAMPORT & HOLT LINE at speed, flashing past the Windsor line platform at Clapham Junction. Photograph Peter Groom.

35026 LAMPORT & HOLT LINE taking water at Yeovil Junction, 6 July 1959. Photograph H.C. Casserley, courtesy R.M. Casserley.

35027 PORT LINE

Entered traffic 11 December 1948 to order No.3393 in unlined Malachite Green.
Named at Southampton Docks 24/4/50 by Mr W. Donald, Chairman of Port Line.

Tenders
3288 11/12/48
3349 14/4/49
3130 20/3/65

Boilers
1117 11/12/48
1098 26/11/54
1101 10/5/57
1115 5/10/63

Allocations
Bournemouth 12/1948
Stewarts Lane p/e 25/3/50
Bournemouth p/e 4/6/55

Works: 1

25/3/49-14/4/49**D**	14,116 Malachite Green, yellow lining
17/4/50-21/4/50**NC**	77,548 repainted BR Blue
1/6/5013/7/50**LI**	80,171
23/10/50-27/10/50**NC**	90,086 at Ashford Works

Works: 2
(Mileages = since last General Overhaul)

29/4/52-31/5/52**LI**	143,359 miles
12/5/53-16/5/53**NC**	187,298 miles Driving axle examined for flaws at Ashford Works
27/10/53-21/11/53**LI**	202,186 miles Sliding covers for whistle and manifold valves, repainted BR Green, front casing removed
6/5/54-8/5/54**LC**	223,024 miles
15/10/54-26/11/54**GO**	238,806 miles, ten modifications and modified balanced crank axle, boiler pressure reduced, modified balanced crank axle to DRG.W.11247/A
26/8/55-3/9/55**LC**	34,979 miles
3/4/56-28/4/56**LI**	61,282 miles, seven modifications, one test, plain coupling rods, TIA recorder removed and connections blanked off
28/3/57-10/5/57**GO**	124,515 miles, seven modifications, five tests, rebuilt having run 363,351 miles, safety valves resited, new left-hand side cylinder, anti glare shield
18/11/57-30/11/57**NC**	52,446 miles, six tests
7/1/59-24/1/59**LI**	120,504 miles, 'T2282, 2292'
26/4/60-14/5/60**LI-HI**	202,733 miles, AWS and speedometer fitted, Briquette container, Cylinder lubrication adaptors, bogie and pony truck spring gear
6/10/61-4/11/61**LI**	291,452 miles, 'T2305'
8/2/62-10/2/62**LC**	298,480 miles, 'T2305'
24/8/62-19/10/62**LC**	At Bricklayers Arms shed, 2nd BR tender emblem
9/8/63-5/10/63**GO**	375,836 miles, spark arrester fitted, 942 Steel, 144 monel metal, 26 flexible and 16 roof stays renewed 6 fusible plugs, 2 complete backs and 2 1/2 diaphragms to syphons, 124 new tubes 'Stewart and Lloyds' 40 new superheaters
3/9/65-15/10/65**LI**	475 steel stays riveted over, 6 fusible plugs, 49 new tubes 'Stewart and Lloyds' 4 new superheaters

Experiments listed on back of BR9215 card: 2081 2150 2242 2264 2277 2281 2282 2292 2296 2305 2307

Withdrawn September 1966 having run 872,290 miles, 508,939 as a rebuild, stored at Eastleigh shed 11/66-4/67 and at Woodham Brothers, Barry 5/67-12/82. When preserved went first to the Swindon & Cricklade Railway and was eventually restored at the old Swindon Railway Works. Currently at Southall shed.

35027 PORT LINE in Folkestone Warren with the Golden Arrow, March 1952. The train had been something of a showcase for the Southern's new Britannia Pacifics, 70004 WILLIAM SHAKESPEARE and 70014 IRON DUKE but an alarming failure on the former late in 1951 – coupling rods fractured on both sides while working the 'Arrow' – and a rash of similar incidents among the class meant Merchant Navys and light Pacifics took over the train.

35027 PORT LINE in blue, at Dover Marine. Not many of the class could be found working on the Eastern Section but for a while 35025-35030 found themselves either at Dover or Stewarts Lane sheds where they all worked in original form. They were, it has been said '...beyond doubt the most technically advanced class of engines to be used extensively in Britain.' So was rebuilding a retrograde step? The arguments continue.

PORT LINE now in green, with casing ahead of cylinder removed, at Folkestone Junction station, 1 July 1954. Photograph J. Davenport, Initial Photographics.

35027 PORT LINE at Nine Elms, attended by men above (trimming the coal) and below. This is 17 August 1956, with less than a year to go to rebuilding. Photograph J. Robertson, www.transportrreasury.co.uk

An impressively brooding rebuilt PORT LINE, up from Bournemouth and in the yard at Nine Elms, in August 1959. V.G. Gilchrist, in charge at Nine Elms at this time, wrote in March 1994 that the decision to rebuild the engines had been a mistake. He knew the engines before and after rebuilding; the originals in his care rarely lost time or failed and he never experienced a chain failure. He could detect no difference in coal consumption before or after rebuilding. This is horse's mouth stuff and cannot be ignored; the more one looks, the more it becomes clear that, as E.S. Youldon put it at the same time, 'the originals were nowhere near as bad as they were sometimes painted and the rebuilds not as wonderful...' Photograph W. Hermiston, www.transportrreasury.co.uk

Bournemouth's 35027 PORT LINE was rebuilt March-May 1957, having run 363,351 miles and had to be fitted with a new left-hand side cylinder as part of the work. Just a month after leaving works the new 35027 is on the up Royal Wessex at Shawford, just north of Eastleigh, on 15 June 1957. Photograph Les Elsey.

PORT LINE, impressive in the shed yard at Nine Elms, 21 September 1957. Photograph Stephen Gradidge.

PORT LINE with the down Bournemouth Belle, passing Clapham Junction on 9 March 1964. Photograph Stephen Gradidge.

Profoundly filthy, 35027 has the 4.30pm from Waterloo approaching Vauxhall on Saturday 7 August 1965. PORT LINE was a Bournemouth loco from June 1955 until withdrawal; it survives and awaits a second overhaul to working order in preservation. Photograph Peter Groom.

PORT LINE in severely straitened circumstances, waiting to leave Waterloo for Nine Elms in 1966; horrible chalked front numberplate. On the platform it seems a footplateman is talking to a fitter; greasetop cap, 'bait' (lunch) box and a newspaper he might get a chance to read. Trouser bottoms fixed to prevent the unwelcome ingress of coal dust. The BR class 5 4-6-0 loco in the background will perhaps couple up to 35027 to save time back to Nine Elms Photograph P. Hocquard, www.transporttreasury.co.uk

35028 CLAN LINE

Entered traffic 23 December 1948 to order No.3393 in Malachite Green livery.
Named at Southampton Docks 15/1/51 by Lord Rotherwick, Chairman of Clan Line.

Tenders
3344 23/12/48
3345 11/7/56
3126 6/3/65
3342 21/10/65

Boilers
1118 23/12/48
1120 3/12/54
1094 24/10/59
1121 1/2/64

Allocations
Bournemouth 12/1948
Dover p/e 29/10/49
Stewarts Lane p/e 25/3/50
Nine Elms p/e 14/6/59
Weymouth p/e 14/9/64
Nine Elms p/e 17/4/67

Works: 1

1/1/51-13/1/51**NC**	93,312 repainted BR Blue	
30/1/51-28/2/51**LI**	93,888	
24/9/51-20/10/51**HC**	117,419 new left-hand side cylinder	
8/2/52-21/2/52**LC**	128,856	

Works: 2
(Mileages = since last General Overhaul)

14/5/53-12/6/53**HI**	167,052 miles, sliding covers for whistle and manifold valves, repainted BR Green, front casing removed
22/4/54-24/4/54**NC**	199,651 miles, trailing truck modified
25/10/54-3/12/54**GO**	222,813 miles, T2132, boiler pressure reduced, safety valves resited, 124 new tubes 'Stewart and Lloyds' 40 new superheaters, internal firebox, 6 lead plug holes welded
28/2/55-5/3/55**NC-LC**	17,640 miles
19/9/55-24/9/55**LC**	39,809 miles
5/6/56-7/7/56**LI-HI**	65,605 miles, six modifications, plain coupling rods, TIA recorder removed and connections blanked off, 375 steel riveted over, 6 fusible plugs, 32 new tubes 'Howell' 3 secondhand welded superheaters
12/12/56-5/1/57**LC-HC**	82,645 miles
6/8/58-6/9/58**LI**	143,009 miles, two modifications. pipe and clips to TIA Doser tank, 420 steel stays riveted over, 6 fusible plugs, 16 new tubes 'Stewart and Lloyds' 33 new superheaters
21/8/59-24/10/59**GO**	178,192 miles, ten modifications, four tests, BR type AWS fitted, rebuilt having run 401,005 miles, 2nd BR tender emblem, PV spindle pockets, 263 monel metal, 1,039 steel and 16 roof stays renewed, 6 fusible plugs, 2 neck patches and 2 back end patches fitted and welded to syphons, Barrel seating fitted
2/6/61-28/7/61**LI**	94,908 miles, three tests, speedometer fitted
31/8/62-1/9/62**NC**	152,100 miles, three tests
13/3/63-7/5/63**LC**	178,743 miles, at Bricklayers Arms shed
4/12/63-1/2/64**LI-GO**	210,376 miles, spark arrester gear fitted, 'T2296, 2341'
20/9/65-21/10/65**LC**	88,814 miles
12/7/66-21/7/66**LC**	131,226 miles
	Experiments listed on back of BR9215 card: 2204 2296 2305 2307 2318

Withdrawn July 1967 having run 794,391 miles, 393,386 as a rebuild. Purchased by Merchant Navy Locomotive Preservation Society straight out of service, since its first trip back on the main line in April 1974 [which the author was on] has been one of the most consistent main line steam performers. Now fitted with air braking equipment and increased coal capacity. Has its own web site!
Mark Arscott writes: *'It was November 1965 that three enthusiasts first got together to plan the preservation of a Merchant Navy. The main requirement was £2,500, then a shortlist of engines that were in good order, both boiler and mechanical. 35022 was chosen and condemned almost immediately; second choice was 35028 laid up at the back of Nine Elms in February 1967 with a cracked Bissel truck. Fortunately Eastleigh decided to send a specialist welder to effect the repair, after which the loco returned to service. In the autumn of 1966 the artist David Shepherd was becoming interested in steam and preservation. Through his contacts with the Army and the Commanding Officer at Longmoor Camp, where the Army operated a large railway for training purposes, a berth was arranged for CLAN LINE and on 13 August 1967 she was duly towed to Liss for transfer to Longmoor. So began the engine's second life. It is interesting to note that the MNLPS have now owned 35028 for longer than BR ever did! Its exploits since have been well recorded. All contributions gratefully accepted.'*

35028 CLAN LINE, perhaps the best-known of the class, at Stewarts Lane on 6 June 1950. Its malachite green livery is worn, shoddy even, and it was only named after emerging pristine in blue from a non-classified repair (which seems to have been solely a repainting) in January 1951. It thus ran with concealed nameplate for about two years. No emblem on tender and no smokebox shedplate. CLAN LINE was named at Southampton Docks on 15 January 1951 by (appropriately) Chairman of Clan Line Lord Rotherwick. Photograph R.E. Vincent, www.transporttreasury.co.uk.

In the depths of the Warren, a blue CLAN LINE on 13 June 1951. It would be October before exhibition-finish 70004 WILLIAM SHAKESPEARE, fresh from the Festival of Britain, arrived to take up Golden Arrow duties and the subsequent tribulations of the Britannias put those (real or related) of the Bulleids in the shade.

Since 1951 Stewarts Lane had had two Britannias, 70004 and 70014 for the prestigious Golden Arrow but the former was at Crewe for the whole of April 1954 (see *The Book of the Britannia Pacifics* for instance) and with 70014 otherwise occupied the job went to CLAN LINE. Here is 35028 on 4 April 1954, at the rather incongruously primitive Folkestone Junction shed coal stage, which otherwise served 0-6-0Ts. From September 1952 Folkestone Harbour was used for the 'outward' steamer service rather than Dover, leaving Victoria at 1pm and arriving Folkestone Harbour at 2.38pm. The main line engine was uncoupled in the sidings at the head of the incline down to the harbour allowing the train to descend the 1 in 31 gradient in charge of one or more R1 class 0-6-0Ts – later 57XX panniers. Meanwhile the main line locomotive retired to the little Folkestone Junction shed for servicing before running to Dover Marine with the empty train (now brought back up to the main line) to await the arrival of the 'inward' steamer from France. Photograph A.R. Carpenter, www.transporttreasury.co.uk

35028 CLAN LINE in BR dark green with the 10am Victoria-Dover boat train at Bickley, 16 July 1955. Photograph D.W. Winkworth.

On the Eastern Section, it is believed.

With the '9am Victoria' at Bromley South, 30 March 1957. Photograph D.W. Winkworth.

35028 with an up boat train from Dover, routed via Chatham; the period is prior to July 1956 when the tender was changed to the one ex-35020 in special livery. There is no hint of the upheaval to come with the enlargement to four tracks in 1959. The signals in the far background are the up homes for the junction at the rear of the train where a spur goes off to join the SER up fast at Chislehurst. The third track over to the left is the return down spur from Chislehurst.

35028 CLAN LINE with the down Golden Arrow at Petts Wood, 13 June 1959. It was the last Merchant Navy to be rebuilt and the unmodified tender was the only one to get the later crest Photograph Peter Groom.

CLAN LINE departing Folkestone Junction with an up boat train for Victoria (via Tonbridge) on 28 February 1959; 34103 CALSTOCK now in the background. Photograph D.W. Winkworth.

35028 CLAN LINE at Exmouth Junction on 17 August 1960. It was driven off, almost, into preservation with little thought that something like a third of the class would eventually rise from the dead (though some are far from fully 'alive' yet – give it time). Photograph W. Hermiston, www.transporttreasury.co.uk

Down Bournemouth express approaching Farnborough, at the very end of the electrified section, on 31 May 1963. Another example of 'part-fitted' AWS, with protector plate but no battery box. Loco still has small pockets; had large pockets from February 1964. Photograph Peter Groom.

35029 ELLERMAN LINES

Entered traffic 19 February 1949 to order No.3393 in Malachite Green livery
Named at Southampton Docks 1/3/51 by Mr. A.F. Hull, Chairman of Ellerman Lines.

Tenders
3347 19/2/49
3129 11/7/52
3113 10/65 [not shown on Engine Record Card]

Boilers
1119 19/2/49
1122 4/12/54
1090 19/9/59
1103 9/11/63

Allocations
Bournemouth 2/1949
Dover p/e 29/10/49
Nine Elms p/e 4/6/55
Weymouth p/e 14/9/64

Works: 1
6/3/50-24/3/50**LC**   54,522 repairs to tyres and wheel flanges damaged in derailment, London Bridge
16/1/51-7/2/51**LI**   87,391 prepared at Eastleigh Works for naming ceremony at Southampton Docks, last of class to be officially   named
17/4/51-25/4/51**NC**   88,761 repainted BR Blue having been repainted only seven weeks   previously, to work train for Danish Royalty in May, 420 steel stays riveted over, 6 fusible plugs, 30 new tubes 'Howell'

Works: 2
(Mileages = since last General Overhaul)
11/6/52-11/7/52**LI**   134,360 miles Repainted BR Green, modified cab lining, front casing removed, 240 steel stays riveted over 6 fusible plugs, 15 secondhand welded tubes 2 new superheater tubes
12/5/53-16/5/53**NC**   171,203 miles Driving axle examined for flaws at Ashford Works
3/7/53-10/7/53**HC**   173,024 miles
19/10/53-24/10/53**LC**   184,679 miles Cab side painted green and lined out minus the black 'splash skirt'? See photograph. Boiler record card: Internal examination 2/54 extended to 9/54
28/10/54-4/12/54**GO**   224,999 miles, nineteen modifications, 'T2242, 2246', boiler pressure reduced and safety valves resited
27/10/55   On this day according to R.O. 35029 arrived on Brighton shed and later moved to the Works. Left for Nine Elms on 7/12/55, not steamed between those dates, not shown on Engine Record Card
25/4/56-26/5/56**LI**   65,667 miles, nine modifications, TIA recorder removed and connections blanked off
14/11/56-1/12/56**LC**   93,453 miles, 'T2246'
30/7/57-24/8/57**LI**   121,219 miles, six modifications, 'T2207'
25/8/58-13/9/58**LC**   181,115 miles
21/11/58-13/12/58**LC**   190,401 miles, new right-hand side cylinder
27/2/59-28/3/59**LC**   194,924 miles
30/6/59-19/9/59**GO**   203,622 miles, ten modifications, four tests, BR type AWS fitted, rebuilt having run 428,621 miles, 2nd BR tender emblem, PV spindle pockets, anti glare shield, spring links, grease lubrication to pony truck
28/3/60-7/4/60**LC**   38,091 miles, 'T2296, 2312, 2318'
8/5/61-3/6/61**LI**   96,837 miles, speedometer fitted, five tests
26/11/62-14/12/62**LC**   177,167 miles, three tests
10/9/63-9/11/63**LI-GO**   208,458 miles, spark arrester gear fitted, 120 monel metal riveted over, 1,126 steel renewed and 220 roof stays renewed, 6 fusible plugs, 2 diaphragm patches fitted and welded, 2 short casing sides L and R sides fitted and welded
1/7/65-18/8/65**LC**
Experiments listed on back of BR9215 card; 2207 2242 2246 2296 2305 2307 2312 2318

Withdrawn September 1966 having run 748,343 miles, 319,722 as a rebuild, stored at Weymouth shed 9/66-4/67 and at Woodham Brothers, Barry, 5/67-1/74. Now a sectioned exhibit at the National Railway Museum York.

35029 at Stewarts Lane on 6 June 1950, nameplate still covered though half, oddly, has fallen off. Its name is thus LINES! It was never based here and has worked up from Dover shed which had a couple of the big Pacifics for the Night Ferry, duty no.430 at this shed. Dover men had the up and down working which at the time was the only through train from the Continent via the ferries. As on CLAN LINE seen earlier, the malachite green with which it emerged from Eastleigh is wearing a bit thin on 35029; naming did not take place until 1 March 1951 and again, like CLAN LINE, ELLERMAN LINES had received a coat of blue for the occasion. Photograph R.E. Vincent, www.teransporttreasury.co.uk.

35029 ELLERMAN LINES at Nine Elms shed on 14 October 1956; it had moved there from Dover the previous year. There is a record from late in 1953 of the cab side being 'repainted green and lined out minus the black splashskirt'; this was because it was about to be paired with the coal weighing tender. In practice this failed to materialise, so the cab lining after a while returned to normal for a high sided tender. Photograph R.J. Buckley, Initial Photographics.

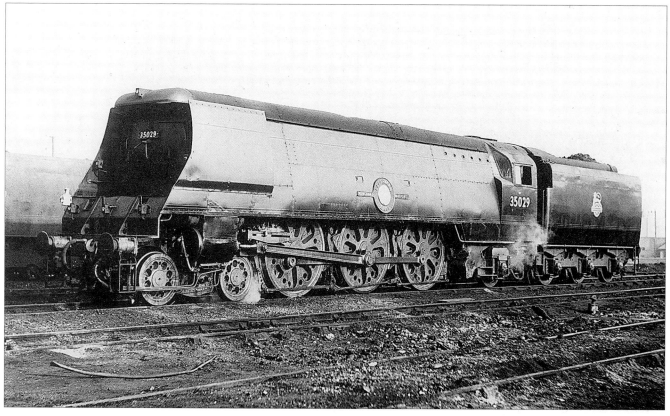

35029 ELLERMAN LINES with a down Folkestone boat train passing Knockholt, 14 August 1954. Photograph D.W. Winkworth.

Nine Elms' 35029 ELLERMAN LINES leaving Weymouth with the 5.35pm service to Waterloo, 4 June 1960. AWS protector plate, no battery box. Tender is no.3129, which was modified with 35029 when it was rebuilt the previous year. Photograph Peter Groom.

35029 had moved to Nine Elms in June 1955; here it is in that splendid wasteland of a yard about 1964-65 – the 70G plate means the period is after it moved to Weymouth in September 1964. AWS fully fitted. Photograph www.transporttreasury.co.uk

35029 ELLERMAN LINES wreathes its train and a fair swath of the surrounding land in its exhaust, at Brockenhurst on 18 March 1963. Photograph Stephen Gradidge.

35030 ELDER-DEMPSTER LINES

Entered traffic 1 April 1949 to order No.3393 in Malachite Green livery, front skirting and cylinders painted black.
Named at Southampton Docks 5/6/50 by Mr. G.H. Avezathe, a Director of the Company.

Tenders
3348 1/4/49
3345 8/65 [not shown on Engine Record Card]

Boilers
1120 1/4/49
1113 22/10/54
1111 23/4/58
1122 5/5/62

Allocations
Bournemouth 4/1949
Dover p/e 29/10/49
Nine Elms p/e 21/6/55
Weymouth p/e 14/9/64
Nine Elms p/e 17/4/67

Works: 1

17/5/50-26/5/50**LC**	44,978 repainted BR Blue and '...after being specially re-painted and cleaned in the works at Eastleigh' for naming ceremony, all exposed metal parts well burnished. 150 steel stays riveted over, lead plugs
25/6/51-28/6/51**NC**	83,683 fitted with indicator shelter
22/11/51-21/12/51**LI**	96,111 360 steel stays riveted over, lead plugs, 30 new tubes 'Howell' Boiler record card: Internal examination extended to 4/55.Ref C40/2293
21/4/53-16/5/53**HI**	151,982 sliding covers for whistle and manifold valves, repainted BR Green, front casing removed, 24 monel metal, 152 steel and 15 roof stays renewed, lead plugs, 30 new tubes 'Howell' 9 new superheaters

35030
(Mileages = since last General Overhaul)Works: 2

29/3/54-10/4/54**NC-LC**	187,845 miles
20/9/54-22/10/54**GO**	207,897 miles, twelve modifications, boiler pressure reduced
1/12/55-14/12/55**LC**	42,332 miles, 'T2204'
5/9/56-22/9/56**LI**	79,586 miles, seven modifications, 'T 2204'
1/6/57-6/7/57**LC**	116,168 at Bricklayers Arms shed
12/3/58-23/4/58**GO**	143,459 miles, nine modifications, three tests, resited safety valves, rebuilt having run 351,234 miles, 2nd BR tender emblem
12/5/59-23/5/59**LC**	78,964 miles
12/5/60-28/5/60**LI**	133,410 miles, AWS and speedometer fitted
11/1/61-28/1/61**LC**	181,590 miles, 'T2285, Metcalf's steam heat couplings (new test)'
27/3/62-5/5/62**GO**	230,583 miles
12/11/63-21/12/63**LI-HI**	85,908 miles, spark arrestor fitted, 'AWS gear made operative'
2/66-15/3/66**LC**	

Withdrawn July 1967 having run 850,876 miles, 499,642 as a rebuild, stored at Nine Elms shed 7/67-4/68.

The last Merchant Navy, 35030 **ELDER-DEMPSTER LINES** with black skirt at the front, just emerged at Eastleigh and delivered to the shed yard in 1949; malachite green, nameplate covered. Next to it is light Pacific 34037 **CLOVELLY**. The next year, in sparkling blue, 35030 was at Southampton Docks for its naming ceremony. Photograph A. Scarsbrook, Initial Photographics.

The Bournemouth Belle winding its way past Millbrook yard behind 35030 ELDER-DEMPSTER LINES on 2 August 1958. The abandoned entrance gate to the dock lines marks a wartime connection, removed at the end of hostilities. Photograph Les Elsey.

An archetypal Merchant Navy view, all power and noise, at Waterloo on 23 June 1963. The headboard looks to have been dropped lately – sheds and crews usually treated such items as unnecessary clutter! Photograph Prorail UK (Durrant)/ www.transporttreasury.co.uk

35030 ELDER-DEMPSTER LINES on shed at Eastleigh about 1960. It had been rebuilt in 1958. Photograph J. Davenport, Initial Photographics.

35030 ELDER-DEMPSTER LINES at Weymouth shed on 6 September 1966. Just three of the class got the electrification warning 'flashes', 35026, 35028 and 35030. They were the ones, the SR authorities expected, that would be used for charters under the wires on the LMR. Photograph John Scrace.

SHAW SAVILL parked amidst the weeds at Eastleigh while its centre drivers get attention – presumably this was during the axle examination episode after the Crewkerne incident of 1953.

Appendix
Down The Years

*T*he Book of the Merchant Navy Pacifics was first published in 2001 by Irwell Press. That book, in another time, was restricted as to space and, well, we can always do with more photographs of these wondrous machines. Moreover it has also proved possible to upgrade 'The Record' to include details of the liveries and tenders which is now the usual in these books and to add a few further details of modifications. A number of corrections to the text and tables have also been made.

The Merchant Navy Pacifics had emerged from the mists of war yet we know more about their construction than any other of the big Pacific classes that passed into BR service. This came about because their activities were made public through official channels both to the trade journal *The Railway Gazette* and to the enthusiast *Railway Observer* and SLS *Journal* throughout 1941. Some pains had been taken for their names to remind the travelling public of the war effort and what was the point of that if their existence and activities remained secret? Beyond that, Bulleid's extremely thorough paper to the Institution of Mechanical Engineers in December 1945 was immediately afterwards serialised in *The Railway Gazette*, parts of which appear in this volume.

21C1 (2 for the bogie, 1 for the trailing wheel, C for the driving wheels and 1 for the number of the engine – this was perverse even by slippery continental standards!) was officially launched in February 1941 right in the worst of the War when things were not going at all well. How did Bulleid get away with introducing such a revolutionary design at such an austere time? Well he did, perhaps using the term 'fast mixed traffic' helped. Still we must be grateful; but for this chink in the country's armour of total war, we might have ended up with another thirty 8Fs! In fact, the new Pacific was lauded as a welcome tool in the war effort; the Minister of Transport hailed it as 'a link in the prosecution of that effort'. To the ordinary man in the street (even streets south and west of the Thames) they would appear as 'streamlined' locos after the fashion of the LNER and LMS express locos so celebrated in the press and in newsreels in the 1930s. But they weren't 'streamlined' at all – the (oval, not round) smokebox door presented as flat a face to the onrushing air as any loco anywhere. 'Streamlining' wouldn't have gone down at all well; would have seemed frivolous (rightly so) in those

desperate days and the expression 'air smoothed' was used instead, whatever it might mean. As the initial report on CHANNEL PACKET put it slightly apologetically: *Streamlining – another and more accurate description would be 'air-smoothed'.*

The first recorded date of 21C1 being steamed was 17 February 1941; this was followed by journeys to Winchester and down the line to Bournemouth West. After unveiling the nameplate of 21C1 CHANNEL PACKET at Eastleigh the Minister of Transport Lt.Colonel J.T.C. Moore-Brabazon donned an engineman's cap and drove the new loco past his audience. It then powered a short ride during which luncheon was served, and made a return trip to Alresford on the Alton line. A number of trial trips were completed during March including runs as light engine to Bournemouth and Salisbury and one test train of twenty coaches with a tare weight of approx 650 tons, a train it seemed to handle with some ease. April 22nd saw 21C1 work a goods train of sixty wagons from Eastleigh to Salisbury.

With nameplates covered, the second engine, 21C2, worked the down evening goods Salisbury to Southampton every evening from 5th to 10th June 1941 and officially entered traffic on June 16th; it was named at Victoria station on 4th July. A marked feature of the two Merchant Navys was the fitting of cast plates for running numbers and the giant SOUTHERN plate on the tender.

21C3 (to traffic 13/9/41) had some detail differences with numbers and lettering in Southern yellow instead of cast brass plates on the cab sides, tender sides and the casing above the front buffer beam. All letters were black lined near the edge. High on the cab side was a small window above the main window to illuminate the mechanical lubricator. Weight saving, after the experience of the first two, was essential, so the frames had numerous lightening holes cut in them while the air smoothed casing was made in 'limpet' board rather than sheet steel.

21C2 worked to Exeter on 26th December 1941 and suffered valve gear problems on the way. It was taken off its train at Axminster and was towed to Eastleigh works. The resulting modification was the addition of a balancing pipe between the ends of the steam chests.

On 9th January 1942 21C3 was in charge of the 11.07am semi-fast West of England train from Salisbury;

Honiton Bank was taken with 'a steady acceleration'. There was considerable slipping on starting from Seaton Junction; the Bulleid Pacifics acquired a reputation for slipping when starting away, especially at Waterloo station where the sanders could not be used in case they interfered with the track circuit. It was a truly memorable sight. 21C3's arrival at Exeter was greeted with some wonder, it seems, for it was one of the first appearances of the startling new type on a passenger train. 21C3 was busy for the next few weeks on 15 coach trains (two return trips a day) between Salisbury and Exeter, to some notable timings apparently. Then came a number of ordinary passenger trains on this route, then duties from Waterloo to Southampton and Bournemouth.

About the spring of 1942 it was ordered that all locos leaving works, including new ones, would be painted black and that included 21C8 which entered traffic on 16th June. 21C5 was the first one repainted black, for its naming ceremony. It was unlined and unvarnished with shaded green and yellow lettering.

The delivery of the first batch to order no.1068 finished with 21C10 BLUE STAR entering traffic on 31st July 1942. By that summer they were recorded in regular use and a visitor to Yeovil could note the following in a single period of observation:
21C7 on the 9am Waterloo that left Salisbury at 11.07am.
21C8 worked the 12.55pm Salisbury to Exeter slow.
21C3 through train to Brighton, 12.30pm from Exeter.
21C4 on a down pick up goods!

From new the first ten spent time at Salisbury or Exmouth Junction sheds; some stayed in the West until withdrawal while the first transfer away was 35005, to Nine Elms in November 1948. Unused to Pacifics, observers continued to report their propensity to slip when starting; even their exhaust was unconventional: 'a peculiar three beat exhaust, one loud, two soft.' On slower working it was a definite 'chuffety-chuff' which is still quite noticeable on say, light Pacific 34046 BRAUNTON to this day. At speed you could hardly discern the separate exhaust beats.

The 10.30pm arrival into Waterloo from the West of England was at this time a regular duty for the new Pacifics; the loco then worked the 1.35am down newspaper train. All ten were in regular service on the West of England main line and one day at Waterloo at the end of July 1942 seems to have been fairly typical, seeing:

21C7on the 1.35am paper train from Waterloo.

21C9 on the 8.54am from Waterloo.

21C3 on the 11.02am from Waterloo.

21C6 on the 2.50pm from Waterloo.

This last departure was another regular duty; 21C8 was often on it, the up working being the 11.09 semi-fast from Salisbury, an easy job for a Merchant Navy.

On 2nd December 1942 21C10 (named a couple of weeks later) worked the 12.50pm Waterloo right through to Exeter Central by way of a test, it seems; it was one of those fearsomely loaded wartime trains formed of twenty bogies and its working was 'entirely successful'. On 13th December 21C10 worked through from Exeter and was only half an hour late at Waterloo despite a special stop at Clapham Junction. The regular train was the first twelve coaches and when ready 21C10 pulled them forward and backed on to the other eight in another platform – these were kept empty all the time to save drawing up at intermediate stations. The special stop on the up trip was to shunt the eight empty coaches into the sidings at Clapham Junction and leave them there. Trains of twenty coaches would, it seems, never become usual in wartime despite the need for vastly increased capacity because of the limitations of platforms and so on but it did prove how capable the engines were.

21C4 was machine gunned by a German fighter on 18th November 1942; luckily (the crew probably did not see it this way) it was working a goods train.

The oil baths were a problem of sorts right through the lives of the Bulleid Pacifics – though it is quite probable that accounts over the years have overstated their shortcomings. Motion failures were far from unknown on other locomotive types of course, and some classes were (relatively) notorious for failure of the inside motion. The fact that Bulleid's chain motion was not perfect cannot mean that it should be condemned as an abject failure. It's probably unfortunately true that Bulleid failures often involved an element of drama absent in 'conventional' failures. In December 1942, even without the intervention of the Luftwaffe, disaster struck 21C6; it had lost the contents of it oil bath and came to a stand after slipping furiously on the lost oil; to pile disaster upon mishap a fire began in the boiler lagging. The oil bath itself had distorted; Eastleigh was obviously pondering the problems (it never ceased doing so, probably) of the new chain gear and how to keep its contents secure. A new pattern oil bath was arrived at and fitted to 21C6 in the spring of 1944, though as we know it did not solve all the problems, nor did the use of a higher grade of oil. All the parts moving round in the oil baths also suffered wear and tear, including the

chains, a major reason (the SR claimed) for the rebuilding.

There were complaints of poor visibility in certain conditions and in 1943 beginning with 21C10 the casing at the top was modified; soon smoke deflectors were fitted. *The Railway Observer*, a shadow of its peacetime self but still valiantly recording the passing scene, so far as it could, noted the following Merchant Navy duties, part of the summer timetable that had started on 3rd May 1943:

Salisbury departures: 6.50am, 8.42am, 12.46pm, 4.48pm.

Waterloo arrivals: 9.11am, 11.09am, 2.42.pm, 6.32pm.

Waterloo departures: 12.50pm, 2.50pm, 5.00pm, 10.50am next morning.

Salisbury arrivals: 2.39pm, 4.42pm, 7.08pm, 12.33am next morning.

The 10.50am, made up of *sixteen* coaches midweek, was worked to Exeter by a Merchant Navy; the up train was split at Clapham Junction, the Plymouth portion of six coaches detached and worked (by one of the empty stock pilots, presumably) into a platform alongside the remaining ten coaches at Waterloo. The only two of the class still in green were the first two built; in the final month of 1943 21C1 was repainted black and 21C2 was so dealt with the following June.

21C1 had casing at the smokebox end altered, so that it looked similar to 21C10; the main difference was that the plate in front of the chimney did not bend downwards and was 'horizontal with a point in front of the chimney.'

Early in 1944 21C5 had the front end of the casing similarly altered, to tackle the problem of drifting smoke that tended to obscure the driver's vision. Before the end of the year it was reported that the next batch of ten had been ordered (along with the first of the light Pacifics); indeed the first three had been laid down at Eastleigh. The first, built to rder no.1189 was 21C11, delivered on 30th December 1944. As would all ten of this batch, it went new to Nine Elms shed where crews were already familiar with them, the five that had been working up from Salisbury for over 2½ years. 21C11 was first recorded in London on 11th January 1945, arriving on the 6am train from Southampton; its first express job seems to have been the 9.30am Waterloo-Bournemouth. On 22nd January 1945 the second Nine Elms Merchant Navy, 21C12, was on the 9.54am Waterloo-Basingstoke stopper, an unusual duty for the class you'd think but it could be turned here as Basingstoke shed had a 70ft turntable installed in 1943 to replace the 55ft one. The same duty was covered again at the end of the month but 21C12 failed at Woking and was replaced by an M7! It was something serious, for the Pacific was laid up at Guildford shed where it stayed for a few days before it was taken to Eastleigh. Here it was

repainted in workshop grey 'with three parallel white lines running along the length of the engine and tender.'

The Railway Magazine of July and August 1945 carried illustrations of the improved cab comfort of the second batch; 'the cab side sheets' it recorded, 'are turned inwards for about 12 inches at the back so forming shield recesses on both sides of the cab for protection from draughts'. The coal space on these tenders was narrowed so the crew, when running in reverse, like on the long run backing down from Nine Elms shed to Waterloo, had an adequate view between the coal space and the curved tender side-sheets'. The new arrangement also gave better protection from the weather; the front tender windows were 'hinged so that the space between the coal space and the tender side-sheets may be used for the stowage of fire irons'.

On 23rd March 1945 21C16, nine days after entering traffic, was on the 9.54am Waterloo-Basingstoke, regarded as the regular test run for the locos. For its naming, 21C12 had been repainted green with three parallel yellow lines running the length of engine and tender. The new Merchant Navys, based at Nine Elms, were working passenger trains to Bournemouth and Salisbury. 21C2 was fitted with a speedometer during the summer of 1945 and 21C3 had the smokebox door repainted minus the familiar SOUTHERN plate. The Southern now began to repaint the class in malachite green. The reason for 21C2 getting the speedometer was a series of trials on the Eastern Section where 21C1, when new, had worked a number of trial trips. August 13th saw 21C2 work the 8.35am Victoria-Ramsgate to allow Stewarts Lane men to familiarise themselves with the loco before a series of trials on August 14th-16th, two return trips each day between Victoria and Dover Marine working ten Pullmans and two corridor coaches. What was envisaged was the restoration of the boat trains and on 23rd October 1945 a continental service ran once again from Victoria to Dover Marine. It left Victoria at 8am on Tuesdays, Thursdays and Saturdays with the return from Dover Marine on Mondays, Wednesdays and Fridays. The inaugural train was worked by 21C17 BELGIAN MARINE. At the end of the year 21C3 was the first of the original ten to be repainted green.

1946 was the first full year to see twenty Merchant Navys at work, all on the Western Section. Stewarts Lane didn't have any on its books until the 1950s, though 21C1 was loaned for a short while in April 1946 to cover the reintroduction of the Golden Arrow. Nor would there really be a time when Eastleigh Works would not have some of the class 'inside', until the rundown of the mid-1960s.

21C1 was ex-works on 9th April 1946, reportedly repainted green again, and it carried on the front the disc with the arrow shot through it and those famous arrows either side of the casing. Familiarisation included light engine running from Stewarts Lane to Ashford in early April 1946. Two days later a trial run with the train was made from Victoria to Dover. Departure time from Victoria was 10.am with arrival at Dover at 11.40am; the Golden Arrow was resumed on 15th April 1946 and one unofficial report had CHANNEL PACKET attaining 98mph near Paddock Wood. 21C1 returned to Exmouth Junction shed the same month.

On 22 September, when 21C2 on the down ACE passed 21C4 on the up Devon Belle between Sidmouth Junction and Honiton an incident (to use current terminology) took place. The right-hand Devon Belle wingplate became loose, hit the down ACE loco and got wrenched off. The plate banged about between trains and some windows were broken – but luckily nothing worse occurred.

21C2 was at Eastleigh shed in June 1946, awaiting entry to the works, when it was noted that the speedometer was disconnected and the recorder box, located in the cab, was covered by a plate. This would mark the ending of the first speedometers. Another first for the class saw 21C17 BELGIAN MARINE at Hamworthy Junction on 20th July 1946 with *The Railway Observer* asking if any of the class had yet worked through to Weymouth.

On 14th August the Continental 8.46 am departure from Victoria was in the charge of a Nine Elms Merchant Navy, 21C19 FRENCH LINE C.G.T., 'in a very clean condition'. This was normally a King Arthur duty and the loco, it was believed, was there for the delight of some *personnes tres important*. It was at this time that the smoke deflectors received modifications, following complaints from drivers of drifting smoke. The new version was about three foot longer than the original.

During the last week of September 21C14 was working a load of sixteen coaches on coal tests Exeter Central-Waterloo and return. 21C4 replaced 21C14 at Nine Elms on these tests and working was extended to both Bournemouth and Salisbury. This loco also had a trial visit to Southampton Docks on 4th October 1946, the first recorded visit of a Merchant Navy. Later it worked an all Pullman train on 16th October 1946 to the docks for the first sailing of R.M.S. Queen Elizabeth. At the same time the Bournemouth Belle started to run again and on 7th October 1946 21C18 was at the head and the new 87 minute schedule to Southampton Central was 'well maintained'. The 'Belle' got going only in fits and starts; on 22nd October it had only two or three Pullmans but the 'consist' was restored to thirteen Pullmans behind 21C20. Later 21C14 failed on the up train and Bournemouth's Lord Nelson 864 SIR MARTIN FROBISHER took over. 852 SIR WALTER RALEIGH had charge

of the Belle later the same week and Bournemouth Nelsons seemed to predominate on the train thereafter. It was reported, in fact, that the new Pacifics were 'not at all common' in the London area which was doubly curious given that ten were at Nine Elms – in fact quite a few were in Eastleigh Works in late 1946.

1947
January 19th 1947 saw 21C13, 21C140 and the electric loco CC1 work trials with fifteen empty coaches including an LMS dynamometer car between Brighton and Norwood, nearly 500 tons in weight. During January the last of the second batch, to get malachite green was 21C11. In June 1947 the short-lived Pullman (famously with an observation car) The Devon Belle was inaugurated and although advertised as running non-stop to Exeter it was well known that at Wilton a stop was made to change locos. The inaugural trips on 20 June 1947 were worked between Waterloo and Wilton by Merchant Navy Pacific 21C15 ROTTERDAM LLOYD on Nine Elms duty 6 which carried a special bufferbeam-mounted head board as well as side 'wing' boards fixed to the smoke deflectors. From Wilton to Exeter Central 21C3 ROYAL MAIL took over while in the up direction to Wilton 21C4 CUNARD WHITE STAR had the train. ROTTERDAM LLOYD, after servicing at Salisbury, took it back to Waterloo. High operating costs prevented the train from being a lasting success; the Plymouth portion was withdrawn in 1950, the train ran at weekends only in 1952 and was withdrawn at the end of summer 1954, to be replaced by an ordinary restaurant car express.

21C8 was involved in an accident at Waterloo on 10th June 1947, running into a stationary electric train and sustaining severe damage to the front end. It was taken off to Eastleigh for repair. It left at the end of August with a V shaped cab similar to that carried by the light Pacifics – this would become standard on the Merchant Navys as they passed through works.

1948
The allocation on 1st January 1948, at the dawning of the new BR era, was:
Exmouth Junction 21C1-21C5 (35001-35005)
Salisbury 21C6-21C10 (35006-35010)
Nine Elms 21C11-21C20 (35011-35020)
During the year a third and final batch of ten was ordered under building lot no.3393 though the final two were not delivered from Eastleigh until 1949. Those new this year were divided thus: Exmouth Junction 35021-35024, Bournemouth 35025-35028. This was the first time any had been allocated to Bournemouth shed and from new they did not carry the numbering system introduced by Bulleid. They were instead numbered in the new order of things and the first twenty were duly

brought in line. April saw 35005 on trial with the Berkeley mechanical stoker and 21C19 now renumbered 35019 have its cab altered to take water scoop-equipped LMS tender no.10219 ready for the Locomotive Exchanges. To make sure everything functioned 35019 worked the 10.54am Waterloo-Basingstoke on 17th April 1948 and on 4th May had charge of the 1.05pm Bournemouth West-Waterloo. 35017 was also fitted with an LMS tender, no.10123, for the Exchanges. The locos must have presented quite a sight, in malachite green and the tenders in LMS black with BRITISH RAILWAYS in white on the tender sides. 35018 was fitted with a Flaman speed recorder and a modified cab for the Exchanges but as it was to work only on home territory it kept its tender. It worked the up and down Atlantic Coast Express, the 10.50am from Waterloo and the 12.40pm from Exeter Central. A fourth, 35020, was also fitted up with modified cab, Flaman speed recorder, uniquely extra long smoke deflectors and LMS tender no.10373 for the Exchanges – as a spare, seemingly, for it was not used.

By 8th June 35017, 35019 and 35020 had finished with the Locomotive Exchanges, been through works and had their original tenders back. While 35005 was undergoing the trials with the mechanical stoker 21C2 was on loan to Salisbury shed from Exmouth Junction. Eventually 35005 was transferred to Nine Elms shed permanently, from November 1948. Sadly, BR renumbering meant the loss of the smokebox door circular plates for the first twenty Pacifics and their replacement by the familiar Gill sans number plates. Of course 35021-35030 carried smokebox number plates from new.

First of the final batch, 35021, emerged from Eastleigh Works equipped with a wedge shaped cab in September 1948; it left fitted with a light Pacific tender no.3333 while its own was being completed at Brighton Works. The tenders had been 'sub-contracted' there but were delayed. Five of the new batch were to come out with the tenders of their lesser brethren, to be eventually united with their intended a few months later – see *The Tender Tale* for instance.

35021, 35022, 35024, 35026 and 35027 were all delivered new in unlined malachite green but soon 35021, 35022 and 35027 received full malachite livery. 35024 and 35026 became blue however, as did 25 of the others in due course.

1949
T.I.A. water treatment was now being fitted; a standard feature of SNCF locos *Traitement Integral Armand* had been used on the light Pacifics before the Merchant Navys and was replaced by the BR 'doser tank' system in the 1950s. The last of the class, 35030 ELDER DEMPSTER LINES was delivered in April 1949. 35025-35030 went new to Bournemouth in place of Lord Nelson

The new malachite reflects the sun off 35021 (with Battle of Britain 5,500 gallon tender) at Eastleigh; see also page 78.

4-6-0s on main line duties to Waterloo. The running in turn was the 1pm stopping train to Weymouth and part of duty no.383 the 11.02am semi-fast Bournemouth West to Waterloo. They did not stay that long at Bournemouth with 35028-35030 moving to Dover shed in October 1949 and 35025-35027 to Stewarts Lane in March 1950. The principal duties of course for those sent to the Eastern concerned the Golden Arrow and the Night Ferry. They were replaced at Bournemouth by light Pacifics, then becoming available in considerable numbers.

35024 was ex-works on 12/2/49 in BR Blue with three red bands and the lion and wheel emblem on the tender sides; now with its own 6,000 gallon tender no.3346 it proceeded to Brighton shed for inspection by members of the Railway Executive. 22nd February saw it travel to Eastleigh via London as the class were banned from travelling over Ford Bridge. It again entered Eastleigh to receive smaller numerals; the red lining was replaced with two black and white lines while the Lion and Wheel emblems were again applied to the tender sides.

By late May 1949 35021-35024 of Exmouth Junction shed were fitted with the wooden battens on the smoke deflectors to carry the Devon Belle boards.

1950
Allocation August 1950 was:
Nine Elms 35005 35010-35020,
Exmouth Junction 35001-35004 35021-35024,
Salisbury 35006-35009,
Stewarts Lane 35025-35028,
Dover 35029 35030.

35002 spent the Festive season in Eastleigh Works being released w/e 7/1/50 but in BR blue, having lost its cast brass number and Southern plates from the side of the tender while 35019, also repainted blue, still had the speedometer fitted that was used in the Loco Exchanges.

Monday 6th February saw a revolutionary development, for through loco workings were instituted Waterloo-Exeter, ending the changeover of locos at Salisbury on all trains. Up till then Exmouth Junction only rarely penetrated to Waterloo, while London locos did not often get past Salisbury. Now six minutes were allowed at Salisbury to take water and change crews while cleaners from Salisbury shed were often available to swarm over the tender and get the coal forward.

35021 had the Royal train on 1st June 1950, on reputedly the longest non-stop journey on Southern metals – of 118.2 miles between Waterloo and Sherborne where the King and Queen were visiting the school. This exceeded, just, the 117.9 miles non-stop between Devonport and Templecombe for the LSWR boat expresses. The load did not tax the big Pacific, for it was only four vehicles and one Pullman car.

For a week or so in mid-June 1950 Dover's 35030 was seen at Exeter several times. It had been named ELDER-DEMPSTER LINES at Southampton Docks and Eastleigh, it seems, was reluctant to let go of it!

On 31 July 1950, to coincide with the opening of the new passenger terminal building at the Ocean Dock, Southampton, a special train was run from Waterloo consisting of twelve Pullman cars to carry four hundred

guests. 35001 was smartly turned out to work this train with a light blue 'No.1 Ocean Terminal Express' headboard.

35005 was having a time of it; the 8.30am Waterloo-Bournemouth was its regular down working and on 15th September 1950 it failed at Raynes Park, to be rescued by H16 4-6-2T 30517 of Feltham shed which hauled the ensemble to Surbiton where 35005 was put in the sidings. Most of the passengers were placed on the 9.30am departure and the original train was worked forward by 34054, 81 minutes late. Then 35005 failed on the same train a week later near Woking, to be replaced this time by U class 2-6-0 31798 of Guildford shed which worked through to Bournemouth. It was October before 35005 could be hauled to Eastleigh, by N 2-6-0 31875.

By November 1950 35001 had been repainted BR blue again, polished and checked over for another Royal duty on 21st November 1950 when the Queen of Netherlands visited this country. The Royal entourage travelled from Dover to Victoria but a defect on 35001 saw 35004 take its place. Doubtless 35014 NEDERLAND LINE was considered – we can only presume it was not in tip-top nick.

The autumn of 1950 saw some locos borrowed from Eastern Section sheds with one Merchant Navy, 35028 CLAN LINE working the 12.30pm from Exeter Central (the up ACE) on 21st October 1950, a working the loco would have on a regular basis in later years.

By the end of the year 35005 had a self cleaning smokebox; 35001 now had a V shaped cab and boiler no.1107 without thermic syphons was being prepared at Eastleigh 'as an experiment to compare the steaming capabilities of both types of boilers.'

1951
The last Merchant Navy to be named was 35029 ELLERMAN LINES at 106 berth in Southampton New Docks on 1st March 1951. It had only been repainted for the ceremony a few weeks earlier but was back in the works for its second coat of BR blue to work a special train for Danish Royalty in May, a Pullman from Dover Marine to Victoria with the loco carrying a special headboard though the return trip was made from Liverpool Street to Harwich. At last, at the end of April 1951 35005 was free of the mechanical stoker, which wasn't used again. During the year the engines were reclassified from 7P to 8P.

The BR blue livery was short-lived and the Southern Region dropped it as soon as it could; in May 35024 was in BR dark green followed the following month by the repainting of 35002 and then 35018.

Badges and emblems had to be kept up to date; 35012, ex-works w/e 1/9/51 had the replica of the shipping company's house flag altered to conform with the new flag of the company.

Apparently 35012 with its self cleaning smokebox (fitted w/e 17/2/51) was a bad steamer because of it. 35019 was fitted with a single blastpipe and chimney; it burnt less coal but was steaming badly and suffering bad time keeping. 35014 had received boiler no.1107 (minus thermic syphons) in the summer and was found to be steaming just as well as when it carried a boiler with the thermic syphons.

1952
35022 arrived at the Rugby Testing Station on 4th March 1952, having run light engine from Willesden and most likely confusing a few spotters on the way. On 22nd March 35002 was at Waterloo station in green livery with a blue tender. On the Eastern Section trials were carried out with partially fitted loads of 30 ferry vehicles and two twenty-five ton 8 wheeled goods brakes – some 700 tons – between Dover Marine and Chislehurst; on 17th February 1952 35030 ascended the bank from Tonbridge to the tunnel without any obvious difficulty.

In February 1952 tender no.3342 with 35021 was modified by the removal of the upper part of the side sheets (the 'raves') so that the profile of the side showed 'a drop of about 18 inches at the middle of the tender' to enable the hose of a water crane to be swung over more easily. The vacuum tanks, positioned behind the coal space, had a protective steel cover fitted above them. The lining was revised 'to form panels in place of the usual continuous lines running the whole length of engine and tender'

The ACE timings saw the 11am departure, Mondays to Fridays,

Waterloo to Exeter Central timed for 3 hours 5 minutes, a cut of 24 minutes on the original schedule. Merchant Navy and crew would have to work just that bit harder and one assumes there had been improvements in the track as well. The service included stops at Salisbury and Sidmouth Junction whereas the best pre-war schedule of 3 hours 5 minutes only included a stop at Salisbury. The up schedule was 3 hours ten minutes, departing Exeter at 12.30pm and arriving at Waterloo at 3.40pm but at Salisbury through coaches from Lyme Regis and Yeovil Town were attached and it also included a through coach from Plymouth, the first since the start of the war. The new schedule was in the hands of 35015 for a while which obtained 'some respite at week-ends by hauling the Devon Belle'. Some respite! The first day of the new schedule saw 35015 haul a train of 375 tons gross and although 88mph was reached on the descent to Salisbury a 3 minute late arrival was recorded.

On 1st May 1952 a test run behind 35028 left Victoria at 9.02am and returned from Dover at 1.33pm with a mixed bag of rolling stock for the planned 92 minute schedule for the Golden Arrow. A maximum of 90mph was reached near Sandling Junction on the down journey and on the up 92mph at Pluckley.

1953
24th April 1953 was the day that 35020, in charge of the 2.15pm Plymouth-Waterloo suffered a broken middle driving axle near Crewkerne which led to the temporary withdrawal of the class and the input of 'foreign' locos to cover their duties – as detailed in the text. Most of the class were back in service at the beginning of June and their days in works are noted in *The Record*.

35029 was noted on 14th November 1953 with the whole of the cab side painted green and lined out, the black 'splash-skirt' being omitted. Pacifics with modified tenders had the cab black 'splash-skirt' removed. Lining extended over the entire cab sheet and the numerals were lowered to be level with the small BR totem on the tender. (35029 did not in fact have a modified tender until September 1959). As mentioned already, 35029 was expected at the time to be paired with the coal weighing tender but this never came to pass.

Allocation 10th December 1953:
Nine Elms 35010-35021,
Exmouth Junction 35001-35005 35022-35024,
Salisbury 35006-35009,
Stewarts Lane 35025-35028,
Dover 35029 35030.

1954
From 8th February 1954 35008, 35011 and 35012 were transferred to Bournemouth, the first from Salisbury and the others from Nine Elms, to work

the Royal Wessex which had been introduced in the summer of 1951 to coincide with the Festival of Britain. It was made up of the modern BR Mark 1 stock in 'plum and spilt milk' livery and served Bournemouth, Swanage and Weymouth. The Merchant Navys didn't stay long; 35011and 35012 moved back to Nine Elms in May 1954 and 35008 moved onto Exmouth Junction in August.

After 21st October, for a while the Eastern Section was short of Merchant Navys with Nine Elms 35012 working the Night Ferry from 22nd to 28th October. Some of the Merchant Navys were in shops or were on their way to Eastleigh namely 35027-35030. Next recorded appearance of a Merchant Navy was another 'on loan' from Nine Elms 35015 ROTTERDAM LLOYD in charge of the 10am down boat train on 13th November. *Trains Illustrated* reported that at the beginning of November Nine Elms' 35012 and 35015 were both at work on the Eastern Section.

On 2nd November 1954 35009 failed at Woking while in charge of the 2.30pm from Exeter and the train was rescued by M7 30246 which ran bunker first with the train to Waterloo. On 11th November 35023 on the up ACE was brought to a halt by a broken leading axle on the tender at Broad Clyst and was drawn back to Pinhoe by the loco off the 12.35pm Exeter-Broad Clyst. 35009 was sent up from Exmouth Junction shed to work the train forward to Waterloo. Then on 10th December 35025 was in trouble when it broke a coupling rod soon after leaving Honiton on the 9am Waterloo train. Salisbury's 30449 SIR TORRE off the 11.46am semi-fast from Templecombe drew the train back into the station and worked it on to Exeter. On 27th December, 34044 dropped a lead plug at Pinhoe while in charge of the 4.16pm Exeter-Waterloo and its fire had to be thrown out. 35006 (waiting to work the 4.56pm departure) was sent from Exeter Central but 35003 was also despatched from Exmouth Junction shed and 'won the race'. 35006 returned to Central; 34004 was left in a siding at Pinhoe and 35003 worked on to London.

1955
Allocation 13th June 1955:
Nine Elms 35005, 35010-35012, 35015-35021, 35025, 35029, 35030,
Bournemouth 35022, 35027,
Exmouth Junction 35001-35004, 35008, 35013, 35023, 35024,
Salisbury 35006, 35007, 35009,
Stewarts Lane 35014, 35026, 35028.

On 14th October 1955 another Merchant Navy came to grief at Woking, 35016 on the down Bournemouth Belle. M7 30110 was coupled on and this combination worked forward to Basingstoke where 30788 SIR URRE OF THE MOUNT of Eastleigh shed took over. There was a bad failure on 16th November 1955 at Gillingham, Dorset, again involving 35016 on the 9am Waterloo-Exeter. Presumably some catastrophic slipping was involved, for all four coupling rods were broken or buckled and outside connecting rods buckled too. There was enormous difficulty in moving 35016 to a siding at Gillingham; in the end it had to be lifted to remove a damaged axle before it could finally be towed to Eastleigh.

On 15th October 1955 35006 of Salisbury and 35029 of Nine Elms were undergoing repairs at Bricklayers Arms but this was not recorded on the BR9215 forms.

On 27th October 1955 35029 arrived at Brighton shed and moved over to the works; this was the first reported instance of a Merchant Navy in for repairs there; the visit is not recorded but was not a non-classified of some sort. It did not leave for Nine Elms until 7th December 1955 and had not steamed between these dates.

In mid-December 35015 was at Bricklayers Arms shed with its driving wheels down, though this *is* in *The Record*.

1956

The most important event for 1956 was the first rebuilding, of 35018 BRITISH INDIA LINE; it emerged from Eastleigh in February in its new form. For all the design though and rebuilding effort and expense it probably seemed a poor deal to the driver. Crews understandably had no interest in the wider view and to drivers it must have seemed that they had to oil all round and underneath whereas before, they hadn't. 35018 had run 504,900 since new over 10½ years and upon withdrawal 8½ years later (September 1964) the figure was 451,644 miles after rebuilding so in which form did BR get the better of the bargain? On 10th February it did a trial return trip Eastleigh-Botley and on the 12th ran up to Nine Elms light, limited to 30mph for inspection at Waterloo on 13th; it returned, again light, on the 14th. Its first rostered job was Eastleigh duty no.253 on 17th February, taking over the 9.54am Waterloo at Eastleigh and the 1.29pm Fareham-Bournemouth West at Southampton Central. Disaster struck and by early evening it was passing St.Denys, tender first and dead hauled by M7 30376. It went straight into the works at Eastleigh for attention due to a 'piston valve failure resulting in a bent radius rod at Lyndhurst Road.' The problem repeated itself on 27th February 1956 at Farnborough when working the 7.22am from Eastleigh. Later 35018 made its debut on the Bournemouth Belle and on March 28th with a load of 520 tons gross this Pullman train reached Southampton in 92½ minutes (net time 86½ minutes) but covered the next distance to Bournemouth in 34 minutes, ahead of the schedule time of 39 minutes. The first report of 35018 on

the lines to the West was 26th and 27th April 1956 when it worked the 9am Waterloo-Exeter and 4.30pm return. The next day, 28th, it was back on the Bournemouth Belle. A correspondent quoted in *Trains Illustrated* a conversation with the crew of rebuilt 35018: she was 'all right' but 'not what she was, you have to keep pushing her'. Which wouldn't have done their career prospects much good!

The second rebuild, 35020, had as its first duty the 7.03am Southampton Docks-Waterloo; 11.30am Waterloo-Bournemouth; 5.05pm Bournemouth West-Waterloo and 10.30pm back. Whit Monday, June 11th saw the start of trials with 35020 and the WR dynamometer car between Exeter and Salisbury and until 22nd the loads varied from 12 to 16 bogies with two return runs fitted in between 8.40am and 5.30pm. On 25th and 27th 35020 took the dynamometer on the up ACE from Exeter. One report was that the rebuilds were 'markedly superior in fuel economy' but then they were testing a near new loco with a very good steam raising boiler.

On 8th February 1956 35015 failed near Woking, a place that seemed to have unhappy associations for the class. Hauling the up Bournemouth Belle it dropped three plugs and the train was pushed into Woking by a class 700; the train was terminated there and later on an M7 took the empty stock to Clapham Junction.

At the end of September 1956 a second Merchant Navy visited Brighton when 35018 came down the main line from Nine Elms; it went first to the shed and was at the Works for a valve and piston exam 25/9/56-4/10/56, returning to Nine Elms on 10th October on the 1.45pm special from Hassocks to Selhurst Dock. The train consisted of a four car EMU with a goods brake van.

On 1st November 1956 35002 on the 6pm Waterloo-Exeter suffered an injector failure near where else but Woking and was stuck in the down fast platform there for half an hour before the inevitable M7, this time 30675, was attached. Other traffic had to use the down slow. The combination struggled to Fleet where the M7 had to stop to raise steam and struggled again on to Basingstoke arriving 87 minutes down. Here the M7 was replaced by H15 4-6-0 30474. On 3rd November it was 35027's turn to be in trouble, on the 11.05 from Bournemouth; it had to be rescued at Basingstoke by 32331 BEATTIE the surviving N15X 4-6-0 which worked the train up to London and returned on the 7.54pm Waterloo-Basingstoke rather than the normal balanced working, the down Royal Wessex.

1957

Allocation 1st January 1957:
Nine Elms 35005, 35011, 35012, 35014, 35016-35021, 35029, 35030,
Bournemouth 35010, 35022, 35025, 35027,

Exmouth Junction 35002-35004, 35008, 35013, 35023, 35024,
Salisbury 35006, 35007, 35009,
Stewarts Lane 35001, 35015, 35026, 35028.

Summer 1957 saw the instigation of the two hour Bournemouth expresses, in the charge of rebuilt Merchant Navys, the trains limited to twelve coaches and a maximum of 400 tons. This required 35026 being transferred in to make five rebuilds based at Bournemouth. By now it had no.3130 the 6,000 gallon long wheelbase tender which had a large cover over the vacuum reservoirs. The duties covered by the Bournemouth Merchant Navys involved the Royal Wessex, Bournemouth Belle and two of the new two hour duties so there was little margin for error with those five; the thirteen light Pacifics on the shed's books doubtless substituted when necessary.

1958

Weymouth was originally built by the GWR in 1885, a standard straight road shed with a 65ft turntable added in 1925 and a typical GWR coal stage. It had long been used by Southern Region locomotives but from 23rd February 1958 it became part of the Region, coded 71G. Accordingly there were more through workings from Waterloo and Pacifics became common.

Rebuilt 35015 was on the 11.28am Hither Green-Feltham goods train and the 2.22pm return during the first week of March 1958 running in after 'local repairs' which presumably meant Feltham.

During the year reports circulated that 35001-35005 were not going to be rebuilt, the main reason being the design of the frames; this was illogical however and 35002 was duly ushered into Eastleigh at the end of March 1958 followed by 35004 in May.

35003, not yet rebuilt and a long time Exmouth Junction engine, was on the up ACE on 31st August 1958. On these originals the valance between cylinders and buffer beams had long been cut away for safety reasons. One drawback on the originals was the siting of the mechanical lubricators on a platform directly under the smokebox door which could allow dust and ash to contaminate the oil, especially when men were cleaning out the smokebox. On the rebuilds the mechanical lubricators were placed conventionally on the running plates alongside the boiler, allowing easier access. They were however, vulnerable to char from the chimney descending all the time a loco was working. Out of the frying pan into the fire?

A drawback on the rebuilds was the narrow step and running plate alongside the smoke deflectors which made carrying equipment awkward; the handrail did not run the full length down the side of the deflectors though hand holds were cut level with the running plate

1959
Allocation May 1959:
Nine Elms 35005, 35012, 35014, 35016-35020, 35029, 35030,
Bournemouth 35002, 35010, 35021, 35022, 35024, 35025, 35027,
Exmouth Junction 35003, 35008, 35009, 35011, 35013, 35023, 35026,
Salisbury 35004, 35006, 35007,
Stewarts Lane 35001, 35015, 35028.

1960
June 18th saw the first Surbiton to Okehampton car carrier formed of seven GUVs (to transfer the cars) and three coach set no.564 made up of a BSK, CK and BSK. It was worked out of Surbiton goods yard by 35029, as far as Exeter Central.

1961
On 27th December 1960 there was a severe landslide near Hook which forced diversions and resulted in sights like 35019 on 13th January hauling the 3.45pm milk empties from Clapham to Basingstoke via Reading. On Sunday 8th January the 9.30, 10.30, 11.30 and 12.30 Waterloo-Bournemouth trains were worked by 34017, 35029, 35030 and 35018 respectively via Alton to Winchester and although single track with passing loops the SR were lucky to have such a route that could take the heaviest of locos and trains. 35018 was of course hauling the down 'Bournemouth Belle' and was piloted by U class 31628 to work the 1 in 60 gradient from Alton up to Medstead and Four Marks though it was all downhill then to Alresford.

Trains Illustrated in June 1961 mortified the linesiders with a chilling, unbelievable report that one of the Merchant Navy Pacifics, possibly 35029, would be withdrawn the following winter '...to provide spares'. It seemed insane; it had only been rebuilt in 1959 (even so it only lasted till September 1966 – it is now, bizarrely and rather sadly, a sectioned exhibit at the National Railway Museum).

On 30th July 35010, now an Exmouth Junction loco was on an Exeter to Salisbury local of three coaches; a phenomenon unknown to us at the London end . Even the big Pacifics, it turned out, sometimes worked such filling-in jobs in the West, between more exacting turns of duty.

In 1961 the Atlantic Coast Express timings were accelerated with 35028 on the 'inaugural' run: Waterloo-Salisbury 79.01 minutes, Salisbury-Sidmouth Junction 70.38 minutes and Sidmouth Junction to Exeter Central 15.2 minutes.

1962
The Merchant Navys were still intact and still seemed set for a fine future. Exmouth Junction's 35013 was a rare sight in Chichester yard on 2nd March;

days later it was in for a non-classified repair so perhaps Eastleigh shed was making use of it before entry to the works.

During the year it was decided to revert to the original red backgrounds on the nameplates; 35012 was the first Merchant Navy to be dealt with during its General 7/3/62-21/4/62. On 2nd June Salisbury's ever faithful 35006 was on one of the shed's regular heavy goods turns, the 8am Salisbury-Exeter. The crew worked the train all the way and returned with the up Brighton passenger; 35006 would have returned on the 2.30pm Exeter-Waterloo crewed by Exmouth Junction men, handed back to the owners at Salisbury. The return working was the 10.15pm non-stop fitted goods.

The shadows were lengthening however and 1963 dawned with no Arthurs, Schools or Nelsons; indeed the wondrous variety of SR steam had all but ended and the diet was now largely Bulleid Pacifics and BR Standards. We could still look forward to the spring resumption of the Atlantic Coast Express, with its mile-a-minute bookings each way between Salisbury and Sidmouth Junction now ranking as 'the hardest steam turn in the country'. On 30th March 35013 was on the up train with a load of 380 tons gross; it left Exeter two minutes late, was on time at Salisbury (exceeding 80mph three times) and some of the banks were climbed at 60mph or thereabouts.

A major change (a disaster in fact) in 1963 was the transfer of all SR lines west of Salisbury to the Western Region; the future for these closed in immediately and carried on closing. Exmouth Junction was recoded 83D from 9th September 1963 and was abandoned within two years, on 1st June 1965. The locos allocated also became WR property, awkwardly, though the new owners had no intention of keeping any of them running a minute more than they had too, or of spending any but the very minimum amount of money on them. Locos when absolutely necessary were still repaired at Eastleigh despite their listing as WR locos. The West of England trains were rapidly becoming dieselised, using worn-out locomotives already beyond their best on the WR main lines. Performance was poor and often awful but getting rid of steam and soon after the lines themselves was the name of the game.

1964
Allocations at 1st January 1964
Nine Elms 35001, 35012, 35014-35020, 35024, 35028-35030,
Bournemouth 35002, 35005, 35008, 35011, 35021, 35023, 35027,
Exmouth Junction 35003, 35009, 35010, 35013, 35022, 35025, 35026,
Salisbury 35004, 35006, 35007.

The first unprecedented/dismal change noted this year was 35015 'stored

unserviceable' in the first few days of January 1964; on 11th January 35003 was at Eastleigh Works marked 'for scrap' but it entered the works a day or two later for a light casual repair and survived two more visits to see out the last days until July 1967. This was of course the beginning of the demise of the class in BR service for the first two were withdrawn in February 1964; 35002 and 35015, set aside dumped at Nine Elms shed. This was also the time, when so many steam locos were being withdrawn, that the works gave up on their traditional role of breaking up locos and many were sold to outside scrap merchants. A lot of the SR locos went to yards in South Wales but 35002 and 35015 somehow seem to have ended up in Yorkshire and disappeared around December 1964 rather after the fashion of the Roman Ninth Legion. Withdrawals continued with 35006 and 35018 in August 1964, 35009 and 35025 in the September and 35001 in November. Times were certainly changing; on 27th July, *Trains Illustrated* reported the astonishing use of 35005 on a block coal train for the Chessington branch. Rightly it was 'believed to be unprecedented'.

The last Atlantic Coast Express ran on Friday 4th September 1964; the down train was hauled by 35022, in immaculate condition and the headboard was in place, a practice that seemed to have ceased during the previous year. Delays in the London area caused a loss of four minutes but the train was right time at Salisbury. On the up train Salisbury men relieved Exmouth Junction men with the former working home on the 7pm from Waterloo; the latter took over the 3pm from Waterloo which left Salisbury at 4.45pm. Warship diesels were now a regular feature at Waterloo though in October 35029 (now a Weymouth loco) was noted on three or four Exeter trains. Exmouth Junction, it will be remembered, was still open, and did not close till June 1965.

From mid-September 1964 all Pacifics were transferred away from Nine Elms and it became the stabling/servicing point for locos working into London from Weymouth/Bournemouth and Southampton – a most unexpected turn of events. it was presumably done in response to staff shortages in London. The deportees were:
35001, 35003, 35004, 35010, 35013, 35014 to Bournemouth
35005, 35007, 35012, 35016, 35017, 35019, 35020, 35022, 35024, 35026, 35028-35030 to Weymouth.

As late as 19th November 35030 was in charge of the 1pm Waterloo-Exeter and it covered the 49 miles from Yeovil to Exeter in rattlingly traditional manner, in 47 minutes; Yeovil to Axminster, 22 miles was covered in 18 minutes with a maximum of 92mph near Crewkerne.

21C19 FRENCH LINE CGT ex-works at Eastleigh. M. King Collection.

1965

Allocation at May 1965
Bournemouth 35003, 35004, 35008, 35010, 35011, 35013, 35021, 35023, 35027, Weymouth 35005, 35007, 35012, 35014, 35016, 35017, 35019, 35022, 35026, 35028-35030.

By May the allocation still showed these 21 still in service so they were holding up well – but it couldn't last and a number were withdrawn throughout the rest of 1965. 35004 went in October 1965 after an unfortunate slipping episode, 35005 went the same month, 35016 and 35021 in August and 35019 in September. Inevitably strange things happened; 35014 worked into Redhill via Woking and Guildford in March, developed a hot axlebox and was left on Redhill shed. It was due to return to the Western Section but was still on Redhill shed in April. It eventually left light for Nine Elms on 23rd April.

Another final steam special ran on the Salisbury-Exeter line on 7th March, non-stop each way between Waterloo and Yeovil Junction, behind 35022. *The Railway Magazine* speculated that 35005 could possibly be cannibalised for spares but this could now be read as a generalised likelihood. A few days later it was noted at Winchester in charge of the Royal Wessex!

Still, in that summer of 1965, the main Waterloo and Bournemouth expresses were operated by Merchant Navys which was making the line pretty unusual in Britain by then. On 6th July 1965 two Merchant Navys were to be found at Feltham yard having worked

in on goods trains, 35014 and 35019, an unimaginable occurrence in years past

During the summer 35010 was at Eastleigh shed, so grimy that the numbers were unreadable; 21C10 was chalked on the smokebox. In September the RCTS paid an official visit to Eastleigh works noting just eight steam locos though there were three Merchant Navys, receiving attention; according to our Record these were 35004 26/8/65-1/10/65**LC**; 35008 13/8/65-1/10/65**LI** and 35027 3/9/65-15/10/65**LI**.

At the end of the year it was rumoured that twenty Britannias were coming from the LMR to replace the Merchant Navys on the Bournemouth line and like an earlier rumour about the Stanier Pacifics it all came to nothing.

1966

Withdrawals in 1966 were 35010 September, 35011 February, 35017 July, 35022 May, 35027 September and 35029 September. 35003, 35008, 35013 and 35023 were transferred to Weymouth in October.

June 5th saw 35028 leave Victoria (now long steam free) on a circular tour via Redhill, Guildford and Staines to Kensington Olympia where 80154 took over. This was the 'Surrey Rambler' organised by the Southern Counties Touring Society and is similar to a route often taken by the preserved 35028 through the Surrey Hills nowadays but from Staines, returning to Victoria.

35029 waiting on the 9.20pm Waterloo to Bournemouth Central became trapped on 23rd June as some vans were derailed and '...blocked the

exits from platforms 10 and 11 and so locked the train in'. So stock was summoned from Clapham Junction and with 73115 KING PELLINORE in charge departed at 10.30pm

'The *seventh* 'last steam to Exeter' ran on Saturday 15th October 1966.

1967

From mid-April 1967 35003, 35007, 35008, 35012, 35013, 35023, 35028 and 35030 were transferred back to Nine Elms from Weymouth but the reasoning, a few months before the finish of Southern steam is unclear. According to official records 34089 602 SQUADRON was officially the last steam engine to be repaired at Eastleigh Works, leaving on 30th September 1966 but other light Pacifics were dealt with after that date plus 35003, for a non-classified repair in January 1967.

On 6th January 1967 35012 had charge of the 08.35 train from Waterloo only to fail on arrival at Weymouth, reportedly with a cracked driving wheel. If true, it was astonishing that it was not withdrawn; a week later it was under the crane at Weymouth shed. This was one of the Merchant Navys transferred to Nine Elms p/e 17/4/67 but as its withdrawal date is given as April 1967 it must have been withdrawn soon after moving back and was stored at Nine Elms for a number of months before moving back to Weymouth and eventual scrapping doubtless at some grim South Wales yard.

The Railway Observer reported that from 3rd April some of the trains on the Bournemouth line were operated by electric traction; only eight steam passenger workings (including the Channel Island boat train both ways) were diagrammed in and out of Waterloo by now. Yet on one reported run 35028 left Southampton with ten vehicles; it was through Eastleigh in nine minutes and following a long relaying restriction in the Shawford area, accelerated the whole way up the bank passing Roundwood at 66mph and then 'gave a splendid display east of Basingstoke to arrive in Waterloo 13¾ minutes early'.

To do justice to the final weeks of steam on the Bournemouth line would be impossible here – a number of exhaustive accounts have gone forensically into every working and it must be the most intensely examined period of working in British railway history. Argument can rage over contradictions that amount to minutes. The last Merchant Navy workings can be summarised from John Bird's excellent *Southern Steam Sunset:*

Sunday July 2nd
Down trains
9.55am Waterloo to Weymouth special 35008; 12.20 Waterloo to Bournemouth special 35028.
Up trains
4.30pm Weymouth to Waterloo special 35028; Weymouth to Waterloo special 35008, piloted by 35007 Weymouth to Bournemouth.
Monday July 3rd
Down trains
8.35pm Waterloo to Weymouth 35028, replaced by 34021 at Bournemouth; 4.03pm Brockenhurst-Christchurch 35030.
Up trains
12.34pm Bournemouth to Waterloo 35023, 5.30pm Weymouth to Waterloo 35007
Tuesday July 4th
Down trains
8.35am Waterloo to Weymouth 35028; 11.38 Waterloo to Basingstoke parcels assumed worked by 35023; 3.01pm Bournemouth to Weymouth 35030; 9pm Bournemouth to Weymouth (the 6.30pm ex-Waterloo) 35028; 7.06pm Basingstoke to Eastleigh 35023.
Up trains
6.49am Salisbury to Waterloo 35023; 5.49pm Weymouth to Bournemouth 35028; 7.35pm Bournemouth to Waterloo 35030.
Wednesday July 5th
Down trains
2.45am Waterloo to Bournemouth 35030; 4.40am Waterloo to Woking 35008; 6.30am Woking to Salisbury assumed worked by 35008;
8.35am Waterloo to Weymouth 35007; 9pm Bournemouth to Weymouth (6.30pm ex-Waterloo) 35007.
Up trains
6.43am Weymouth to Bournemouth 35028; 12.34pm Bournemouth to Waterloo 35028; 2.45pm Weymouth to Westbury (tomato special) 35003; 4pm Weymouth Quay to Waterloo

35030; 6.38pm Salisbury to Waterloo 35008; 5.30pm Weymouth to Waterloo 35023; 5.49pm Weymouth to Bournemouth 35007.
Thursday July 6th
Down trains
8.10am Waterloo to Weymouth Quay 35030; 8.35am Waterloo to Weymouth 35008; 9pm Bournemouth to Weymouth (6.30pm ex-Waterloo) 35008.
Up trains
4pm Weymouth Quay to Waterloo 35003; 5.30pm Weymouth to Waterloo 35007; 5.49pm Weymouth to Bournemouth 35008.
Friday July 7th
Down trains
8.10 am Waterloo to Weymouth Quay 35023; 8.35am Waterloo to Weymouth 35003; 9pm Bournemouth to Weymouth (6.30pm ex-Waterloo) 35003.
Up trains
7.49am Weymouth to Waterloo 35008; 12.34pm Bournemouth to Waterloo 35008; 4pm Weymouth Quay to Waterloo, 35023 banked by 41320 Poole to Branksome;
5.49pm Weymouth to Bournemouth 35003.
Saturday July 8th
Down train
8.30am Waterloo to Weymouth 35023.
Up train
4pm Weymouth Quay to Waterloo 35023.
Sunday July 9th
Down train
2.30am Waterloo to Poole 35030.
Up train
2.07pm Weymouth to Waterloo 35030.

Saddest train of all, the 2.07pm Weymouth to Waterloo, the final steam express on the Southern Region of BR, worked throughout by 35030, the highest numbered Southern steam loco on 9th July, arriving at Waterloo ten minutes early at 5.46pm. And that was that.

What about today's survivors?
35005 CANADIAN PACIFIC now owned and kept on the Mid-Hants Railway.

35006 PENINSULAR & ORIENTAL S.N. Co. In the final stages of restoration at Toddington on the Gloucestershire-Warwickshire Railway.

35009 SHAW SAVILL. Dismantled and owned by Ian Riley.

35010 BLUE STAR Stored at the Anglian Railway Museum at Chappel and Wakes Colne station in Essex.

35011 GENERAL STEAM NAVIGATION. Currently kept at Sellindge, near Ashford, Kent a scheme to restore this locomotive has been launched.

35018 BRITISH INDIA LINE. Now owned by Ian Riley.

35022 HOLLAND AMERICA LINE. Stored at Southall shed, as spares for 35027.

35025 BROCKLEBANK LINE. Now kept at Sellindge along with 35011, work

is to resume on the overhaul of this locomotive.

35027 PORT LINE (along with 35022) is owned by Jeremy Hosking and kept at Southall shed where it is planned to be returned to main line condition.

35028 CLAN LINE. A regular performer on the main line since 1974 it is regularly seen on rail tours in the South of England.

35029 ELLERMAN LINES. This one will never work again for it has been sectioned and is a working exhibition in the National Railway Museum in York.

Acknowledgements to Keith Gunner with respect to withdrawal and disposal details; the project www.whatreallyhappenedtosteam.co.uk aims to research and publish definitive and accurate details of the fate of all BR steam locos withdrawn between 1957 and 1968. For more information and to see how you can help, please visit the project website.

35001   Withdrawn from Bournemouth. Withdrawal date 22.11.1964. Sold to Birds Commercial Motors, Morriston.
35002   Withdrawn from Nine Elms. Withdrawal date 23.2.1964. Sold to Slag Reduction, Rotherham.
35003   Withdrawn from Nine Elms. Withdrawal date 9.7.1967. Sold to Cashmore, Newport.
35004   Withdrawn from Bournemouth. Withdrawal date 31.10.1965. Sold to Cohen, Ringwood. Cut up at Eastleigh shed
35005   Withdrawn from Weymouth. Withdrawal date 10.10.1965. Sold to Woodham Bros., Barry.
35006   Withdrawn from Salisbury. Withdrawal date 16.8.1964. Sold to Woodham Bros, Barry.
35007   Withdrawn from Nine Elms. Withdrawal date 9.7.1967. Sold to J.Buttigieg, Newport.
35008   Withdrawn from Nine Elms. Withdrawal date 9.7.1967. Sold to J.Buttigieg, Newport.
35009   Withdrawn from Exmouth Junction. Withdrawal date 1W.9.1964. Sold to Woodham Bros, Barry.
35010   Withdrawn from Bournemouth. Withdrawal date 11.9.1966. Sold to Woodham Bros, Barry.
35011   Withdrawn from Bournemouth. Withdrawal date 6.2.1966. Sold to Woodham Bros, Barry.
35012   Withdrawn from Nine Elms. Withdrawal date 23.4.1967. Sold to Cashmore, Newport.
35013   Withdrawn from Nine Elms. Withdrawal date 2.7.1967. Sold to J.Buttigieg, Newport.
35014   Withdrawn from Weymouth. Withdrawal date 26.3.1967. Sold to Cashmore, Newport.
35015   Withdrawn from Nine Elms. Withdrawal date 23.2.1964. Sold to Slag Reduction, Rotherham.
35016   Withdrawn from Weymouth. Withdrawal date 8.8.1965. Sold to Hayes, Bridgend.
35017   Withdrawn from Weymouth. Withdrawal date 17.7.1966. Sold to J.Buttigieg, Newport.
35018   Withdrawn from Nine Elms. Withdrawal date 9.8.1964. Sold to Woodham Bros, Barry.
35019   Withdrawn from Weymouth. Withdrawal date 5.9.1965. Sold to Cashmore, Newport.
35020   Withdrawn from Weymouth. Withdrawal date 14.2.1965. Cut up at Eastleigh Works.
35021   Withdrawn from Bournemouth. Withdrawal date 8.8.1965. Sold to Birds Commercial Motors, Bridgend.
35022   Withdrawn from Bournemouth. Withdrawal date 22.5.1966. Sold to Woodham Bros, Barry.
35023   Withdrawn from Nine Elms. Withdrawal date 9.7.1967. Sold to J.Buttigieg, Newport.
35024   Withdrawn from Weymouth. Withdrawal date 24.1.1965. Sold to I.C.Woodfield, Newport.
35025   Withdrawn from Exmouth Junction. Withdrawal date 1W 5.9.1964. Sold to Woodham Bros, Barry.
35026   Withdrawn from Weymouth. Withdrawal date 26.3.1967. Sold to Cashmore, Newport.
35027   Withdrawn from Bournemouth. Withdrawal date 18.9.1966. Sold to Woodham Bros, Barry.
35028   Withdrawn from Nine Elms. Withdrawal date 9.7.1967. Sold for preservation to Merchant Navy Locomotive Preservation Society.
35029   Withdrawn from Weymouth. Withdrawal date 11.9.1966. Sold to Woodham Bros, Barry.
35030   Withdrawn from Nine Elms. Withdrawal date 9.7.1967. Sold to J.Buttigieg, Newport.

Withdrawal dates are 'on' dates, with the exception of 35009 and 35025 which are '1W', which are 1 week ending dates.

The notes above do not include dates of actual scrapping for the locos sold to private contractors since these are rarely known with any certainty.

MERCHANTS IN COLOUR

35001 CHANNEL PACKET at Dorchester South in September 1964. Even the mightiest loco had still to reverse its passenger train into the up platform at Dorchester. The Merchant Navy would have worked up from Weymouth (the main line from there curves in from the left) stopped out of sight to the tight and reversed into the 'terminus' or up platform, where 'Packet' is standing. Note the typical Bournemouth line head code carried by 35001, one of few, incidentally, to work on the Eastern Section. George Powell.

CHANNEL PACKET, near Dorchester it is thought. It moved to Bournemouth shed only a couple of months before withdrawal, which came in November 1964. It understandably enough looks rather down at heel, on a train bound for Weymouth in former GWR territory. George Powell.

35024 with boarded name EAST ASIATIC COMPANY as it appeared ex-Eastleigh works on 2 February 1949 in blue with three crimson bands. Paired with new 6,000 gallon tender decorated with hand painted emblem – transfers not yet available. Cab number is yellow Gill sans. The crimson lines failed to win official approval so were changed to two black lines edged in white, emerging thus on 3 March 1949. After a few further adjustments this became the standard Merchant Navy livery for all repaints until May 1951. S.C. Townroe, Colour Rail.

Poor ROYAL MAIL in deplorable external 'BR grey' livery, tender emblem buried under grime, heading west from Andover Junction. It's a truism that almost none of us will model them in this state – yet it was an all too typical condition during those last years of service. A long time Exmouth Junction loco, it passed to the WR (in name only) when the shed there was cast into outer darkness and it eventually moved to Bournemouth, in September 1964. ROYAL MAIL was one of the last survivors; its last recorded working was on 7 July 1967, on the 21.00 Bournemouth to Weymouth. Peter Coster.

That's better! 35005 CANADIAN PACIFIC at Southampton Central; lining out clearly visible, red backed nameplate, mechanical lubricators on running plate, 8P classification on cab side along with yellow triangle denoting water treatment, speedo prominent. Outside of the ashpan rather burnt but well, what do you want? Peter Coster.

35005 CANADIAN PACIFIC at 'Bomo'. It went to Bournemouth shed not long after rebuilding and is here running light engine at the Central station; the shed yard is over on the left. 35005 is one of the few survivors to have steamed since 1967. Peter Coster.

35003 ROYAL MAIL in standard BR blue, among the wastes of Nine Elms, in the early 1950s. It went to BR green in August 1953. Colour Rail.

35020 BIBBY LINE in standard BR blue at Eastleigh shed after a part repaint in June 1951. Speedometer removed but bracket remains, as does the extra long smoke deflector. P.C. Short, Colour Rail.

35008 ORIENT LINE, in action at the head of a rake of green coaches, always green, which is how we best remember them. 35008 spent most of its rebuilt life at Bournemouth shed and survived until the bitter end. Its final working appears to have been the 07.49 Weymouth-Waterloo on 7 July 1967; it was stored at Nine Elms awaiting its ultimate fate. Michael Poulter.

ORIENT LINE at Southampton Central; semaphores upstanding in foreground. Merchant Navy Duty no.383 at one time covered the 10.30 am passenger from Waterloo, arrive Weymouth at 13.45 with the balanced working 17.30 from Weymouth arrive Waterloo at 20.51. The working notes to the duty read: *Nine Elms men work down, Bournemouth men relieve at 12.45, work to Weymouth and dispose. Weymouth men work the 16.50 light engine from Weymouth loco and are relieved at Southampton at 19.14.* [Was this the time the photo was taken?] *Eastleigh men work to Waterloo to be relieved by Nine Elms men at 20.51 who work and dispose the loco.*

35001 at Exmouth Junction in June 1949. Well, its last repaint was in April 1946 and it shows! Repainting when normally due would have meant renumbering to 35001 and the loss of the SOUTHERN tender plate and the 21C1 plate, and the Southern rather preferred to cling on to these as long as possible. W. Boot, Colour Rail.

35011 GENERAL STEAM NAVIGATION on the Bournemouth Belle at Weybridge; goods shed in the background, long since demolished and the original booking hall, burnt down late in 1987. Richard Derry recalls: *Though most of the class were rebuilt before serious development of the frontal lobe took place I can remember the Merchant Navys in their original condition. 'The Belle' always passed Weybridge before 1pm on a weekday and this spotting area, like most in the locality, was reached on the faithful push bike.* The impressive signal gantry controlled the down running lines and the crossings to the Virginia Water branch and the crossing from down slow to down fast. When rebuilt 35011 was an Exmouth Junction loco; in 2011 it is a long way from becoming a runner again. M. King Collection.

35013 BLUE FUNNEL on a short, perhaps local train somewhere in the West Country; usual Exeter line headcode. After the rebuilding of the class the vast majority of the workings were on the South Western section as shown here. 35013 was always based at 'South western' sheds and lasted until the end of Southern steam. Michael Poulter.

35013 BLUE FUNNEL at Eastleigh; it was rebuilt in May 1956 and is here back in works for a week in July 1956, for adjustments, though the term hardly seems to do justice to a complete removal of the wheels. Notice lining on boiler, running plate and cylinders and the black backing to the nameplate. The name 'proper' occupies only the top half of the circle of the nameplate; *CERTUM PETE FINEM,* which could have been a safety warning for all we knew; *KEEP OFF YOU LOT* even, is squeezed in the lower part. M. King Collection.

A resplendent 35023 HOLLAND-AFRIKA LINE at Exmouth Junction shed. 35023 has been serviced, watered and turned ready for the return working of the Atlantic Coast Express to Salisbury in July 1957.

35017 BELGIAN MARINE working an SLS special which on consulting John H. Bird's *Southern Steam Sunset* turns out to have taken place on 23 May 1965. The society ran the train from Birmingham, hence the maroon coaches. 35017 worked the train Salisbury-Exeter-Bristol-Westbury where 7029 CLUN CASTLE took over and worked it back to Birmingham with 34051 WINSTON CHURCHILL having worked Birmingham to Salisbury. The photograph above shows the train at Semley and below leaving the same station under roadbridge No.297; of the three locos involved 35017 did not survive into preservation. Peter Coster.

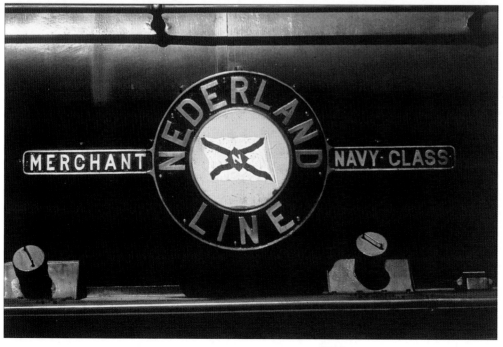

Nameplate backgrounds are something of a can of worms. The Merchant Navys were red until April 1952 when official instructions were issued that the backgrounds should be black instead. These appear never to have been rescinded. As it turned out, Motive Power Depots often had other ideas and would repaint them RED. All Pacifics were rebuilt with black backgrounds but that red had a way of creeping back in... Colour Rail, M. King Collection.

35020 BIBBY LINE at Woking, August 1964, EMU in platform road. This was another fine 'spotting' place available through a cheap after-school early evening steam-hauled outing from Waterloo, for a good 'bag' – see *The Steaming Sixties* colour series by Irwell Press, *No.6, From Woking to Weymouth*. On a down West Country working, BIBBY LINE was the second rebuild, of April 1956. A Nine Elms loco for most of its life it was equally at home on Bournemouth or Exeter workings. John Eyres.

35021 NEW ZEALAND LINE with the Bournemouth Belle, at Weybridge station once again. The footbridge here was taken down one Christmas (!) day a few years later to provide a road to a new sewage works by the River Wey. This is pre-1959 when 35021 was rebuilt though the raves have been removed from the tender which will be no.3342. The line on the right, minus third rail, ran past the generating station and behind the down platform but was seldom used by the late 1950s. In the background is a Virginia Water branch train with behind it what looks like a 700 'Black Motor' 0-6-0 shunting the up goods yard with a cattle wagon and an army lorry in the train. There appears to be at least eleven Pullmans in the 'Belle' and the time would be about 12.55pm. The return up working would pass at about 6.20pm. M. King Collection.

35022 HOLLAND AMERICA LINE (remember, no hyphen!) on a down train approaching Dorchester in September 1964. It is about to roll left to the Weymouth line; the 'terminus' platform seen at the beginning occupied by 35001 is to the left of those further rails. Old ballast on the very right indicate the site of the late engine shed. George Powell.

HOLLAND AMERICA LINE at Seaton Junction and about 1964, from the feel of it. In its rebuilt state the loco was first at Bournemouth shed before returning to Exmouth Junction for a second time in March, 1960. Sadly since withdrawal this loco is just a basic hulk and looks like it will serve as spares for 35027 PORT LINE. Peter Coster.

And another one goes red... Colour Rail.

35023 HOLLAND-AFRIKA LINE (with hyphen) blowing off at Nine Elms shed maybe about 1959. One glance at the frightening power of the steam from the safety valves and the frail asbestos sheeted roof will reveal why engines liable to blow off were NOT parked inside. Though not visible the tender still has the first emblem – see again *The Steaming Sixties* colour series by Irwell Press, *No.6, From Woking to Weymouth* for a similar picture taken on the same occasion. George Powell.

35023 HOLLAND-AFRIKA LINE going away on Honiton bank, after March 1960 when it was transferred from Bournemouth to Exmouth Junction. Surviving to the end of Southern steam its final recorded working was on 8 July; the 16.00 Weymouth Quay-Waterloo, the last steam worked up Channel Island boat train. Chalked on the smokebox was **THE END THE LAST ONE**. On 22 July 1967 it was noted in the 'New shed' at Nine Elms with 35028; unlike CLAN LINE, however, it was never to work again. Peter Coster.

35023 HOLLAND-AFRIKA LINE at Wimbledon with a Bournemouth line train on what looks like duty no.436, the 06.43 Weymouth depart, arrive Bournemouth Central 08.25. George Powell.

35014 NEDERLAND LINE; nice and clean as you'd expect for an Eastleigh Open Day, with the rods 'set down' in the correct manner. Sadly the chalk board cannot be read. 35014 was withdrawn in March 1967. M. King Collection.

35029 ELLERMAN LINES on the approach to Southampton Central. It was one of the class that spent a while working out of Dover shed in the early 1950s on the lines in Kent. Now, dismally, it is sectioned, in the National Railway Museum at York. A terrible fate; the senior BR Officer assigned to pick out a suitable locomotive on behalf of the NRM was ever after reluctant to admit to it, except to close friends after a few drinks. Michael Poulter.

35030 ELDER DEMPSTER LINES at Waterloo, with that new London skyline steadily rearing up on the rubble of the Blitz. Here 35030 holds the attention of a father and son – who quite possibly required a bit of comfort with that ear-splitting safety valve going off. Peter Coster.

Waterloo in 1952; tender cut down hence cabside has a low pitched number to match. Colour Rail